D-DAY

THE WORLD WAR II INVASION THAT CHANGED HISTORY

ALSO BY DEBORAH HOPKINSON

We Had to Be Brave: Escaping the Nazis on the Kindertransport

Dive! World War II Stories of Sailors & Submarines in the Pacific

Courage & Defiance: Stories of Spies, Saboteurs, and Survivors in World War II Denmark

Titanic: Voices from the Disaster

Up Before Daybreak: Cotton and People in America

Shutting Out the Sky: Life in the Tenements of New York, 1880–1924

D-DAY

THE WORLD WAR II INVASION THAT CHANGED HISTORY

by

DEBORAH HOPKINSON

SCHOLASTIC FOCUS

NEW YORK

This book was originally published in hardcover by Scholastic Focus in 2018.

ISBN 978-0-545-68250-3

10 9 8 7 6 5 4 21 22 23 24

Printed in the U.S.A. 40
This edition first printing 2020

Book design by Abby Dening

For CH,
in love and friendship

And for all
who have struggled and sacrificed
for equality, freedom, and justice

USS *Nevada* blasts at a foe from the English Channel.

Therefore, my lords, omit no happy hour

That may give furtherance to our expedition;

For we have now no thought in us but France.

WILLIAM SHAKESPEARE,
HENRY V, ACT I, SCENE 2

June 6, 1944—just past midnight off the coast of Normandy

" 'Look, men, look! It's the fleet.' " At the sergeant's voice, paratrooper David Kenyon Webster peered out the window of the rumbling C-47 plane and caught his breath. " 'Man, oh man.' "

The clouds had slid off the moon to reveal an extraordinary sight. "Five hundred feet below, spread out for miles on the moonlit sea, were scores and scores of landing barges, destroyers, cruisers, and attack transports," said David. "They were bearing the infantry slowly east, like a flood of lava, to a dawn assault on the shingle shore of Normandy."

He turned back around. "I stared at the men opposite me in the racketing, vibrating, oil-reeking, vomit-scented darkness . . . My stomach tightened and filled with ice, and a voice told me to get ready.

" 'It's coming,' the voice said, 'it's coming.' "

Not much longer now. The paratroopers of E Company, 506th Parachute Infantry Regiment, 101st Airborne Division, were set to jump before 1 in the morning. They had just a few hours to clear the way for infantry soldiers landing on Utah Beach at dawn. Their mission: to destroy German gun nests and take control of four causeways leading off the beach over a mile of lowlands the enemy had flooded as a defensive measure.

These tracks were the only ways off the beach. If Americans controlled them, the thousands of soldiers landing on the beachhead would be able to move inland, seal off the base of the Cotentin Peninsula, and move north into it to capture the port of Cherbourg. It could make the difference between gaining a real foothold in France—or being stalled on the shore, giving Germany more time to rush in reinforcements for a counterattack.

David's plane was over land now. The drop zone was close—at least David hoped it was the drop zone. The paratroopers struggled to their feet and lined up. The plane lurched to avoid tracer bullets. They'd been spotted! David lost his balance, stumbling into the man behind him.

"Oh God, I prayed, get me out of here. I don't want to blow up in the sky and burn to death. I don't want to die like a mouse in a can on a garbage dump fire. I want to die fighting. Let's jump, let's jump. Let's go, go, go!"

The plane rolled again. "I smelled the smoke and oil and puke and gagged on my supper as it rose in my throat." David clamped his teeth shut. He refused to get sick. "The plane slammed up and down, zigzagged, rattled and roared, threw up from side to side with such violence that several of us fell down again, cursing the pilot . . . It was all I could do to remain upright and not dissolve into a gutless, gibbering blob of fear."

The lieutenant shouted at them to go. Two men tripped and fell in the doorway. "There was a wild, cursing tangle as others fought to lift them and push them out, and then the line moved again, sucked out the door like a stream of water."

David shuffled closer to the opening and looked down at the ground. Only it wasn't ground. It rippled and reflected like water. It *was* water. He couldn't jump out into that. "But this was D-Day and nobody went back to England and a lot of infantry riding open barges seasick . . . were depending on us to draw the Germans off the causeways and gun batteries."

David Kenyon Webster had turned twenty-two four days before. Now he grabbed both sides of the door and hurtled himself into the sky.

"I fell a hundred feet in three seconds, straight toward a huge flooded area shining in the moonlight." David had always feared a water landing; his heavy equipment could easily drag him to the bottom before he could get free. And now all he could see was water rushing up at him.

"Just before I hit, I closed my eyes and took a deep breath of air. My feet splashed into the water. I held my breath, expecting to sink over my head and wondering how I was going to escape from my harness underwater—and hit bottom three feet down. My chute billowed away from me in the light wind and collapsed on the surface. I went to work to free myself from my gear."

David's rush of relief was short-lived. The night erupted with a long, ripping burst of sound. Machine-gun fire! He dropped to his knees in the black, cold water. Staccato bursts shattered the silence again—splutters and pops and *burrrp-burrrp-burrrp* stutters. It was real, David knew, too real.

And then, slowly, he realized that it wasn't that close to him. For the moment, he was safe. He got up, assembled his rifle, which had been broken apart for the jump, and rammed on his bayonet. Where was everyone? Not just his friends, but the other regiments? He couldn't see anyone else.

David was ready to find his way out of the swamp. But where to go? "Lost and lonely, wrestling with the greatest fear of my life, I stood bewildered . . . Where is the drop zone? Where are the other regiments?

"Six regiments jumped tonight, and I am alone in Normandy."

Like most of the paratroopers dropped behind Utah Beach in the early hours of June 6, David felt isolated in those first moments.

Yet, in fact, he was part of the largest military invasion in history, involving 156,000 military personnel on D-Day. Its goal was nothing less than the Allied defeat of Adolf Hitler's Nazi Germany, a tyrannical, evil regime based on hatred, racism, and persecution of Jewish people. With Hitler at its helm, Germany had occupied free countries, carried out unspeakable atrocities, and sent millions of innocent people, including about six million Jews, to their deaths in the Holocaust.

Hitler had to be stopped. The future of humanity and free democracies was at stake. This was not an invasion for conquest, but for a cause.

Yet despite careful, meticulous preparations; long months of training; and the sharpest military minds in the world, nothing about D-Day was certain.

In those first treacherous hours, no one, not the U.S. president, the British prime minister, the supreme commander, not any general, and especially not young soldiers like David Kenyon Webster, could know whether this great endeavor would succeed—or fail.

TABLE OF CONTENTS

June 6, 1944—just past midnight off the coast of Normandy ix

What Is D-Day? xix

And What's a Regiment, Anyway? xxii

PART 1 THE PLAN

CHAPTER 1 Operation Overlord 3

CHAPTER 2 Invasion Preparation: Toy Soldiers Come to Life 17

CHAPTER 3 Meet the Supreme Commander (and His Dog) 30

PART 2 THE GODS OF WAR

CHAPTER 4 The Weatherman 45

CHAPTER 5 "D-Day Calling" 52

CHAPTER 6 The Decision to Go 59

PART 3 NIGHT INTO DAY

CHAPTER 7 Across the Channel by Sea 81

CHAPTER 8 Before the Jump 88

CHAPTER 9 Pegasus Bridge 100

PART 4 UTAH

Voices from the Airborne Divisions 124

CHAPTER 10 Crickets: Normandy before Dawn 130

CHAPTER 11 Scenes from a Chaplain's D-Day 139

CHAPTER 12 Crash-Landing into Normandy 144

CHAPTER 13 First Battles 157

CHAPTER 14 Approach from the Sea: Voices from the Beachhead 166

CHAPTER 15 On Utah Beach: Starting the War from Here 177

PART 5 OMAHA

USS Augusta *3:35 a.m., off the Normandy Coast* 197

Voices from Omaha Beach 202

CHAPTER 16 Some Kind of Prayer 211

CHAPTER 17 A Scene of Havoc and Destruction 220

CHAPTER 18 A Thin, Wet Line of Khaki 232

CHAPTER 19 "29, Let's Go!" 244

CHAPTER 20 The Rangers at Pointe du Hoc 261

PART 6 AFTERMATH: MORE THAN COURAGE

Voices after D-Day 277

CHAPTER 21 The Miracle of a Toehold 288

QUARTERMASTER'S DEPARTMENT

World War II Timeline 306

Glossary 308

Key People in This Book 311

Look, Listen, Remember: Links to Online Resources 314

Bibliography 321

Source Notes 331

Photo Permissions 347

Index 349

Acknowledgments 372

About the Author 375

WHAT IS D-DAY?

The Allied invasion of Normandy, France, on June 6, 1944, is often simply called D-Day. Many people are curious: Just what does that "D" stand for?

The "D" in D-day, like the "H" in H-hour, is a military term used to plan the day and hour of an operation. As you'll see here, the proposed date for the invasion of Normandy changed several times. In the end, D-Day took place on June 6, 1944, and it's become known by that name.

There are so many stories to tell about D-Day. Hundreds of books have already been written, but no single title can cover this complex undertaking, capture what it meant to those who were there, or illuminate its full meaning and significance today.

I wrote this book hoping to provide an introduction to D-Day and what it was like for just a few of those who took part. And while thousands of Allied troops from the United States, Great Britain, and Canada participated, the stories here primarily focus on the experiences of Americans at Utah and Omaha Beaches. (One exception is the extraordinary British capture of Pegasus Bridge.)

I hope seeing history through the eyes of those who were there will encourage you to read more. To this end, you'll find lists of books and online resources in the "Quartermaster's Department" in the back and in recommendations called "Look, Listen, Remember" scattered throughout.

The narrative also includes sections called "Briefings," which provide additional context, including "Reader's Invasion Briefings." Like soldiers getting briefed before a mission, you'll be briefed in advance: The Overlord, Utah, and Omaha briefings appear before the relevant sections.

Dispatches are first-person accounts. A free press was as crucial in World War II as it is today, and in the "Reporter's Notebook" sections you'll meet some of the men and women who reported the war.

A note about numbers and statistics: Casualty figures reported for D-Day vary widely, as do the number of troops who took part. Not all deaths were recorded in a timely fashion and true figures may never be known. I have chosen to use figures from the D-Day Museum in Portsmouth, England, which reflect research undertaken by the National D-Day Memorial in Virginia, as well as the work of esteemed D-Day historian Joseph Balkoski. Links to both organizations, in addition to the exceptional National World War II Museum in New Orleans, whose staff members were enormously helpful in the preparation of this book, can be found in the

"Quartermaster's Department" in the back. (A *quartermaster* is in charge of supplies and provisions.)

As the last survivors pass from this world, one way to honor and remember them is to learn as much as we can about their courage, commitment, and enormous sacrifices. I hope this book inspires you to believe in—and work for—a future in which each life on our planet is valued and respected, and where democracy that embraces diversity, justice, and equality thrives.

Remember them.

—Deborah Hopkinson

AND WHAT'S A REGIMENT, ANYWAY?

The names and organization of military units used today have their roots in battles dating back several centuries. Although there were some variations in numbers on D-Day, the following table from the U.S. Army provides a general overview of how units are organized. In reading about World War II, you may notice that the term "regiment" is sometimes omitted. For instance, the "4th Infantry" is understood to refer to the "4th Infantry Regiment." However, since readers may be unfamiliar with military terminology, I've chosen to use it throughout.

Airborne divisions were usually smaller than infantry. On D-Day, some units had additional personnel attached to them to perform specialized tasks, such as demolition of beach obstacles, and so these numbers are just a general guideline. You'll often see the symbols used on military maps. The information is from an unclassified army pamphlet entitled *Organization of the United States Army.*

ELEMENT	SYMBOL	NUMBER OF SOLDIERS
Squad/Section	·/··	9–10
Platoon	··	16–44
Company/Battery/Troop	I	62–190
Battalion/Squadron	II	300–1,000
Brigade/Regiment/Group	X/III	3,000–5,000
Division	XX	10,000–15,000
Corps	XXX	20,000–45,000
Army	XXXX	50,000+

PART 1

THE PLAN

"The great Allied invasion of Normandy on 6 June 1944 was the most complex and daring military operation in the history of modern warfare, the culmination of more than three years of conception, often contentious debate, and the most prodigious military planning ever undertaken. Its success was a testament to the cooperation of allies with fundamentally opposing military and political philosophies, as well as the indomitable courage of men called upon to fight and die on the battlefield."

CARLO D'ESTE, historian

"The target date for Overlord is May 31, 1944. Will the Channel run red with blood?"

HARRY BUTCHER, aide to the Supreme Commander

CHAPTER 1

OPERATION OVERLORD

What had to happen for thousands of young paratroopers like David Kenyon Webster to jump out of an airplane, and for tens of thousands more to cross the English Channel to struggle ashore on the beaches of Normandy? Where does the story of D-Day begin?

We could begin on September 3, 1939, when Great Britain and France declared war on Hitler's Nazi Germany after it invaded Poland. We might trace D-Day's roots to May 1940, when British forces were overpowered and retreated to Dunkirk, France. There, to prevent certain defeat, troops were evacuated by naval ships and a flotilla of civilian boats of all sizes. Britain had wanted to return to France ever since.

Or we might begin with the surprise Japanese attack on Pearl Harbor in Hawai'i on December 7, 1941. The next day, President Franklin D. Roosevelt signed the declaration of war against Japan; the United States declared war on Germany and Italy on December 11, which widened the global conflict and gave Great Britain, at last, a powerful ally in the fight against Hitler. By the time the United States entered the war, Hitler had Europe in his grip: The German Army had invaded

President Franklin D. Roosevelt signing the Declaration of War against Japan, December 8, 1941.

France, the Netherlands, Norway and Denmark, the Soviet Union, and Greece, among others.

Then again, we might start on August 19, 1942, when 6,000 British and Canadian forces launched a raid on the French port of Dieppe. Its failure made it clear the invasion of France couldn't happen right away. Britain alone simply didn't have the needed capacity. The invasion would have to wait until "the German Army had been worn down by the Russians, the Luftwaffe [German Air Force] bled white by Allied air power, the U-boats thwarted, and American war production expanded." In other words, Germany needed to be weakened before there was any hope of winning.

We could begin telling the story of the complex history of planning for the invasion of France at any of these points in time. Instead, though, we will begin on a day largely forgotten in D-Day history, a rather ordinary day: March 12, 1943. That's when a forty-nine-year-old British officer named Frederick E. Morgan stepped into an elevator on his way to a meeting at New Scotland Yard in London.

"Just as the lift was taking off, in jumped Admiral Lord Louis Mountbatten [a top British military official] himself, fresh from discussion with the British Chiefs of Staff, who proceeded to congratulate me vociferously in spite of the presence of a full load of passengers of all ranks," Morgan recalled.

Morgan had absolutely no idea what Mountbatten was talking about. He found out a few minutes later when General Hastings Lionel Ismay, Prime Minister Winston Churchill's chief of staff, handed him a mountain of paper. The stack contained all the previous plans for an assault on Hitler's "Fortress Europe."

The continent was protected by a system of coastal defenses known as the Atlantic Wall. Stretching from Scandinavia to Spain, it included troops, manned gun placements, beach obstacles, and mines—all designed to thwart invading forces.

Now the time had come to make the attempt. An assault across the English Channel had been high on the agenda at the recent January 1943 Casablanca Conference. At this Allied leaders' summit, Churchill and U.S. President Franklin D. Roosevelt agreed the Allies were ready to launch an invasion of France in 1944.

Of course, there was no firm plan in place for any of this. In fact, Morgan was being "invited" to come up with one. The target date was May 1, 1944—less than a year away. It didn't give much time. As for when he should have his plan ready, Morgan was told, " 'No hurry, old boy, tomorrow will do.' "

General Ismay added one final comment on Morgan's task: " 'Well, there it is; it won't work, but you must bloody well make it.' "

Along with his new assignment, Morgan was given a title: Chief of Staff to the Supreme Allied Commander (Designate), a mouthful soon shortened to COSSAC. (In January 1944, COSSAC offices became SHAEF, Supreme Headquarters of the Allied Expeditionary Force.)

Morgan was headquartered at Norfolk House, 31 St. James's Square in London. At first the planning team was just Morgan and a couple of aides. He commandeered an unoccupied space and moved in. "The equipment consisted of a couple of desks and chairs we found in the room, and we were lucky enough also to find a few sheets of paper and a pencil that someone had dropped on the floor."

And with that, Frederick Morgan set out to plan the largest military endeavor in history.

From the start, Morgan and the team he eventually assembled faced enormous challenges. The schedule was brutally demanding: The plan needed to be reviewed by the British Chiefs of Staff in July 1943, just a few months away.

As for who would lead it: Well, no Supreme Commander for the Allied Expeditionary Force had yet been named. In the meantime, Morgan, who had no decision-making power or ability to lobby higher-ups for additional resources, would just have to do the best he could within the parameters he was given.

At least the endeavor, formerly known as Roundup, had been given a new code name, chosen from a list of possibilities by Prime Minister Winston Churchill himself.

It was called Operation Overlord.

Lt. General Frederick E. Morgan,
Chief of Staff to the Supreme Allied Commander.

READER'S INVASION BRIEFING

World War II and the Context for Operation Overlord

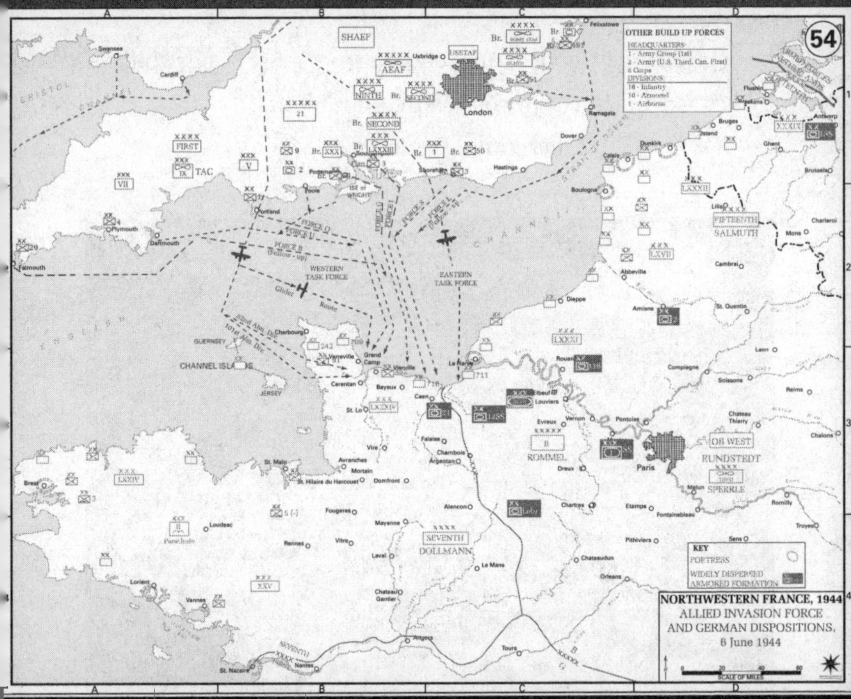

A WWII map of the

WORLD WAR II, sometimes called the Second World War (1939–1945), was the largest conflict in the history of the world. It pitted the Axis powers of Germany, Italy, and Japan against the Allies, which included Great Britain, France, the United States, and the Soviet Union, among others.

Between forty and fifty million people died, including millions of innocent civilians. Many historians believe that the war had its roots in the First World War, which ended in 1918. The peace negotiations following that conflict, especially the 1919 Treaty of Versailles, placed blame and harsh financial burdens on Germany. Adolf Hitler, who opposed the treaty and the postwar government of Germany, rose to power during this time, buoyed by resentment about World War I and a growing German nationalist movement. Under his leadership, the Nazi Party gained control; in 1933, he became chancellor of Germany and before long had assumed the powers of a dictator.

World War II began in 1939, when Germany invaded Poland on September 1. Following this, on September 3, Great Britain and France, both allies of Poland, declared war on Germany. Germany extended her power, invading Norway and Denmark in April 1940. In May, Hitler targeted France, as well as the "low countries" in the coastal region of northwest Europe, invading Belgium, the Netherlands, and Luxembourg in May.

Hitler's extreme racist and anti-Semitic beliefs led to a horrific plan, called "the Final Solution," to annihilate all Jewish people. During the Holocaust, six million Jewish men, women, and children were murdered in unspeakable conditions in extermination camps. Hitler also killed millions of other innocent civilians including activists, people with disabilities, LGBT people, and people of Roma heritage. Another seven million people, including Poles and Ukrainians, were forced into slave labor as part of the German war machine. Underground resistance movements grew up in countries occupied by Germany, and in some cases with support from Great Britain.

Great Britain stood almost alone against Germany in the early part of the war, suffering military defeats and the harrowing bombing of London and other English cities. Although Germany and the Soviet Union had initially formed a cooperation pact, Germany invaded the Soviet Union in June 1941. Later that year, the United States entered the global conflict after Japan, which was aligned with Germany and Italy as an Axis power, attacked Pearl Harbor on December 7, 1941. By the end of 1941, the United States was at war with Japan, Germany, and Italy.

Great Britain now had help in the fight against Hitler in Europe, but the United States needed time to recruit, train, and produce the massive amount of vehicles, ammunition, and equipment necessary to mount a direct attack on Germany, which had built up such a strong defense the European continent became known as Fortress Europe.

In the meantime, throughout 1942 and 1943, in addition to fighting the war against Japan in the Pacific, the United States joined with Great Britain to try to weaken Germany and Italy in North Africa and in the Mediterranean. In November 1942, the

Allies launched their first joint operation, codenamed Torch, ir North Africa. Part of the goal was to control the Suez Cana in order to obtain a supply of oil from the Middle East to pro- duce gasoline for tanks, trucks, ships, and planes. In addition Operation Torch sought to weaken German forces fighting in the area, and eventually move Allied troops northward to invade Sicily and push the Germans from the mainland of Italy.

Under the direction of General Dwight D. Eisenhower, more than 100,000 troops conducted amphibious landings in Novembe 1942 near Casablanca, Morocco, and the Mediterranean coast o Algeria, forcing the withdrawal of German troops, and leaving North Africa in Allied control by May 1943.

When Roosevelt and Churchill met at the Casablanca Confer- ence in January 1943, they decided their next target would be Sicily, in order to take advantage of Allied victories in the Mediterranean. Codenamed Operation Husky, the invasion o Sicily, again under the command of Eisenhower, was launched ir July 1943. On July 25, the Italian dictator Benito Mussolini was arrested.

The Sicilian campaign paved the way for the successful Alliec invasion of Italy in September 1943. By October, the Allies con- trolled most of southern Italy. They then engaged in a long drawn-out series of battles with German forces in Italy until May 1945, which turned into what historian Carlo D'Este called a "bloody stalemate."

Perhaps war correspondent Ernie Pyle put it best: "The wa in Italy was tough. The land and the weather were both agains us. It rained and it rained. Vehicles bogged down and temporary bridges washed out. The country was shockingly beautiful, and just as shockingly hard to capture from the enemy."

Even as Allied leaders undertook these campaigns, they were fully aware that if an invasion of France and northern Europe were to take place in 1944, preparations couldn't be delayed. And so in March 1943, General Frederick Morgan was asked to begin planning Operation Overlord.

The ultimate goal of Overlord was clear and uncompromising: "the utter defeat of Germany." From the outset, planners knew the enemy wouldn't be surrendering anywhere near the coast of France. The Allies would need to break through Hitler's Atlantic Wall of coastal defenses—sea mines, gun emplacements, beach obstacles, and troops.

To win, they'd have to break out of occupied France and pursue the Germans deep into Europe. In other words, the initial airborne and the cross-channel amphibious assault (a part of Overlord codenamed Operation Neptune), was only the first step. Overlord was expected to be a long campaign involving two million soldiers battling their way seven hundred miles to Berlin.

For this reason, Overlord would require a reliable, uninterrupted flow of troops, vehicles, and supplies over a long period of time. (And although planners didn't know it then, it would take eleven months—and more than three hundred days of hard fighting—before Germany surrendered in May 1945.)

With that in mind, Morgan and the Overlord planners knew it was imperative to choose the best invasion site they could find. Two possibilities had already been identified: the Pas-de-Calais region in northern France and the Caen-Cotentin area of Normandy. Calais, a major port since the Middle Ages, had some obvious advantages. It was the closest city to England, an easy reach separated only by the narrow Strait of Dover.

Yet since it was the most obvious spot to anyone looking at a map (including the Germans), Calais was heavily defended.

And so the Overlord planning staff turned their attention farther south, to the coast of Normandy.

This region offered an element of surprise and had fewer German defensive fortifications than Calais. The landings could be followed quickly by the capture of the port of Cherbourg on nearby Cotentin Peninsula. Also, the beaches would be well suited to the massive buildup of equipment and vehicles that would immediately follow the amphibious landings.

Plans barreled forward during the summer of 1943. Morgan met his deadline to present the British Chiefs of Staff an outline in July. Then, in August, when President Roosevelt, Prime Minister Churchill, and Canadian Prime Minister William Lyon Mackenzie King met secretly in Quebec, Canada, they adopted the Overlord plan and approved the May 1 invasion date.

As for the Supreme Commander—there still wasn't one. Even so, troops had to be trained, vehicles and landing craft readied, equipment and ammunition secured. Thousands of complicated logistical problems had to be solved.

"The stop-watch," Frederick Morgan said, "was already ticking."

BRIEFING

A Preposterous Idea: Mulberry Harbors

A port. They needed a port.

A reliable supply line was essential for Allied forces to break out of Normandy, liberate Paris, and pursue the enemy into Germany. As naval historian Samuel Eliot Morison put it, "if momentum is not maintained, an amphibious operation bogs down." In other words, troops could be stranded—and forced to retreat without the supplies, ammunition, and food they needed.

However, the Allies knew that Hitler had paid close attention to defending port towns, and they couldn't count on capturing Cherbourg immediately. It would also take time and heavy equipment to get its harbor functioning again. It was a given that the Germans had laid mines and sunk ships to make it unusable.

And so Frederick Morgan and his team faced what seemed an impasse: "Without at least one port in the first few days . . . the thing was just not on."

Not on. But it *had* to be on. Morgan recalled a meeting one hot summer day as planners tried to grapple with "this immense puzzle." A Royal Navy representative, Commodore John Hughes-Hallett, joked, "'Well, all I can say is, if we can't capture a port, we must take one with us.'"

Take one with us? It sounded incredible, but maybe it wasn't. And when the team members revisited the notion the next day, they decided: "There might be something in this apparently preposterous idea."

And so the British designed and secretly built the Mulberries, two artificial harbors that could be taken along on the invasion. The Mulberries would be placed off the coast of Normandy to create sheltered water and a docking area. "Mulberry A" would ultimately serve the two American beaches (codenamed Omaha and Utah), "Mulberry B" the three British and Canadian landing sites (Sword, Juno, and Gold). The term Mulberry was simply a code name chosen at random.

What began as an offhand remark and a preposterous idea turned into reality—and a spectacular engineering feat that became a key factor in the invasion's success.

LOOK, LISTEN, REMEMBER: To read more about Mulberry harbors visit http://d-dayrevisited.co.uk/d-day/mulberry-harbour.html.

CHAPTER 2

INVASION PREPARATION: TOY SOLDIERS COME TO LIFE

"All my life I had wanted to go to England," said David Kenyon Webster. David had been a Harvard student and aspiring writer before volunteering as an army paratrooper.

As a little boy, he'd worn button shoes like Christopher Robin. He'd grown up reading British adventure stories like *Robin Hood* and *Kidnapped*. "When I played with toy soldiers they were English: sturdy, kilted Scotchman running with fixed bayonets; tall, bright-red guardsmen on parade.

"Finally, in September, 1943, I did go to England. I was a little boy no longer. The toy soldiers had come to life; I was one of them."

David was one of thousands—hundreds of thousands—of American soldiers in England in the preinvasion months. By January 1944, it's estimated there were nearly 750,000 U.S. troops in the United Kingdom, most in eleven divisions, with 15,000 to 20,000 men in each. This number would double by D-Day.

The troops included sailors, soldiers, and airmen. Racial prejudice in the military barred African Americans from combat positions, and it wouldn't be until July 26, 1948, that President Harry S. Truman signed Executive Order 9981 desegregating the military. Nevertheless, African Americans played a critical part in the D-Day invasion and the war in Europe. One historian estimates that of the 1.5 million American servicemen in Great Britain in June, about 134,000 were African Americans. "More than 60 percent of all general service regiments, dump truck companies, truck drivers, and ordnance units were black."

Although exact figures vary, D-Day itself would involve a landing force of some 156,000 Allied military personnel from the United States, England, and Canada. (Additionally, there were some troops from Free France and Norway who had managed to flee their homelands and were serving alongside British forces. Remnants of the Royal Norwegian Navy had also evacuated. According to the Royal Norwegian Navy Museum, about ten Norwegian vessels were part of Operation Neptune.) The invasion also involved about 11,500 aircraft, including 867 gliders. The assault deployed nearly 7,000 ships, including 4,126 landing ships and smaller landing craft.

But those are just numbers. Like David, each soldier and sailor was an individual who had left family, friends, and loved ones behind. The going away was not easy.

"You know those orders are coming. Yet no one is ever prepared for them when they do come," wrote John Mason Brown. He was a well-known drama critic in his early forties when he volunteered in 1942 as a naval officer on the staff of

Admiral Alan Kirk. (Kirk would serve as the senior naval commander for the Western Task Force of the invasion, in charge of landing Americans on two beaches.)

Brown went on, "The Invasion, which is so many things, is also a mountain range of orders; hence of farewells, of empty places at the table, of incomplete Christmases, uncelebrated anniversaries, untaken weekends, and of changed lives here, there, and on the way over."

The journey itself across the Atlantic was fraught with danger. Troops crossed in all kinds of ships. There were convoys and transports sailing under navy protection from prowling U-Boats (German submarines).

Americans also came, Brown noted, "on heavy freighters dipping under breakers, in postcard weather or through black, wintery waters . . . on large ships that race alone, on cruisers, battleships and vessels loaded with explosives."

Watching this influx, Brown said that it made him realize that "to invade Europe we would have to invade England first."

It wasn't just soldiers arriving in England in the months before D-Day, but a mind-boggling inventory of supplies: "our tanks; our jeeps, our stretchers . . . our camouflage and our small stores; our typewriters, our desks . . . our bedding and most of our food."

The French word *matériel* is used to describe military equipment and materials. And production of matériel for this massive undertaking was only possible because of an

African Americans fought discrimination to break into combat positions late in the war. Throughout, they played critical roles in specialized support units and in war production.

extraordinary production effort. More than twelve million American men joined the military during the war, including about nine hundred thousand African Americans and about three hundred and fifty thousand women. With so many men gone, the resulting labor shortage was filled by women.

Six and a half million American women went to work during the war years, filling jobs in factories and shipyards once held by men. During the war years, factories produced machines and equipment on an unprecedented scale. As just one example, in the first three months of 1944, more than 600 C-47 aircraft that would be used to carry paratroopers into Normandy were delivered to an airfield in Fort Wayne, Indiana. From there, crews flew them to England, where they would enter intensive training. By April 1944, there were more than 1,000 of these troop carrier planes in England ready to go.

World War II poster by J. Howard Miller.

This accelerated war production was made possible through what Secretary of War Henry L. Stanton called "the vast reserve of woman power." African American men, who faced discrimination in the military and were essentially barred from combat service, also formed a key part of the civilian and military workforce.

Once the vehicles, planes, landing craft, invasion supplies, and people arrived in England, they needed to be accommodated. John Mason Brown observed, "As we Americans moved in, the British had no other choice than to move over, which is no easy thing to do in your own house."

But they did it. And there was something else, Brown thought, that would lead to success. The British most certainly needed the Americans, but the Americans needed the British, too. After all, the British people had been standing up to the Nazis since 1940. Thousands of soldiers had already died in the war effort. An estimated 40,000 British civilians had also been killed during Germany's bombing raids in England known as the Blitz.

"Had they not stood alone, we might not have been able to stand at all," Brown said. "We were both the stronger when we stood side by side."

BRIEFING

African Americans in World War II

During World War II, American society, including the U.S. military, was still very much segregated, and opportunities and rights for African Americans were severely limited.

Albert E. Cowdrey at the U.S. Army Center of Military History has observed that "For American blacks the war was a time of paradox. The fight against Hitler's homicidal racism was one in which they had a special interest . . . It was also a time of disappointment and growing anger, for the nation failed to integrate its armed forces or grant genuine equality to blacks in uniform."

Although Benjamin Oliver Davis Sr. had become the army's first black general in October 1940, African Americans were not allowed in combat roles until late in the war, and then in a very limited capacity. Overall, more blacks than whites were turned down for the draft.

In another example, black medical personnel seeking to join the navy were turned away. Several thousand black physicians had formed the National Medical Association (NMA), since in many parts of the country African American doctors were excluded from the American Medical Association. In 1940, the NMA formed a committee to lobby for a role in the war effort. Cowdrey notes that "The navy was polite but firm. Except as mess personnel it had no use for any blacks and consequently none for black doctors. The army was more forthcoming." Promises were made to use black physicians with all-black units.

Similarly, while the army gave commissions to about five hundred African American nurses during the war, the navy only gave four. The situation for nurses began to improve slightly over the course of the war, thanks to the efforts of such organizations as the National Association of Colored Graduate Nurses (NACGN), which had the support of First Lady Eleanor Roosevelt.

As a result of systemic racism, in the first years of the war, African Americans in the military were largely limited to noncombat service positions such as engineers, logistics, or transportation, or segregated support units.

According to the National World War II Museum, "By 1945, however, troop losses virtually forced the military to begin placing more African American troops into positions as infantrymen, pilots, tankers, medics, and officers in increasing numbers."

This included the 761st Tank Battalion, which distinguished itself with General George S. Patton, spending more than 180 days in combat. The "Tuskegee Airmen" of the 332nd Fighter Group have become legendary, flying over 15,000 missions. And in Italy beginning in the late summer of 1944, the 92nd Infantry Division battled the enemy in treacherous terrain, earning a reputation for toughness.

Daniel Inouye, the late, beloved senator from Hawai'i (and the highest-ranking Asian American politician in U.S. history) fought in Italy with the 442nd Regimental Combat Team, primarily made up of Japanese Americans. Grievously wounded, Inouye would eventually lose his right arm.

He once shared a special memory of the African American soldiers of the 92nd from his experience in a field hospital. "'I remember a nurse showing me a bottle of blood. It had a name on it—Thomas Jefferson Smith, 92nd Division—and while they were rigging it for transfusion . . . I realized that fighting men did more than fight, that they cared enough about each other and the men assigned to their sector to donate their blood for the time when somebody would need it to sustain life,'" he once said, adding his thanks "'to every man in the 92nd Division who donated blood that helped save my life.'"

In December 1944, facing a shortage of replacement infantry troops in Europe, the U.S. Army called for volunteers to fill infantry positions. The call was opened to all races. About 5,000 African American men volunteered, and 2,500 were accepted, forming fifty-three platoons (led by white officers).

On July 26, 1948, President Harry S. Truman signed Executive Order 9981, which called on all American armed forces to provide equal treatment and opportunities without regard to race, color, religion, or national origin.

Faced with this discrimination, some African Americans walked away at the recruiting door. The eminent historian Dr. John Hope Franklin once described his attempt to volunteer for an office position with the U.S. Navy.

When he was asked about his skills, Dr. Franklin replied that he could type, manage an office, and take shorthand. And then he added, "'And, oh, yes, I have a Ph.D. in history from Harvard.'

"The recruiter then said, 'You have everything but [the right] color.'"

Dr. Franklin replied, "'Well, I thought there was an emergency, but obviously there's not, so I bid you a good day.'

"And I vowed that day that they would not get me, because they did not deserve me. If I was able—physically, mentally, every other kind of way, able and willing to serve my country—and my country turned me down on the basis of color, then my country did not deserve me."

LOOK, LISTEN, REMEMBER: To read more about African Americans in the army in World War II, including six soldiers who were (eventually) awarded the Medal of Honor, visit the U.S. Army Center of Military History: http://www.history.army.mil/html/topics/afam/index.html. Additional resources about African Americans in World War II are listed in the Quartermaster's Department at the back.

REPORTER'S NOTEBOOK

Fog, Blackouts, and Courage

In the early months of 1944, American newspaper journalist Richard L. Tobin crossed the Atlantic to cover the war from London. After just one day at sea, thick North Atlantic fog forced the troop transport ship he was sailing on to stop and wait it out.

The engines were shut off. Danger seemed to lurk all around them. At any moment, the ship could be attacked by marauding German U-Boats.

"In war, one does not use a foghorn; yet we are in the convoy lanes and collision is a momentary threat," Tobin wrote. "The bows of one freight ship after another, bound empty for America, can be seen emerging from the fog, sometimes as close as one hundred and fifty feet away. The ghostly ships come from all angles.

"Idling troop ships are like sitting ducks to hunters. But where a hunter won't shoot a sitting duck, a U-Boat or a German will shoot at anything."

★

In London, Tobin found living conditions far worse than in America. Meat and vegetables were in short supply. Although beef was nearly impossible to get, horsemeat could be had at a shilling a pound—if you could bear to eat it. And as for the meat: Not all the meat was, well, meat.

"The sausages are a joke, filled with sawdust," Tobin said. "Meat is rationed to one decent meal a week. The rest of the time you gulp down flat, doughy mouthfuls that defy identity."

The worst part for the American, though, was getting used to severe blackout conditions. It made Tobin realize how much the British people had endured since September 1940, when German bombers first began their attacks.

"The blackout comes increasingly late, and thank God for it. For when the blackout comes (in winter as early as 3:30 in the afternoon) the bombers come, or at any rate the threat of death," he said. "The blackness is a shroud dropped upon the shoulders of ten millions, the largest city in the world, as completely as the lid on a coffin or the cap on a well."

One night the reporter walked home from his office in that darkness. "This is a timeless world, this black world of mine, for I am the only one in it as I walk. The other shadows are in worlds of their own . . . Only at night in the blackout am I afraid as a child is afraid, afraid of unknown things."

Even though attacks had lessened, many people still slept on underground platforms of London's Tube, or subway. "There, indeed, they sleep, they eat, they talk, and somehow live their nights in an atmosphere of smells, bad air, mosquitoes, infection and unending noise," said Tobin. "Tube sleepers reached a peak on September 27, 1940, at the pinnacle of the blitz. As many as 177,000 Londoners slept far below ground that night . . .

"It took real courage to stand it."

CHAPTER 3

MEET THE SUPREME COMMANDER (AND HIS DOG)

President Franklin D. Roosevelt couldn't make up his mind.

By the fall of 1943, planning for Operation Overlord was proceeding nonstop. September turned into October, then November. The largest military invasion in history was mere months away—but the massive effort had no one at its head. The other Allied leaders had agreed the Supreme Commander would be an American, but Roosevelt still hadn't named one.

At the Tehran Conference of Allied leaders at the end of November, the Soviet Union's premier, Joseph Stalin, couldn't contain his impatience. His nation had joined the Allies after Germany attacked it in June 1941. The effort to push Germany back had already cost the Soviets millions of lives. Everyone knew a Soviet defeat would be catastrophic, enabling "Germany to dominate the whole of Europe . . . and probably force England to capitulate," observed historian Gordon Harrison. For this reason, "it followed that every possible effort should be made by the Western Powers to insure that Russia was not defeated."

Operation Overlord would open a second front in Europe, drawing off German forces and relieving pressure on the

Allied leaders Stalin, Roosevelt, and Churchill at the Tehran Conference, November 28–December 1, 1943.

embattled Soviet troops. But since similar plans had been floated for 1942, Stalin was anxious that his partners wouldn't follow through this time. The lack of a commander was a troubling sign, prompting Stalin to demand, " 'Who will command Overlord?' "

The leading contender for Supreme Commander was General George C. Marshall, Chairman of the Joint Chiefs of Staff. But Roosevelt was reluctant to lose Marshall's expertise and advice in Washington, D.C. There was only one other candidate acceptable to Churchill, and a few days later, Roosevelt flew to Tunis in North Africa to deliver the news personally.

" 'Well, Ike . . . you are going to command Overlord,' " the president said.

"Ike," as he was popularly known then and now, was, of course, General Dwight D. Eisenhower.

In 1943, the future 34th president of the United States was a fifty-three-year-old general with exceptional organizational, political, and military experience. Born on October 14, 1890, in Denison, Texas, Eisenhower was raised in Abilene, Kansas. After graduating from West Point Academy in 1915, he had embarked on a successful military career.

After Pearl Harbor, Eisenhower served in Washington, D.C., as a key planner of American war strategy under George C. Marshall, who recognized his talents and promoted him. In June 1942, Eisenhower was appointed Commanding General of the European Theatre of Operations based in London. In November that same year, he left England to lead Allied campaigns in North Africa and in Sicily. Although the Italian campaign, begun in the fall of 1943, was expected to be a long one, Eisenhower could arguably now be spared for something larger. (In Italy, the Allies had to fight not only the Germans, but bad weather and difficult, mountainous terrain, resulting in slow progress. In the end, it would take twenty months. But Italy also kept portions of the German Army occupied—and away from France.)

Clearly, the invasion of France was the highest priority. In fact, if Roosevelt selected Marshall to head Overlord, Eisenhower expected to be sent back to a staff position in Washington, a prospect he didn't much relish.

Eisenhower liked action and being in the thick of it. Commanding Overlord was exactly what he'd wanted.

★

Eisenhower was scheduled to report for his new post in London in January 1944, after a brief stop in the United States to see his wife, Mamie. Eisenhower decided to spend his final week in the field visiting Allied troops fighting in Italy.

Always eager to take good care of his boss, Eisenhower's close aide Harry Butcher located an old stone hunting lodge in the forested hills near Caserta, thirty-five miles from the front lines, to serve as a temporary headquarters. Butcher was enthusiastic about finding a relaxing retreat, a dream house complete with a fireplace.

But shortly after they arrived, another Eisenhower aide, Sergeant Mickey McKeogh, came rushing down the stairs in fright. He was carrying Telek, Ike's black Scottish terrier, who'd encountered an unwanted stranger in the general's bathroom.

Running to investigate, Butcher discovered a rat perched on Ike's toilet seat. The newly named Supreme Commander wasn't about to tolerate the intruder. Butcher recorded in his diary that Ike put on his glasses, "growled that the light was bad, and carefully took aim and shot."

The first shot missed; the rat jumped to a pipe. Ike was not defeated. "He again took careful aim and shot. He clipped its tail. The rat jumped a foot higher, clinging to the pipe. Again Ike shot. The rat tumbled to the floor after a final shot and lay quivering."

It was, perhaps, a good omen. The Supreme Commander had proved victorious.

DISPATCH

Telek: The (Not So) Supreme Dog

Like other U.S. presidents, including Franklin D. Roosevelt and Barack Obama, Dwight D. Eisenhower was fond of dogs. He received Telek from his staff as a birthday present in 1942, and the two became inseparable.

According to aide Harry Butcher, the name "Telek" came from "Telegraph Cottage," the rented residence outside London where Eisenhower was staying then. Butcher's diary of his three years with Eisenhower is full of stories about the exasperating Telek, who was apparently quite difficult to housebreak. Butcher recounted one morning in Algiers when he stepped out of bed, "and my foot landed in the middle of Telek's puddle." He added, "This war is hell."

Despite this, Butcher had purchased a second dog, named Caacie (pronounced "khaki," her name stood for "Canine Auxiliary Air Corps"). When Telek and Caacie met it was "love at first sight."

However, their offspring, Junior and Rubev, were apparently no better than their father at the potty business. Eisenhower and Butcher brought the two pups back to the United States in early 1944 during Ike's brief visit. The men's wives met them in a hotel in Washington, D.C. The first thing the dogs did was to piddle on the fancy carpets.

★

Ike's dog traveled with him to his various posts. The general was so fond of Telek that when he returned to London to take up his duties as Supreme Commander, he considered asking for a relaxation of Great Britain's six-month quarantine law. Butcher advised against asking for favors, so Telek had to endure months in a kennel. This was rather hard on his master who admitted it was like "'locking up a part of my heart.'"

On Monday, January 24, 1944, Ike went to visit his furry friend, who'd become quite famous by this time. When the press showed up, Ike chided Harry for allowing it. In his usual tongue-in-cheek style, Butcher observed, "However, I cannot control news interest and I have assured him that no one has ever been hurt for loving a dog, but he wants his love life with Telek kept private.

"However, he is rapidly learning that there is little privacy available in the life of *the* Supreme Commander."

BRIEFING

Secrecy, Deception, and Crossword Clues

The Supreme Commander may not have been able to keep his affection for his dog private, but from the outset, secrecy and deception were vital components of the success of D-Day.

As early as July 1943, Overlord planners decided that a cover operation needed to be implemented side by side with preparation for the actual invasion. An overall deception plan, with the code name Bodyguard, covered all Allied operations against Germany for 1944. Under that umbrella was Fortitude, code name for deception activities related to the invasion. It had three primary goals:

1. To make Germany believe the main assault would take place in or near the Pas-de-Calais area.
2. To keep the enemy in doubt as to the date and time of the invasion.
3. To keep German land and air forces contained in or near the Pas-de-Calais for at least fourteen days.

Fortitude included a number of tactical strategies. Double agents and inaccurate leaks of information were used to try to persuade German intelligence the Allies would need more time to prepare an assault, and, therefore, wouldn't launch an invasion until late summer.

One ingenious aspect of Fortitude involved the construction of a false army both on paper and in real life with the use of inflatable tanks and landing craft. Under the leadership of General George S. Patton, a fictitious unit of infantry and armored divisions was created. In order to further try to persuade Germany that Calais was the target, the phantom force (complete with its own insignia) was stationed near Dover, the closest English city across the Channel.

Dummy lighting was even erected around Dover to give the impression it would be the main embarkation site. Inflatable tanks and landing craft were also used to help fool any German reconnaissance planes flying overhead.

As the invasion date drew closer, the need for secrecy grew in intensity. There were some famous security scares, including the mysterious appearance in newspaper crossword puzzles of code words associated with D-Day, including the terms *Omaha, Utah, Mulberry,* and even *Overlord* itself.

Military authorities questioned the man who created the clues, a teacher in Surrey, England. He turned out to be innocent. Apparently the teacher routinely polled his students for ideas—and the boys were hearing the words (without knowing their meaning) from American soldiers stationed nearby.

An officer in London who had too much to drink caused a scare as well. On May 23, 1944, Eisenhower aide Harry Butcher recorded in his diary: "Another case of loose talk has been reported to Ike. This time it concerns a naval officer who is said to have mentioned at a cocktail party places and dates of the assaults . . . Ike said this breach of security is so serious it practically gives him the shakes."

LOOK, LISTEN, REMEMBER: Read about the "Crossword Panic" at http://www.historic-uk.com/HistoryUK/HistoryofBritain/Crossword-Panic-of-1944/.

. . . he which hath no stomach to this fight,

Let him depart.

WILLIAM SHAKESPEARE,
***HENRY V*, ACT 4, SCENE 3**

PART 2

THE GODS OF WAR

"Failure would have brought disaster of the most crushing dimension. It is told that even the great British lion-heart [Churchill] lost many an hour's sleep . . . tortured by thoughts of the Channel clogged with British and American corpses."

FREDERICK MORGAN, Overlord planner

" 'I thank the gods of war we went when we did.' "

DWIGHT D. EISENHOWER,
Supreme Commander, Allied Expeditionary Force

CHAPTER 4

THE WEATHERMAN

The names of many of those who helped make D-Day a success are etched in history books: Eisenhower, Roosevelt, Churchill, a host of generals and officers, and a heartbreakingly long list of soldiers, sailors, paratroopers, and specialists, some of whom lost their lives that day.

You have to look a bit harder to find the name of J. M. (James Martin) Stagg. He wasn't even officially in the military. Yet one day in October 1943, this forty-three-year-old Scotsman found himself on a path that would bring him into the inner circle of key decision-makers.

Stagg, a civilian meteorologist, was called into a secret meeting with his boss, who told him an invasion of France was in the works. The military was looking for someone to advise the Supreme Commander on weather conditions. Stagg assumed he was being asked to recommend names. But that wasn't it.

"'I intend to nominate you,'" his boss told him.

A few weeks later, Stagg entered Norfolk House, which would soon be occupied by Eisenhower and his SHAEF (Supreme Headquarters Allied Expeditionary Force) staff. It was a confusing place, especially to a nonmilitary man.

James Martin Stagg.

There were "Unpronounceable groups of letters on each door of the long corridors," Stagg said. Once he figured out the letters he realized he was seeing the incredible scope of the operation, including departments for "beach landing craft, glider and parachute movements, long-range naval gunnery, heavy bombing, communications, security, post-invasion plans and all the multifarious services needed for supplying food, fuel and armaments for a vast invasion force."

Stagg's first task was to discover what sort of weather would be ideal for the invasion. Each group seemed to have different needs. Take the matter of tides: The army wanted to land the first assault team at high tide; the navy wanted low tide so beach obstacles could be seen and destroyed by a wave of demolition experts.

(In the end, planners compromised with beginning the assault on a rising tide. For instance, at Omaha, H-Hour was set for 6:30 a.m., one hour after low tide. Demolition experts would be among the first to land. Their job would be to destroy metal beach defense obstacles that would still be visible then. Later, as the tide rose, these lethal objects designed to damage the underside of boats would be covered and impossible to see. The next wave of landing craft was scheduled for 7:00 a.m., with more to follow at ten-minute intervals.)

Realizing perfect conditions would be impossible, Stagg rephrased the question: " 'What are the least favorable conditions in which your forces can operate successfully?' "

Everyone agreed they needed a period of several days when the weather was "quiet," rather than stormy. Heavy mist or fog wasn't good for landing troops at night by glider or parachute. Low winds and calm seas would reduce the danger to soldiers disembarking from landing craft. Good visibility would be important, too, so ships offshore could locate and bomb onshore targets.

Still, reflected Stagg, "If every one of the requirements that I had been given was to be insisted on it was easy to deduce that Overlord might not get under way for another hundred years or more."

In the end, Stagg decided to take all he'd heard and come up with the most essential criteria. He also examined past weather records, which revealed some important information:

The chances for optimum weather conditions were twice as good in June as in May. As it turned out, he wasn't the only one thinking about changing the invasion date of May 1.

James Stagg got his first glimpse of the Supreme Commander at SHAEF shortly after Dwight D. Eisenhower arrived in London in mid-January 1944. Mounting a platform wearing a crisp, well-ironed uniform, Eisenhower addressed a group of officers. Looking around, Stagg realized he was the only one *not* in uniform. (Eventually he was given one along with a temporary commission as a Group Captain.)

Ike made a favorable impression on the weather forecaster. "With a broad smile, an athletic movement like a gymnastic instructor about to give his first lesson . . . he looked in first-class mental and physical condition," said Stagg. Stagg was also impressed with the acceleration of activity at SHAEF headquarters: Eisenhower was forging ahead.

In fact, the new Supreme Commander was making critical changes and improvements to the original invasion plan. These included strengthening the actual assault forces by adding two more divisions, for a total of five. (Allied infantry divisions numbered between 15,000 to 20,000 men on D-Day, while airborne divisions were about half that size.) Adding more divisions would require more time, and on Eisenhower's recommendation to the Combined Chiefs of Staff, D-Day was postponed to a "favorable period" in June, with the final decision left to the Supreme Commander.

Eisenhower, as well as British general Bernard Montgomery, who would take overall command of all ground forces, recommended expanding the number of beachhead landing sites. There would now be five, spanning a total of about fifty miles: two British (codenamed Sword and Gold), one Canadian (Juno), and two American (Omaha and Utah).

As far as weather, Eisenhower had new requirements in that arena, too: He wanted assurance four days in advance that the weather on D-Day itself would not prohibit the landings. He also wanted a reliable weather forecast for two or three days following the invasion.

Stagg was flabbergasted. He even came close to warning out loud that "it could not be done. All the meteorological brains of the U.S. and British (and any other) weather services put together could not produce a reliable forecast of English weather" for so long a time period. This was, of course, long before weather satellites. With the instruments of the day, reliable weather forecasting more than a day or two ahead wasn't feasible.

Stagg decided to remain silent. Maybe, he thought, when the actual time came, the requirements would be relaxed.

Or maybe not.

BRIEFING

Choosing D-Day: A General and a Historian Weigh In

"One of the knottiest problems that affected all levels of planning was timing the assault—the selection of D-day and H-hour," observed historian Samuel Eliot Morison, who wrote a fifteen-volume history of U.S. naval operations during World War II.

Weather, of course, was a key factor. So was the length of the day. "It was essential that initial assault forces cross the English Channel during darkness, and the problem was to get enough darkness."

The tides were especially critical. Since there were extreme variations between high and low tides on the Normandy beaches, General Omar Bradley, commander of the U.S. First Army on D-Day, observed that in choosing D-Day Eisenhower was "at the mercy of the tides."

After much deliberation, planners decided to set H-Hour at a rising tide. The assault would begin with demolition teams that would be allotted thirty minutes to begin destroying beach defenses before the water became too deep. Landing craft would follow at high tide. This would allow boats to come in close to shore and reduce the distance soldiers needed to cross while exposed to fire and out in the open.

The lunar cycle left only six days each month when these tidal conditions were right. "The first three fell on June 5, 6, and 7," said Bradley. "If bad weather forestalled invasion on all three days, the assault would have to be put off for two weeks. If bad weather again prevented our going during that second June phase of the moon, there was no alternative but to delay the invasion until July."

A long delay would present additional challenges. Once the assault troops were briefed, it would be hard to ensure that more than a hundred thousand people could keep a secret for another month. And according to Bradley, that wasn't the worst of it.

"Even more frightening than the problem of security was the likely effect of a month's delay on Allied operations in France," he said. "Not only would that long a postponement shorten by one third the time left for our summer campaign, but it would shove us one month nearer the deadline for seizing a Channel port before the advent of stormy weather.

"We were told we could not bank on the Channel for beach unloading after September 1. If the Germans were to hang on to Cherbourg for 50 or 60 days after a July D-day landing, we might be seriously pressed for wintertime maintenance of our troops ashore."

In the end, wrote Morison, "The final choice, like the plan itself, had to be a compromise."

CHAPTER 5

"D-DAY CALLING"

It was the end of May, and for soldiers like David Kenyon Webster, the waiting was unbearable. He'd been in England now for eight months, a paratrooper in the 506th Parachute Infantry, 101st Airborne Division.

Then, at last, something happened. He and the others were herded onto buses to the train—the train that would take them farther south, to a staging area near the English Channel. And across the Channel lay France. As the train passed green meadows, brooks, and small towns and villages, David imagined the train's whistle refrain:

" 'D-Day calling, D-Day calling, D-Day calling.' "

D-Day was calling, and the Allies were ready to answer that call. The long months of planning, production, drills, and training had been to one purpose. More than 175,000 men—American, British, and Canadian—were gathered in the south of England. Of

Father Francis L. Sampson (left).

these, 156,000 would take part in the first assault on D-Day. A fleet of 5,000 ships lay in readiness, along with 50,000 vehicles and 11,000 planes—all prepared to undertake one of the greatest military operations in history.

Everywhere he looked, Father Francis L. Sampson could sense anticipation. Father Sampson was a Roman Catholic priest and chaplain to the 501st Parachute Infantry Regiment, 101st Airborne Division. The men he served—he sometimes called them "his boys"—were headed for Utah Beach.

"The war room at division headquarters was under guard; airfields were beehives of activity; long convoys of trucks were heading for the southern ports of the isle; we had the most realistic dry run yet, traveling to the airfields in trains, loading the planes and boarding them fully equipped."

Rumors were flying fast and furious, and Father Sampson found his chapel fuller than normal. There was a seriousness of purpose in the men's faces, reflected in the longer letters home—serious letters, as soldiers' thoughts turned to the action to come and loved ones left behind.

"We were ready," Father Sampson observed, "as ready, we felt, as we ever would be."

He sensed that same spirit when General Eisenhower came to visit troops before the big day. "As General Eisenhower passed among the men with his friendly grin and informal chats, it is difficult to say whether he gave them more confidence than they gave him as they grinned back."

Ike was, thought Sampson, the GI's "right guy," who

"refused to show in his face the terrible burden of the decision for which he accepted full responsibility, nor did he betray a certain apprehension he must have felt."

Photographer Robert Capa was getting ready to travel with troops. (He would provide some of the most searing shots of Omaha Beach—and of war—ever taken.) "Every piece of our clothing had to be gasproofed, waterproofed, and camouflaged in the many various colors of our future landscape."

The famous war correspondent Ernie Pyle recalled that at his briefing, all the war correspondents were told to prepare a

A Catholic chaplain conducts Mass for D-Day troops about to embark for Normandy.

will. "Everybody in the room laughed—you know, one of those cackly, mirthless laughs of a man who is a little sick at his stomach."

The journalists laughed even harder when, after they were told to take only what they could carry on their backs, with the rest of the luggage to be forwarded to them later in France, a novice asked whether they should carry their steel helmets and gas masks or not.

Obviously, that steel helmet wouldn't do him much good packed away.

The war correspondents didn't know to which unit they'd be assigned—or when the final call would come. And though they tried to maintain a sense of humor, there were times when they grappled with the danger before them.

"And in more pensive moments we also conjectured on our chances of coming through alive," reflected Pyle, who was tragically killed on assignment before the end of the war. "I began having terrible periods of depression and often would dream hideous dreams.

"All the time fear lay blackly deep upon our consciousness. It bore down on our hearts like an all-consuming weight."

Like the soldiers, the war correspondents had a battle kit that included "a shovel to dig foxholes, seasickness capsules, a carton of cigarettes, a medical kit, and rations." In fact, Ernie Pyle heard one officer joke that the Germans would have to come to them, since they were so loaded down with equipment it was hard to move.

The journalists had been living in hotels or flats in London, and, they agreed, they'd all gotten a little soft. But soon they would be starting "the old horrible life we had known for so long—sleeping on the ground, only cold water, foxholes, and dirt.

"We were off to war again."

REPORTER'S NOTEBOOK

American Women Reporters

American women also covered World War II, continuing a long tradition of female war correspondents. In 1846, Margaret Fuller became the first European correspondent for the *New York Tribune* covering conflicts in Italy.

Novelist Mary Roberts Rinehart reported on World War I, as did Peggy Hull, the first woman correspondent officially accredited by the war department. Women who reported from the field in World War II included Helen Kirkpatrick, Iris Carpenter, Catherine Coyne, and Mary Welsh.

Welsh described the moment she found out about D-Day. "I had an arrangement with a military friend . . . that he would telephone me as soon as he knew that the invasion was launched. We were joshing one evening about what confrontations would 'curl our hair' and since he thought his telephone was probably tapped by either British or American sleuths, we decided that his message to me would be something about hair curlers . . .

"At about 4 a.m. on June 6 my military friend rang to say, 'Take the curlers out of your hair and get going,' I had no curlers but I got going."

Welsh didn't actually get to Normandy until July. But reporters such as Lee Carson and Martha Gellhorn weren't inclined to wait for permission. Carson, who is credited with being the first Allied war correspondent to enter Paris after its liberation in

August 1944, is said to have talked a pilot into giving her a seat on a plane on D-Day, making her the first woman reporter to reach Normandy.

Martha Gellhorn snuck on board a hospital ship a day or two after D-Day, traveling with six American nurses newly arrived in England. "There were four hundred and twenty-two bunks covered with new blankets; and a bright, clean, well-equipped operating room, never before used. Great cans marked 'Whole Blood' stood on the decks. Plasma bottles and supplies of drugs and bales of bandages were stored in handy places.

"Everything was ready and any moment the big empty hospital ship would be leaving for France."

LOOK, LISTEN, REMEMBER: To read more about Lee Carson, Martha Gellhorn, and other women war correspondents, visit the American Air Museum in Britain online at http://www.americanairmuseum.com/person/240041; BBC news at http://www.bbc.com/news/magazine-27677889; and the Library of Congress online exhibit Women Come to the Front: War, Women, and Opportunity at https://www.loc.gov/exhibits/wcf/wcf0002.html.

CHAPTER 6

THE DECISION TO GO

The Supreme Commander still had one vital decision to make. He had tentatively chosen Monday, June 5, as D-Day. But that date *could* change—depending on the weather.

At the end of May, Eisenhower and his staff left London for the Advance Command Post at Southwick House, a stately mansion in the south of England closer to the embarkation points. In order to provide weather briefings, chief meteorological officer Stagg would go, too.

He and Lieutenant Colonel Donald Norton Yates, chief of weather services for U.S. Strategic Air Force in Europe and a member of the SHAEF staff, would have camp beds in a tent among the trees. The two men got along well—a good thing, too. Together they'd hold twice daily phone conferences with teams of American and British weather forecasters, and then present a consensus to the Supreme Commander and the other leaders.

But as the date set for the invasion grew closer, it soon became clear the forecasters couldn't agree on anything.

★

CHAPTER 6

By Friday evening, June 2, Stagg felt sick as he grasped the phone and listened to the other weather experts debate the forecast for Monday.

"In less than half an hour I was expected to present to General Eisenhower an 'agreed' forecast for the next five days which covered the time of launching of the greatest military operation ever mounted," he said. "No two of the expert participants in the discussion could agree on the likely weather for even the next 24 hours."

While some of the experts were optimistic, Stagg was not. To him, the weather patterns looked ominous. He knew that poor weather conditions could mean more deaths—and total failure. And so when he entered the briefing room, Stagg went with his gut: The prospects for Monday weren't good. General Eisenhower pressed. Would Tuesday offer better conditions? Wednesday? Stagg couldn't say.

Twenty-four hours later, Stagg had no better news. The weather still looked unsettled, with winds and with low visibility, though at least now, the other forecasters agreed with Stagg. As he gave his report, Stagg could sense the gloom as he spoke. "General Eisenhower sat motionless, with his head slightly to one side resting on his hand, staring steadily toward me."

The next meeting was set for 4:15 a.m. Sunday. Some ships had already sailed. If D-Day was to be postponed, they would have to be turned around, subjecting the sailors to more hours of seasickness.

"The tension in the room was palpable," recalled Stagg of that early morning meeting.

At Eisenhower's nod, he gave his assessment: The bad forecast hadn't changed. General Eisenhower made his decision. The invasion would *not* take place Monday. Postponing such a huge operation wasn't an easy thing to do.

"Within an hour hundreds of vessels and tens of thousands of troops would be turned back in their tracks. For at least 24 hours the whole vast operation was in a state of suspension," reflected Stagg. Worse still, if by Sunday night the forecast was no better, the whole assault would have to be put back two weeks for the tides and moon to be right.

General Eisenhower spent most of Sunday alone in his trailer or pacing as he scanned the skies. At one point, he took a walk with reporter Merrill "Red" Mueller, who said it seemed to him each of the general's four stars must " 'have weighed a ton.' "

And then James Stagg spied a glimmer of hope. Poring over weather charts on Sunday, he noticed conditions changing rapidly: There might be a break in the stormy weather on Tuesday between the passage of a cold front and a low depression.

That could mean an interlude of fair weather—an interlude long enough to allow the first critical assault landings on Tuesday, June 6. Invading that day would also have the benefit of surprise. Given Monday's rain and wind, the Germans wouldn't expect an assault the next day.

It would be up to Stagg to make the case. "If the Supreme Commander could be persuaded to take advantage of it, it might be a heaven-sent break."

First, though, he had to consult with the other forecasters. And if Stagg thought they'd share his interpretation of the charts, he was wrong. At the first phone conference on Sunday, experts spent two hours arguing about the data. Stagg persevered, making his arguments. A few hours later, the others had come around to his view.

There probably had never been a more important weather prediction in history as the one James Stagg made on that Sunday evening. If he was wrong, and the invasion failed because of weather, the fate of Europe hung in the balance.

Stagg presented his forecast to Eisenhower and the others, declaring, " 'I am quite confident.' "

General Eisenhower turned to Bernard Montgomery, commander of all Allied ground forces. " 'Do you see any reason why we should not go on Tuesday?' "

Stagg remembered Montgomery's answer: " 'No, I would say—*Go*.' "

Stagg and Yates withdrew but waited in the hall in case they might be needed again. They hadn't been standing there long when Eisenhower appeared. " 'Well, Stagg,' he said, 'we're putting it on again; for heaven's sake hold the weather to what you told us and don't bring any more bad news.' "

Very early on Monday morning, Stagg confirmed his forecast once more. Eisenhower's decision would stand. There would be no turning around. As dawn broke, Yates and Stagg returned to their tent, exhausted but awake. "We could not sleep, Yates and I, but we knew we had now done all we could do for the great operation."

Captain James M. Stagg has been called one of the "unsung heroes" of D-Day, someone Eisenhower had learned to trust: " 'a man of sharp mind and soft speech, detached, resolute, courageous.' "

After the war, Stagg observed that new developments in technology and weather forecasting would have transformed the decision-making process during those fraught days of early June. But as it turned out, he *had* been right. June 6 was one of the best—and only—days where weather conditions favored an assault.

On June 19, a ferocious, unexpected storm hit the beaches of Normandy, destroying the Mulberry harbor offshore near Omaha Beach and damaging many vehicles. Noted one historian, "If the invasion had been postponed for two weeks . . . the fleet would have sailed into one of the worst storms in Channel history."

After the storm, Eisenhower sent James Stagg a note of gratitude from France, which included the words, " 'I thank the gods of war we went when we did.' "

DISPATCH

Ike's Other Message

On the evening of Monday, June 5, Dwight D. Eisenhower visited paratroopers of the 101st Airborne Division as they prepared to make the jump into Normandy.

"Ike wandered through them, stepping over packs, guns, and a variety of equipment such as only paratroop people can devise, chinning with this and that one. All were put at ease," recalled aide Harry Butcher.

Eisenhower's Order of the Day was handed to each soldier, sailor, and airman. In it, he wrote, "I have full confidence in your courage, devotion to duty and skill in battle. We will accept nothing less than full Victory!"

But the Supreme Commander had also composed another message—a message that, thankfully, never had to be used. On July 11, he gave it to Butcher.

"This afternoon Ike called me into his office and handed me a sheet of notepaper on which he had scribbled a message," recalled Butcher. "He said he had found it in his wallet. After reading it, I told him I wanted it. He reluctantly assented, saying that he had written one in [a] similar vein for every amphibious operation but had secretly torn up each one. The note:

"'Our landings in the Cherbourg-Havre area have failed to gain a satisfactory foothold and I have withdrawn the troops.

My decision to attack at this time and place was based on the best information available. The troops, the air, and the Navy did all that bravery and devotion to duty could do. If any blame or fault attaches to the attempt it is mine alone.'"

Supreme Commander Dwight D. Eisenhower gives the order of the day to paratroopers.

READER'S INVASION BRIEFING

Overview of Overlord

OPERATION OVERLORD: Operation Overlord plan took more than fourteen months to complete and involved hundreds of staff, all of whom worked without the benefit of today's computers and technological tools. The plan called for an initial assault force numbering nearly 160,000, followed by two million Allied soldiers to be deployed in France in the two months following D-Day.

Prior to H-Hour, which began at 6:30 a.m. and varied at each beach, approximately 13,000 paratroopers and glider troops attempted to land behind German lines to help prepare for the ground soldiers. (Overlord planners used Double British Summer Time, or GMT+2, a special wartime daylight saving system that set clocks ahead two hours.) About 5,000 vessels of all types were deployed to carry troops, supplies, vehicles, and equipment across the English Channel. The mission was supported in the air by more than 11,000 aircraft dropping 13,000 bombs.

INVASION LOCATION: The coast of Normandy in the Bay of the Seine, a wide, north-facing inlet of the English Channel, shaped more or less like a rectangle. It sits south of the port of Calais. The total landing area was about fifty miles long.

One way to envision the invasion area is to hold out your left hand, parallel to the floor with your palm facing you and your thumb pointing to the ceiling. Your thumb is the Cotentin Peninsula, with Cherbourg at the top and Utah Beach at the base. Stretching along the top of your index finger toward your fingertip are the other four beaches: Omaha, Gold, Juno, and Sword. Also near the tip would be the city of Caen and the two bridges leading to it. Your hand itself is France. The D-Day objective was to reach a few miles inland in most places. If we call each of your fingers ten miles, then you might think of it as the width of one finger—in other words—off the beach and a little way inland.

PARTICIPANTS: Allied forces included American, British, and Canadian troops, with some Norwegian and Free France participants.

FIVE LANDING BEACHES: There were five landing beaches, from east to west: Sword, Juno, Gold, Omaha, and Utah. Utah Beach, on the Cotentin Peninsula (sometimes called the Cherbourg Peninsula), was the most isolated, westernmost sector, separated from the five-mile stretch of Omaha Beach by the mouths of two rivers, the Douve and the Vire. One key objective after landing was to capture and clear the port of Cherbourg, since the Mulberry harbors were temporary solutions.

BRITISH AND CANADIAN FORCES: Sword, Juno, and Gold

SWORD BEACH was the easternmost landing site and closest to the city of Caen, about nine miles away. The British Army was

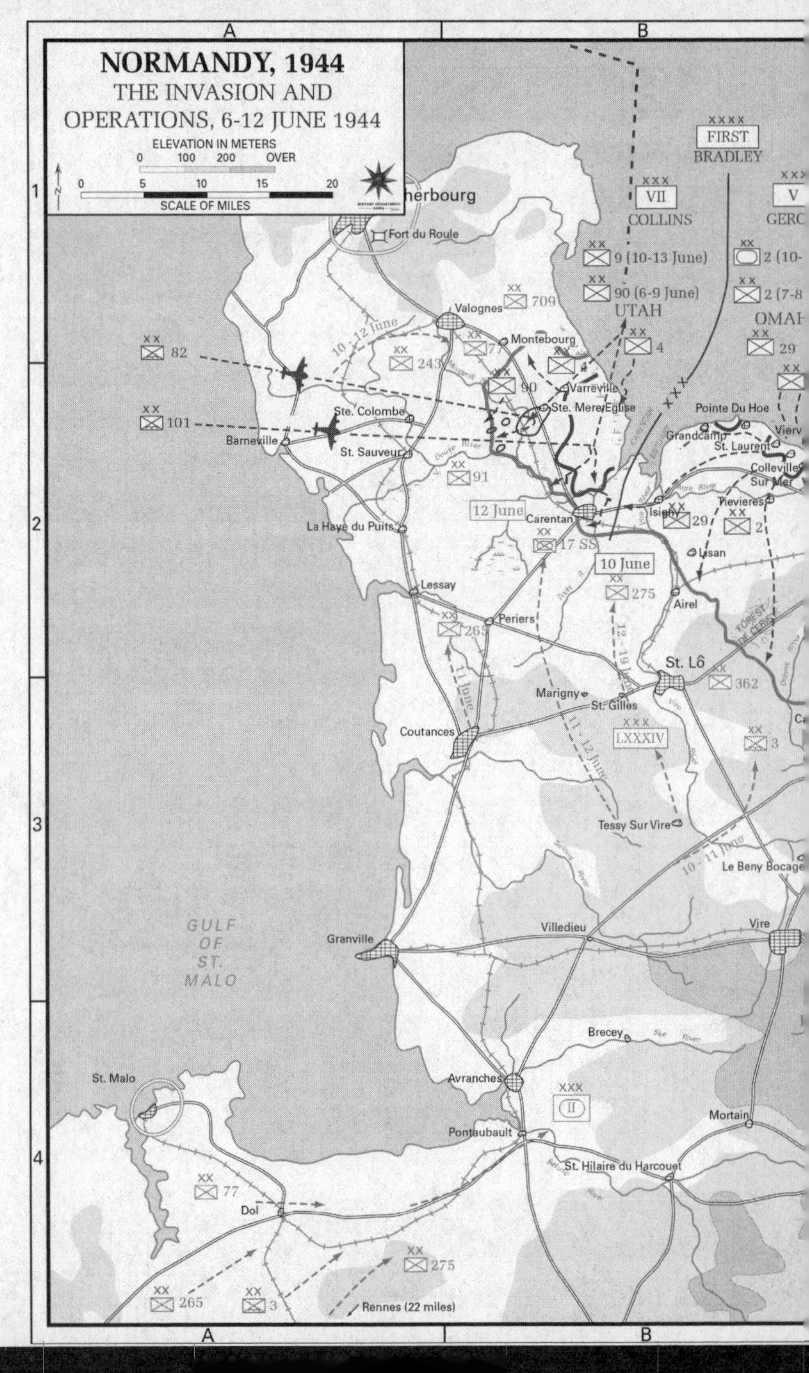

Overview of ... Operations.

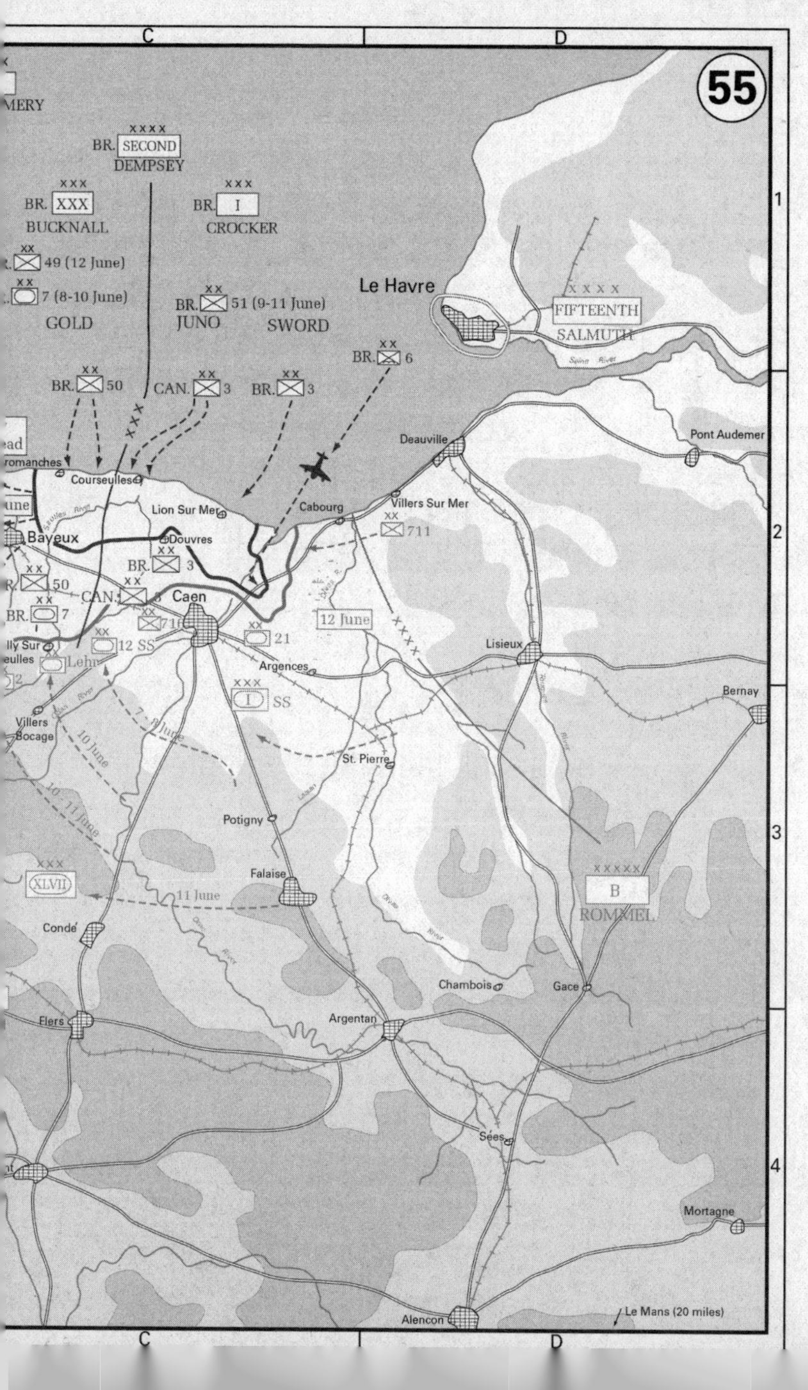
55
C
D
BR. SECOND
DEMPSEY
BR. XXX
BUCKNALL
BR. I
CROCKER
49 (12 June)
7 (8-10 June)
BR. 51 (9-11 June)
GOLD
JUNO
SWORD
Le Havre
FIFTEENTH
SALMUTH
Seine River
BR. 6
BR. 50
CAN. 3
BR. 3
Deauville
Pont Audemer
Courseulles
Lion Sur Mer
Cabourg
Villers Sur Mer
711
Bayeux
Douvres
BR. 3
50
CAN.
Caen
BR. 7
716
12 June
21
12 SS
Lehr
Argences
Lisieux
I SS
Bernay
Villers Bocage
7 - 8 June
10 June
St. Pierre
10 - 11 June
Potigny
XLVII
Falaise
11 June
B
ROMMEL
Condé
Chambois
Gace
Flers
Argentan
Sées
Mortagne
Alencon
Le Mans (20 miles)
1
2
3
4

responsible for taking the five-mile stretch of beach and linking up with Canadians at Juno Beach and American forces from Omaha to the west. While casualties were low on shore, Allies met resistance farther inland.

JUNO BEACH was the second landing site from the east. The six-mile-wide beach was assaulted by Canadians, who took losses in the first wave but succeeded in gaining control. Juno Beach was near a small fishing port, with other villages located inland behind sand dunes. There were houses onshore, occupied by Germans, who were able to fire at troops emerging from the sea, causing high casualties in the first wave. The currents and tides at Juno created difficult conditions for landing craft and tanks, with nearly a third damaged or lost. About 1,200 Canadian soldiers died, out of 21,400 who landed.

By evening, links had been made with the British from Gold Beach to the west, but not with Sword Beach forces. This left a gap of about two miles. A counterattack was launched by the German 21st Panzer Division.

GOLD BEACH Gold Beach lay in the center of the five landing areas. More than five miles long, it included several beach hamlets, with houses containing German defenders. While the wooden houses were vulnerable to bombs and fire, other German guns were located in a concrete bunker on a steep cliff. British infantry carried out the assault at Gold Beach.

(A note to readers: An overview of Omaha and Utah is included here. More detailed briefings also appear prior to the sections devoted to these beaches.)

OMAHA BEACH Omaha was, by far, the deadliest landing site, where Allied soldiers came under unrelenting fire from well-established German defenses. Nine infantry companies were assigned to Omaha. They would come under fire from eighty-five German machine-gun nests, and heavier guns—more than Sword, Juno, and Gold combined. The barriers on the shore were laced with deadly mines.

Not only was Omaha the most heavily defended beach, but tactical errors added to the terrible conditions there. Most of the ships anchored far offshore, meaning that landing craft had to make a slow, dangerous journey through eleven miles of wind and waves. In addition, the prelanding bombings by the Allied air forces had been ineffective, and done little to neutralize German fire power—which was trained relentlessly on soldiers. Finally, Allied intelligence had failed to detect the recent presence of two regiments of the German 352nd Division which had been recently moved into position primarily behind Omaha.

It's no wonder Omaha is sometimes called Hell's Beach.

UTAH BEACH The mission for American troops was to secure and seal off the Cotentin Peninsula, to prevent German reinforcements from moving in, and then to capture the port of Cherbourg, about thirty miles away. Utah Beach was the last landing site added to the Overlord Plan. The initial objectives included taking control of four causeways. These were narrow dirt tracks of high ground over swampy, flooded areas that would allow the soldiers to get off the beach and move inland. The mission also included taking the town of Sainte-Mère-Église and sealing off the base of the Cotentin Peninsula to prevent Germans from sending in reinforcements.

The Utah Beach assault included airborne landings by the 82nd and 101st divisions; the amphibious assault was conducted by troops of the 4th Infantry Division.

LOOK, LISTEN, REMEMBER: You can learn more online about the units that took part in D-Day. At Utah Beach the main forces were the 82nd Airborne Division: http://www.ww2-airborne.us/division/82_overview.html and the 101st Airborne Division: http://www.ww2-airborne.us/18corps/101abn/101_overview.html. The 4th Infantry Division, established in 1917, assaulted Utah Beach: http://www.4thinfantry.org/content/division-history.

At Omaha, the Society of the 1st Infantry Division maintains a website: https://www.1stid.org/historyindex.php. The 29th Infantry Division Historical Society: http://www.29infantrydivision.org/. Descendants of the 2nd Ranger Battalion have a website: http://www.wwiirangers.com/History/History/Battalion%20Pages/2nd%20Rgr%20Bn/second.htm. The Naval History and Heritage Command website includes photos of D-Day: https://www.history.navy.mil/our-collections/photography/wars-and-events/world-war-ii/d-day.html.

GERMAN DEFENSES

Atlantic Wall

As early as December 1941, Adolf Hitler envisioned an "Atlantic Wall," an indestructible line of fortifications and coastal defenses designed to prevent an Allied invasion. Stretching as far north as Norway to as far south as Spain, Hitler's goal was to build concrete structures able to withstand bombing and naval gunfire protecting "a continuous belt of weapons commanding the principal ports and beaches."

In November 1943, Hitler ordered efforts concentrated near the Pas-de-Calais, since the narrow Strait of Dover was considered the most likely invasion site. He also gave Field Marshal Erwin Rommel the task of reinforcing the Atlantic Wall. Rommel envisioned defenses that started with underwater mines, and included beach obstacles, guns, and infantry stationed within several miles of the beach area.

Allied mine sweeping in a vast sea area in the days before the invasion involved nearly 250 vessels from both the British Royal Navy and the U.S. Navy, a task more difficult due to foul weather. On June 5, the USS *Osprey* (AM-56) struck a mine which blew a hole in the forward engine room. "She sank soon after, with a loss of six men, first casualties for the United States Navy in Operation Neptune."

LOOK, LISTEN, REMEMBER: To read more about the German response to D-Day, visit the website of London's Imperial War Museums: http://www.iwm.org.uk/history/the-german-response-to-d-day.

★★★★ DISPATCH ★★★★

Watching History Being Made

As a petty officer in the Women's Royal Naval Service, Jean Watson worked in communications in the Southampton area of England and witnessed the buildup of the naval force.

"The sheer size of the invasion force was mind-boggling," she said later. All the assembly areas "were saturated with Allied troops, tanks, guns and armaments of all shapes and sizes, trucks large and small."

In the signals office, Jean and others were kept busy sending and receiving signals to ships and skippers. And Jean was on duty to send out the final message—the invasion was on.

"Just before going off watch in the morning, my friend and I were given permission to go down to the river to see the last landing craft sail away and I remember thinking, 'I'm watching history being made and I am part of it.'

"I remember too, the awful deathly silence that pervaded the base as we walked back to our quarters. Where there had been thousands of troops, armaments and incessant noise, there was nothing. The tents, the troops, the guns, the ships—all were gone."

SUPREME HEADQUARTERS
ALLIED EXPEDITIONARY FORCE

Soldiers, Sailors and Airmen of the Allied Expeditionary Force!

You are about to embark upon the Great Crusade, toward which we have striven these many months. The eyes of the world are upon you. The hopes and prayers of liberty-loving people everywhere march with you. In company with our brave Allies and brothers-in-arms on other Fronts, you will bring about the destruction of the German war machine, the elimination of Nazi tyranny over the oppressed peoples of Europe, and security for ourselves in a free world.

Your task will not be an easy one. Your enemy is well trained, well equipped and battle-hardened. He will fight savagely.

But this is the year 1944 ! Much has happened since the Nazi triumphs of 1940-41. The United Nations have inflicted upon the Germans great defeats, in open battle, man-to-man. Our air offensive has seriously reduced their strength in the air and their capacity to wage war on the ground. Our Home Fronts have given us an overwhelming superiority in weapons and munitions of war, and placed at our disposal great reserves of trained fighting men. The tide has turned ! The free men of the world are marching together to Victory !

I have full confidence in your courage, devotion to duty and skill in battle. We will accept nothing less than full Victory !

Good Luck ! And let us all beseech the blessing of Almighty God upon this great and noble undertaking.

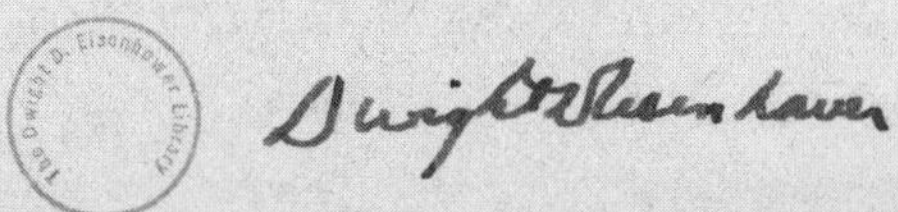

"You are about to embark upon the Great Crusade, toward which we have striven these many months. The eyes of the world are upon you. The hopes and prayers of liberty-loving people everywhere march with you."

GENERAL DWIGHT D. EISENHOWER,
Supreme Commander, Allied Expeditionary Force

PART 3

NIGHT INTO DAY

"'The violence, speed, and power of our initial assault must carry everything with it.'"

GENERAL BERNARD MONTGOMERY

"Of all the themes touched upon by old soldiers who experienced the D-Day invasion, the most common and powerful is the chaos of war. From the perspective of the participants, seemingly nothing on D-Day went according to plan, and yet somehow or other, the invasion worked."

JOSEPH BALKOSKI, historian

"Enlisted men had brought along a wire-haired terrier which belonged to one of the sergeants. It wouldn't have been an invasion without a few dogs along."

ERNIE PYLE, reporter

They're off! The invasion's on!

CHAPTER 7

ACROSS THE CHANNEL BY SEA

"For the first time since Sicily I buckled on a pistol and bent my neck under the weight of a steel helmet," recalled Brigadier General Omar "Brad" Bradley. It was Saturday, June 3, and he was about to board the cruiser USS *Augusta* (CA-31) in Portsmouth, England.

The *Augusta* was the flagship of Rear Admiral Alan Kirk, Commander of the Western Naval Task Force, under the overall command of British Admiral Sir Bertram H. Ramsay. With nearly forty years of navy service, the fifty-six-year-old Kirk was in charge of landing U.S. troops on Omaha and Utah beaches and was the most important American in charge of the Neptune landings.

The *Augusta* would also serve as a command post for Bradley, who commanded troops of the U.S. First Army, slated to land at Utah and Omaha. Bradley had been assigned the skipper's cabin, though it was a fair bet he wouldn't be spending much time there.

Instead, he made his way to a temporary, ten-by-twenty-foot, sheet-metal shed on the afterdeck that would serve as his army war room. A plotting table stood in the center. The walls were papered with maps and charts: a motor map of France, detailed terrain maps of the assault beaches, charts showing the ranges of the enemy coastal guns, and maps pinpointing Allied intelligence on beach defenses and expected locations of German forces.

The first thing Bradley did was check the weather forecast; it didn't look good. There followed anxious hours of waiting. "At midnight I turned in and fell asleep. It was almost six when I was awakened on Sunday, June 4. The weather in Plymouth harbor was soupy and wet; visibility was down and I shivered as I dressed," Bradley said.

An aide walked in with a message: D-Day was postponed for twenty-four hours. Bradley knew the delay would affect his ground forces. "Just as soon as Eisenhower had reached his decision the navy rushed fast destroyers to head off the units that had put to sea and shepherd them back to ports. Now the sharp edge of those troops would be dulled and seasickness would take its toll in another day on the choppy Channel."

Bradley could also imagine how difficult these next hours would be for the Supreme Commander. "For the second time he was to be cornered alone on the single most important yes or no decision of the war. That choice alone might hold the key to success or failure."

Then there came Stagg's heaven-sent weather break and the decision to go. "The Plan had taken over," said Bradley. "For the next 24 hours the fate of the war in Europe was to ride not in the big-hulled command ships but in the wet flat-bottomed craft where GIs were to be seasick on the slippery steel floors as they groaned through the choppy Channel."

★

Monday, June 5. It was time. From the deck of the *Augusta*, Bradley watched an awe-inspiring scene unfold. "Soon the waters of Plymouth harbor churned in a tangle of wakes as hundreds of ships turned obediently into line. As the columns uncoiled toward the Channel the *Augusta* put to sea, rapidly overtaking the awkward, slow-moving craft.

"As far as we could see both fore and aft, ships crowded the British coast line. Overhead their barrage balloons bucked in the wind. Fast destroyers screened us seaward."

Moving toward Normandy.

Bradley realized the unsettled conditions had brought with them another benefit: The usual German naval and air reconnaissance patrols would have been canceled because of the poor weather. This meant the fleet's approach went undetected. "In this capricious turn of the weather we had found a Trojan horse."

"We boarded our ship at midday today after all the troops were loaded," wrote Associated Press correspondent Don Whitehead, one of the reporters who crossed the Channel with the soldiers.

"They lounged on bunks in holds, reading, sleeping or arguing. Some played cards; others rolled dice. In the bottom hold the Army had set up a miniature sponge-rubber model of the beach and countryside which our troops are to attack. Made from hundreds of aerial photographs, the model shows in detail each hedgerow, tree, house, barn, church and lane."

The soldiers' morale was running high, although, Whitehead reflected, "they know what lies ahead of them, that many will die on the beaches of Normandy. They know the Germans are going to throw everything in the book at them to smash the invasion, but still they are grimly confident.

"They feel this is the road back home, home which most of them have not seen in many months."

Traveling with troops headed for Omaha Beach on the USS *Samuel Chase*, photographer Robert Capa divided the soldiers into three groups: those who spent their time playing cards and gambling, some who clustered around models of the terrain doing last-minute planning, and men who hid themselves away to pen letters to loved ones back home.

The soldiers would go ashore with their assigned company. A colonel offered Capa his choice. He was invited to arrive later, in the colonel's boat. Capa's chances of being safe were better in that boat, which would follow the first wave of infantry.

"I am a gambler," wrote Capa later. "I decided to go in with Company E in the first wave."

It was a decision he would never forget.

Soldiers on the USS *Samuel Chase* plan the landing on a model reproduction of Omaha Beach.

On Monday evening, Admiral Kirk asked General Bradley to brief the war correspondents on the First Army's assault plans so they could understand what they were about to witness.

Bradley began, "'To help the amphibious get elements ashore . . . we're going to soften up each of the beaches with an 800-ton carpet bombing. Ten minutes before the first wave touches down, we'll drench Omaha with 8,000 rockets, put another 5,000 on Utah. These rockets should tear up his wire, detonate his mines, and drive him under cover the instant before we land . . . Then promptly at H hour we'll swim 64 tanks ashore . . .'"

The swimming tanks were special DD, dual-drive tanks, which had canvas water wings and an auxiliary propeller. Noted Bradley, "Tactically these DD tanks provided the answer to our need for heavy well-aimed fire against the beach defenses at the moment of touch-down."

If, that is, the DD tanks made it ashore.

Late on Monday, Bradley fell into bed with his shoes on, hoping to catch a few hours' sleep. "Only the lonely wind in the rigging and the wash of water past our sides broke the silence of the night."

To Lieutenant John Mason Brown, also on the *Augusta* as part of Admiral Alan Kirk's staff, those first hours were filled with anxiety and anticipation—and a sense of purpose. "As the skies, until recently so blue, grayed and the Channel became choppy and chill, we on the *Augusta* forgot about the wonders of this English spring. We wanted only to get going.

"Across the Channel were millions of people who in their hearts had not known the spring for four appalling years," Brown went on. "No one could blame them if they felt that even this spring—this glorious spring now turned battleship gray on the Invasion's eve—was late in coming.

"As always, however, it would prove worth waiting for; if only it bloomed according to our prayers and plans."

CHAPTER 8

BEFORE THE JUMP

"It was supposed to be a secret that we were setting off for the Invasion of Europe," said paratrooper David Kenyon Webster.

But, he thought, that secret would be hard to keep from anyone who caught sight of the paratroopers on the train as they journeyed through the English countryside to their final waiting area nearer the coast. The soldiers were burdened down with equipment. They wore helmets with camouflage netting, and carried new ammunition pouches and bulging knapsacks.

There was something else, too, David thought. The "excited way we talked; and the distant look in our eyes meant only one thing: invasion."

And then they were at the airfield waiting to jump into Normandy. Rows of C-47s waited. Some planes would carry the paratroopers. Others would tow gliders full of men and heavy equipment—ammunition, vehicles, and short artillery pieces called howitzers.

Unarmed and engineless, the British Horsa glider and the American Waco CG-4A gliders also carried a dubious nickname: "flying coffins." It wasn't much of an exaggeration. Built by the British manufacturer Airspeed, the large Horsa gliders were named for a legendary fifth-century conqueror of Britain: the word *horsa* is the Old English word for "horse." Horsas were made mostly of plywood. Nearly seventy feet long and twenty feet high, with a wingspan of eighty-eight feet, these giant workhorses of the sky could carry up to 70,000 pounds. (Introduced during World War II, gliders have since been replaced by military transport helicopters.)

One day passed. Another; then another. The soldiers weren't aware of the anxious weather deliberations taking place at Southwick House, a hundred miles closer to the coast. For them, it was just nervous, endless waiting. David could feel the anxiety in the air. "Entertainers and newsmen on deadline can talk all they want to about tension, but they wouldn't know tension if you dipped it in a bucket of water and hit them in the face with it—unless they had spent five days in a marshaling area waiting to start the Invasion of Europe."

The food suddenly got better, and he figured that was a sign. "It was a beautiful load: white bread (our first overseas), great gobs of melting butter, marmalade (from an open keg swarming with yellow jackets, but who cares?), rice pudding and cream, all the coffee you can drink."

The troops were told to help themselves to seconds. Then, as David and his crew mates lounged in their tent with full stomachs, someone poked his head in and announced a movie. "White bread and movies on the same day? Impossible."

But it wasn't the latest Hollywood film meant to entertain

and keep their minds off the battles to come. Instead, it was footage of the enemy in action. The light mood shifted; the men grew somber.

Afterward, a colonel told them, "'We've shown you this picture because we wanted you to see how the Germans fight. Did you watch them closely? Did you see how fast they moved? How they used every bit of the available cover and concealment? Remember those things when you go into combat.

"'Now go get a good night's sleep. We have a lot of things to do in the next couple of days.'"

The following day, one platoon at a time, men crowded into a briefing tent with maps and diagrams and three-dimensional models mounted on sand tables. A captain explained, "'We'll go in about midnight . . . so we'll be all alone that night. I hope none of you men is afraid of the dark.'"

More waiting. And then, just as they were set to go, came a sudden announcement: not tonight, the wind is too high. A reprieve—but for one day only. The men went back to waiting and ate stew, all that was left.

Monday: 5:00 p.m. The order came to put on gear. This time it was real.

"First you put on your cotton underwear. Then you wriggled into your woolen long johns . . . shirt and trousers were next, and over all, a shrunken impregnated jumpsuit," said David. "It was a stifling ensemble for seersucker [i.e., warm] weather, and I prayed, as I buckled on my musette bag and hung my cartridge belt with a canteen, a bayonet, a trench

D-Day uniform and equipment of an American paratrooper.

knife, a first-aid packet, and a pair of stolen wirecutters, that I would not have to make a water landing. I zipped up my jump jacket to the collar and could barely breathe.

"Hot, itchy, stiff, and extremely confined, I broke my rifle down with trembling fingers and put its three pieces into the padded canvas case that would be buckled under my reserve chute. Then I lay down stiffly, like a knight on a sarcophagus, and closed my eyes and tried to think of other things. But I couldn't."

David's thoughts turned to the unknown—to what lay ahead of him across the Channel. He knew there was a chance that this late spring evening might be his last. And if it was?

"What a lousy way to leave the world. Nobody to say good-bye. Nobody who loves you waving from the dock. No friends or relatives at the bedside.

"How quiet it is—and godforsaken lonely."

They waited by their plane, on a runway with C-47s stretching for a half mile. "Our lieutenant lined us up in jumping order and made us count off. There were twenty-one of us altogether."

The sun sank and fell out of sight. The skies darkened. David didn't feel like talking. Every once in a while he got up and went to the side of the airstrip to relieve himself. Everyone was on edge. The minutes dragged unbearably: 8:30 p.m., 9:30 p.m., 10:00 p.m.

At 10:45 p.m., the crew chief climbed down from the plane's metal ladder. " 'Let's go, men,' " he said. " 'It's time to load up.' "

Thirty minutes later, the thunder of engines pierced the quiet. David's plane rumbled down the runway and stopped. "There was a last, terrible, rattling, all-pervading roar, and the plane began to move ahead. Then, gaining speed, it raced down the runway, faster, faster, faster. We held our breath and clung to our seat belts . . . Just when it seemed as if we would never leave the runway the plane's nose lifted and we were airborne.

"The motors' roar faded to a steady drone. With a collective sigh of relief, we relaxed and undid our seat belts. The invasion had begun."

★

Paratroopers in the 508th Regiment, 82nd Airborne Division, prepare equipment for D-Day drop.

Now the waiting would be done by others.

"The war leaders, the high commander, the planners . . . had no choice now but to sit back and wait. They had done what they could to insure that the men who crossed the Channel . . . should have the greatest possible chance of success," wrote army historian Gordon Harrison.

The story of D-Day belongs to paratroopers jumping into darkness, to coxswain fighting the waves, to brave demolition experts, to soldiers fighting for a hold on the beach, to Rangers scaling the cliffs.

The story of D-Day belongs to the men who were there.

nnel.

DISPATCH

From the Air: They Had to Go in Alone

Twenty-two-year-old pilot Bert Stiles was a gifted writer and a student at Colorado College before he joined the Air Force in 1942. As a pilot in a "Fort," a Boeing Flying Fortress B-17 Bomber, he'd been flying preinvasion missions over Europe in the months leading up to D-Day. It was part of the effort to decimate Germany's own air force, the Luftwaffe, and achieve Allied air supremacy.

Like the soldiers and sailors, pilots had been anxiously anticipating the cross-channel assault for a long time. "We waited so long it turned into a joke," wrote Bert. "Each time they woke us up in the night somebody would say, 'It's D-day.' But it never was."

Until it was.

Shortly after midnight on June 6, Bert and the other pilots were dragged out of bed and told to get ready for breakfast, which would be followed by a mission briefing at 2 a.m.

When Bert walked into the room, the first thing he saw was a map of Cherbourg, France. He felt tension in the air. He'd slept for only thirty minutes, but that didn't matter now. Everyone knew. "We were in on it. We were flying in the big show."

The officers laid out the carefully timed invasion schedule minute by minute: ships, tanks, troops, and aircraft. Bert would fly in a squadron of six planes assigned to hit a wireless radio and telephone facility five minutes before troops landed by sea.

They left at dawn. "The moon came through just before takeoff time, a big yellow moon soft on the easy hills," he wrote. "The tattered overcast pulled itself together south of London and became a steady blanket, puffed up here and there in soft overcast . . . There were Forts all over the sky, pointing the same way."

Across the Channel the sky above was clear; below it was socked in. Bert and his crew cursed the clouds. "Then just before we crossed the coast, the overcast thinned out . . . and I saw a curve of landing boats . . . maybe fifteen. And they were really pouring it on. The flashes of the guns were a bright stutter against the gray sea . . . and then we were over them, bomb bays coming open."

Aerial of D-Day morning, France.

Bert and his crew executed their mission: they released the plane's bombs and turned back for England. Their part was done. By then the soldiers had begun the assault.

"We were all thinking about those poor bastards down on the beach. The planes would be over them, and the ships would be behind them but they had to go in alone."

LOOK, LISTEN, REMEMBER: Bert Stiles was a promising author who'd sold stories to prestigious publications, such as the *Saturday Evening Post*, while in college. A veteran of thirty-five bomber missions, he was killed in action on November 26, 1944, at age twenty-three.

In 1952, his mother published Bert's WWII memoir, *Serenade to the Big Bird: A True Account of Life and Death from Inside the Cockpit*. To see Bert's picture and read an excerpt from his book, visit the American Air Museum in Britain (part of the Imperial War Museums) online at http://www.americanairmuseum.com/person/17046.

GLIDER FLIGHT

(Sung to the tune of "The Marine Corps Hymn")

We work and strain and load the plane,
We pray it's loaded right.
The ache and pain come back again,
To plague us through the night.

The bugle blows; it's dark, God knows,
Too dark to find our stuff.
The men in rows are on their toes,
They know it's not a bluff.

We eat our meal and take, not steal,
What we can find around.
We do not feel that this is real,
We doubt we'll leave the ground.

We jam aboard and praise the Lord
And pass the ammunition;
We load the cord and holler, "Gawd,
Another dry-run mission."

The planes go high into the sky,
We'll glide real smooth we hope,
The channel's nigh, we hear a cry,
"It's no dry run, you dope."

PRIVATE TOM DUNNE

CHAPTER 9

PEGASUS BRIDGE

At 9:30 p.m. on the evening of June 5, pilot Roy Howard was at the airfield ready to go. Someone asked if he'd be bringing his glider back later. Roy told him no. In just a few hours, he expected his plane would be sitting on the ground in France—hopefully still in one piece, if he could help it.

This Horsa glider and five others, along with the 180 men they carried, were about to set off on the first, top secret operation of the D-Day assault. Codenamed Deadstick, it would be a "coup de main," a sudden, surprise attack led by Major John Howard and British soldiers from the "Ox & Bucks," nickname of the Oxfordshire and Buckinghamshire Light Infantry.

John Howard, a former police constable, had worked his way up through the ranks to become an officer. When he'd been informed in April that his D Company would spearhead the entire invasion, he'd at first sat rooted to his chair, his mouth dry. But he told the colonel, " 'You can have every confidence in me and my men.' "

That would turn out to be an understatement. Under John Howard's leadership, the operation we now call Pegasus Bridge has gone down as one of the most daring surprise attacks in military history. The mission had two clear objectives: Take and keep control of two vital bridges near the city of Caen on the left flank of the fifty-mile-long Normandy invasion area, east of Sword Beach.

A simple mission really: clear, essential, and unbelievably audacious.

Seizing control of the flanks of the invasion area was critical. This would help prevent the enemy from breaking through gaps to attack vulnerable soldiers as they scrambled out of the sea or fought their way inland. On the western end, this task would fall to American paratroopers dropping into enemy territory behind Utah Beach in the predawn hours.

John Howard's team would handle the eastern flank. As D-Day historian Cornelius Ryan put it, "If their task could be achieved a major artery between Caen and the sea would be severed, preventing the east-west movement of German reinforcements, particularly panzer units, from driving into the flank of the British and Canadian invasion area."

The bridges would have to be captured early, before the enemy got wind of the invasion itself and rushed in reinforcements. That's why Operation Deadstick was set to begin just after midnight, spearheading the entire effort. Three gliders would land near the bridge over the Caen Canal (today known as Pegasus Bridge); the other three would put down near the Ranville Bridge over the River Orne, about four hundred yards away (now called Horsa Bridge).

Much depended on the pilots. If the gliders crashed or missed the drop zone, the attack could fail. Thanks to reconnaissance efforts, the glider pilots had been briefed about what they'd find when they got there. Recalled pilot Roy Howard, "Someone had made a most marvelous sand-table, a perfect model of what was on the ground in Normandy—even down to the last tree and ditch."

Still, landing a glider with an immense 88-foot wingspan in the small corner of a pasture in the dark wouldn't be easy. "If I overshot, I would crush us all against a 14-foot high embankment—if I undershot I would destroy my seven tons of powerless aircraft and its human cargo on a belt of 50-foot-high trees," said Roy Howard, who was set to bring his glider down near the River Orne bridge. "There was simply no room for error."

On the evening of June 5, Major John Howard and his platoons assembled on the runway, waiting for the signal to go. They were joined by the six pilots of the Halifax planes, nicknamed "Hallys," that would tow the gliders to France.

" 'I've got to hand it to you boys,' " one remarked. " 'We've flown on some sticky jobs in our time but what you lot are going to do—well, that takes some guts!' "

"Somehow I found I really did not want to think of our mission in those terms," said Major Howard. So rather than replying, he gave the order for his men to synchronize their watches and then board. "I recall hearing shouts of 'Ham and Jam!' from them all; those were the success signals for the capture of both bridges intact . . . I felt a terrible lump in my throat." ("Ham" was the canal bridge; "Jam" the river bridge.)

The Hallys rumbled down the runway in one-minute intervals, each tugging a glider into the air. John Howard was in Glider No. 1, piloted by Jim Wallwork. Howard and a platoon of about twenty-eight men would take the lead on the attack on the Caen Canal bridge, which was expected to be more heavily defended. It was also more important strategically: The bridge could be raised to allow ships to pass along the waterway.

Once over the English Channel, they were plunged into total darkness whenever clouds obscured the moon. They couldn't see any of the other gliders, or the ships of the invasion so many feet below them. The glider lurched, and Howard concentrated on not getting airsick, something his men liked to tease him about. But, for the first time, he didn't feel sick.

"About forty minutes after take-off, Jim Wallwork saw the white line of surf breaking on the beaches of Normandy," Howard said. The pilot gave a two-minute warning, then called out, " 'Prepare for cast-off.' "

Major Howard ordered all chatter to stop as the glider separated from the Hally and swept down in a steep dive. He realized Wallwork and his copilot wanted to get below the clouds quickly to get their bearings and spot the correct drop zone.

In the back of the glider, Lieutenant Den Brotheridge heaved open the glider door, a risky maneuver but one that would allow them to respond quickly if German soldiers were waiting for them.

"Suddenly we were all aware of the sweet, damp night air

over the Normandy countryside as it filled the glider and we all breathed in, for the first time, the smell of France," said John Howard.

Through the open door he could see cattle grazing. "The patchwork of fields was so similar to the countryside of England, it was hard not to believe that we weren't just on another exercise. The silence was uncanny and all we could hear was the air swishing past the sides of the glider; it was a sound that none of us would ever forget."

But now it seemed to him the glider was coming in too high. The plane was swinging about; the copilot yelled for them to hold on tight. Then Howard saw something remarkably familiar up ahead: the canal bridge, looking exactly like the model they'd studied.

Howard recalled that before they set off, pilot Jim Wallwork had asked where the major wanted the glider put down. "Never imagining that he would take me seriously, I had told him, 'Ideally Jim, right through the wire defenses of the bridge!'

" 'Right-ho, sir,' Jim had replied."

Now Wallwork was fighting with the controls to do just that, adjusting the flap and steering the large plane. It was, wrote Howard later, "the most accurate and skillful landing of his life," a feat called " 'the finest piece of pure flying of World War II.' "

At the time, it didn't feel like that at all. The men lifted their feet off the floor to reduce the chances of breaking a leg on impact. Howard said, "I gritted my teeth and tried to pray but all I could think was 'Please God, please God' as we came to land with a terrific crash."

The glider bounced—once, twice. They'd lost the wheels and were skidding across the ground, sending sparks flying. Then everything stopped.

John Howard felt stunned. "We . . . came to a sudden and stupefying halt with the glider's nose right through the barbed wire defenses, just as I had requested."

The air was filled with dust. The copilots had both been injured and were groaning in pain. There were holes in the glider and the cockpit had been smashed. But outside—outside Howard heard nothing.

"There was silence, complete silence, no gunfire at all—we had achieved our first objective of complete surprise."

The sentries on the bridge must have heard the noise, Howard guessed, but hadn't yet grasped what was happening. Instead they seemed bewildered.

The men raced into action, running toward the bridge. Howard went into position, staking out a prearranged spot to serve as a command post, and trying to dodge machine-gun fire. Den Brotheridge led the charge on the bridge with a platoon of some two dozen men with him. In the darkness, David Wood, platoon leader from the second glider arrived, and Howard sent Wood and his men in.

The sounds of machine guns split the night. And then it was silent again. Within fifteen minutes, the D Company men had thrown grenades into the machine-gun pillbox and captured the bridge.

Pegasus Bridge with Horsa gliders visible in the background.

Pegasus Bridge was not without loss. As he stormed across the bridge, Den Brotheridge was hit by machine-gun fire in the neck and died soon after. He was the first Allied casualty on the ground at D-Day, leaving behind a young wife and an unborn baby.

In the silence, Major John Howard realized he hadn't heard shots from the Orne River bridge. But then came a radio message: It had been captured without resistance.

Glider pilot Roy Howard had brought his plane in close to the target, startling a herd of cattle. The platoon leader, Dennis Fox, raced for the bridge. The British soldiers took it without a shot. Apparently the startled sentries, like the cows, had run off.

The entire operation had taken about fifteen minutes. John Howard ordered the wireless radio operator, Corporal Ted Tappenden, to report their success, but he had a hard time getting through at first.

"I well remember his voice repeating over and over again, 'Hello Four-Dog, Hello Four-Dog, Ham and Jam, Ham and Jam,'" said Howard, "and I am certain I heard Tappenden eventually say 'Ham and Bloody Jam!'"

Their part was done. But everything else was just about to begin. It was still dark when Major Howard heard the sound of droning engines overhead. Planes carrying British paratroopers began to appear and then, suddenly, the sky was full of parachutes.

"It was a sight none of us ever forgot, as they drifted to earth illuminated by the ground flares."

Since 1994, a new bridge spans the Caen Canal. It still carries the name it was given years earlier: Pegasus Bridge, after the mythical winged horse, which serves as the insignia of the British 6th Airborne. The river bridge is now called Horsa, in honor of the Horsa gliders. The original Pegasus Bridge has been preserved as part of the Memorial Pegasus Museum.

Den Brotheridge, the first man killed in action on D-Day, has not been forgotten. Fifty years later, his daughter, Margaret, went to Normandy to visit her father's grave. Den Brotheridge was twenty-eight years old.

LOOK, LISTEN, REMEMBER: See a photo of Pegasus Bridge at http://d-dayrevisited.co.uk/d-day/pegasus-bridge.html and visit the website of the Memorial Pegasus Museum at http://www.memorial-pegasus.org/mmp/musee_debarquement/. The bridge also became famous as part of the award-winning 1962 D-Day film, *The Longest Day,* based on the book by Cornelius Ryan, published in 1959. John Howard served as a consultant to the Pegasus Bridge scenes.

To learn more about World War II gliders, visit the American Society of Mechanical Engineers at https://www.asme.org/engineering-topics/articles/aerospace-defense/the-flying-coffins-of-world-war-ii.

DISPATCH

A Panzer Commander in Caen

Major John Howard's superiors had kept one piece of information from him. British Intelligence had learned that the 21st Panzer Division, a crack force of German panzers (tanks) was stationed near Caen. One regiment of the 21st Division was under the command of Major Hans von Luck.

Monday evening, June 5, found the thirty-two-year-old von Luck poring over papers and maps in a house in a small town east of Caen, preparing drills to keep his troops sharp. A man who liked action, he was tired of waiting for the enemy invasion everyone knew must be coming.

German tank in Normandy.

The day had been rainy, and German weather forecasters had predicted bad weather for Tuesday as well. "So we did not anticipate any landings, for heavy seas, storms, and low lying clouds would make large-scale operations at sea and in the air impossible for our opponents," he recalled.

"About midnight, I heard the growing roar of aircraft, which passed over us. I wondered whether the attack was destined once again for traffic routes inland or for Germany herself. The machines appeared to be flying very low—because of the weather? I looked out the window and was wide awake . . .

"At the same moment, my adjutant was on the telephone, 'Major, paratroops are dropping. Gliders are landing in our section.'"

Von Luck wanted to launch a counterattack, but to do so he needed a direct order from the German Supreme Command. He learned that Hitler was asleep and had left instructions not to be disturbed—instructions no one dared to disobey. "I paced up and down and clenched my fists at the indecision of the Supreme Command in the face of the obvious facts."

Field Marshal Erwin Rommel, who headed defensive efforts in northern France, wasn't available, either. He'd taken advantage of the bad weather to go home to Germany to celebrate his wife's birthday. "If Rommel had been with us instead of in Germany, he would have disregarded all orders and taken action—of that we were convinced," said von Luck.

It was a long, frustrating night. When dawn broke, von Luck got his first glimpse of Allied forces. "In the early hours of the morning, from the hills east of Caen, we saw the gigantic Allied armada, the fields littered with transport gliders and the numerous observation balloons over the landing fleet, with the help of which the heavy naval guns subjected us to precision power."

There would be no chance to throw the Allies back into the sea now. "A successful invasion, I thought, was the beginning of the end."

★

On D-Day, Hans von Luck didn't give up. He eventually got the permission he needed. As a result, elements of the 21st Panzer Division mounted the only armored German counterattack on D-Day. The determined professional soldier survived D-Day and fought in Europe until he was captured by the Russians on April 27, 1945. He spent five years in captivity.

After World War II, Hans von Luck devoted himself to reconciliation and peace, and often gave lectures in Germany and in England. He wanted to build a world where the events that had happened in his country could never happen again.

"The example that young people set us older ones should be followed by all in positions of responsibility: the practice of tolerance, that best of human attributes."

In 1983, Hans von Luck met D-Day historian Stephen Ambrose, who at that time was working on a book on Pegasus Bridge and wanted to interview him. Ambrose subsequently wrote the introduction to von Luck's 1989 memoir, *Panzer Commander*. Hans von Luck also became good friends with his former opponent Major John Howard, who had led the surprise attack at Pegasus Bridge.

In May 1984, the three men met at a café near Pegasus Bridge: one British, one German, one American. Said von Luck, who died in 1997, "For me the moment was symbolic: opponents of forty years earlier sat together as friends."

DISPATCH

Landing! A Frenchwoman's D-Day Diary

Marie-Louise Osmont was no stranger to war. Born in 1890 in Paris, France, she volunteered as a nurse during World War I, driving an ambulance to ferry wounded soldiers from the battlefield to field hospitals.

When World War II broke out, Marie-Louise was a doctor's widow living in the village of Périers. Her house, called Château de Périers, lay close to the city of Caen and three miles from Sword Beach, which would be stormed by British troops in the early hours of June 6.

Some German soldiers assigned to guard the coast simply moved into people's homes. Since 1940, Marie-Louise had endured the occupiers. She felt heartbroken: "for me they represent Invasion, Defeat." Massive German trucks trampled the grass in her yard; men ransacked her lovely vegetable garden. Soldiers even removed her beloved rosebushes to dig foxholes. When the Allied bombing raids became intense at the end of May, Marie-Louise and Bernice, her housekeeper and cook, took refuge in one of the foxholes, where they met two German soldiers.

It seemed to Marie-Louise that even these enemy soldiers were weary of waiting—and of the war. Monday, May 29, was a day of sunshine. The soldiers went on a patrol but spent the rest of the day playing cards and sleeping.

"Everything is idyllic, everything radiates peace . . . and yet the sirens have already howled several times, the never-ending airplanes pass over in tight layers, and perhaps this day will be the last!" she wrote.

"War! All have had enough of it, all look forward enthusiastically to the day when they will return to their homes, most of them are gentle men, dreamers, all of them long for the end and feel powerless. Today they are all gaiety and blissful relaxation; tomorrow, helmeted and carrying machine guns, they may be Death passing!"

★

Marie-Louise awoke on Tuesday morning, June 6, to the sound of planes. That was hardly unusual. But this time felt different. "Little by little the gray dawn comes up, but this time around, from the intensity of the aircraft and the cannon an idea springs to mind: landing!"

Outside, she found the noise deafening. "Coming from the sea, a dense artificial cloud; it's ominous and begins to be alarming; the first shells hiss over our heads. I feel cold; I'm agitated.

"I go back home, dress more warmly, close the doors; I go get Bernice to get into the trench, a quick bowl of milk, and we run—just in time! The shells hiss and explode continually . . . Shells are exploding everywhere, and not far away, with short moments of calm; we take advantage of these to run and deal with the animals, and we return with hearts pounding to burrow into the trench."

Around noon, during a lull, the two women tried to eat lunch. But the battle was too close—the thin walls of the house too dangerous. They grabbed bread and meat and ran back to the trench, falling into the trench just in time. "There's hissing and banging everywhere, our stomachs are churning, we feel suffocated, there's a smell of gunpowder. The afternoon is endless."

Later, she inspected the damage to her house. Slates had been blown off the roof; windowpanes were cracked. That wasn't so bad, but in the gatehouse at the foot of the driveway, where Bernice and her family lived, a shell had exploded in the kitchen.

"The big clock, dishes, cooking equipment, walls, everything is riddled with holes, the dishes in broken pieces, as are almost all the windowpanes," she wrote.

"We realize that if we had stayed there, we would both have been killed."

READER'S INVASION BRIEFING

Utah Beach and the Cotentin Peninsula

BY AIR AND SEA: OVERVIEW OF AIRBORNE AND INFANTRY GOALS

Utah Beach, the westernmost site, was the last landing area to be added to the invasion plan. You might think of it as the gateway to the thumb of the Cotentin Peninsula, with the ultimate

C-47 "skytrains" with paratroopers off Utah Beach.

prize being the port of Cherbourg on the tip. There were two separate parts of the assault strategy: by air and by sea.

First, paratroopers would land in the area behind the beach during the night. Their goals included helping prepare the way for 4th Infantry forces storming Utah Beach by sea at dawn. They were charged with taking control of key points across the base of the Cotentin Peninsula and trying to hold on until reinforcements landing on the beach arrived. The paratroopers would also prepare the way by seizing control of the existing roadways—or what passed for roads. The airborne strategy also included bringing in supplies and equipment by glider.

The Germans had made creative use of existing natural resources in their strategy to defend the Cotentin Peninsula. The terrain, called *bocage*, consisted of patches of small meadows separated by thick hedgerows. Rather than build walls, the enemy had used locks controlling the waters of the nearby Douve and Merderet rivers to flood those meadows, about twelve square miles of land, effectively "bogging down" any potential invaders.

"Utah Beach lay almost in the center of these man-made lakes," explained historian Cornelius Ryan. "There was only one way that the men of the 4th Infantry Division (plus their tanks, guns, vehicles and supplies) could force their way inland."

The troops needed roads—any kind. The paratroopers needed to seize and hold four causeways, raised tracks like rough country roads, which sat above the swampy areas. Controlling the causeways would enable infantry troops from the 4th Infantry Division landing on Utah Beach to move inland.

DETAILS OF THE AIRBORNE MISSIONS BEHIND UTAH BEACH

Two airborne divisions totaling about 13,000 paratroopers made night drops. A total of six landing zones had been chosen, each about a mile and a half long and a half mile wide. Each zone had been given a letter name: A, C, D, O, N, T. To make the task easier for the C-47 pilots, groups of pathfinders had been dropped first to try to identify and mark the zones with colored lights and a radio transmitter. (The pathfinders weren't always successful, and some were killed. In other places, the lights illuminating the landing zones were shot out.)

Except for members of the 505th Parachute Infantry Regiment, most of the young soldiers jumping out of planes that night would be experiencing combat for the first time.

101ST AIRBORNE DIVISION, THE SCREAMING EAGLES

These paratroopers had two primary goals:

- Support troops landing on Utah Beach at dawn by seizing control of four causeways that led inland from the shore. If the Germans controlled them, tanks and soldiers from the 4th Infantry Division wouldn't be able to move off the beach—they could be pinned there under heavy artillery fire.

- The 101st Division was also charged with capturing the town of Sainte-Mère-Église, which lay at a strategic crossroads, with roads leading into the peninsula meeting there.

The 101st Airborne Division began with eleven planeloads of eighteen pathfinders each. Their job was to land about thirty minutes ahead of the main paratroopers and set lights to mark three designated drop zones (A, C, and D).

The pathfinders were then followed by waves of planes. The 101st Division included three parachute infantry regiments: the 502nd (carried by 171 planes), 506th (126 planes), and 501st (135 planes). Last to arrive on D-Day were about fifty gliders carrying medical personnel and equipment, jeeps, gun crews, and guns. Other glider missions followed on June 7.

82ND AIRBORNE, THE ALL AMERICANS

The second division of paratroopers deployed at Utah was the 82nd. It also consisted of three parachute infantry regiments: the 505th (the only unit with previous combat experience), the 507th, and the 508th, as well as glider units to deliver ammunition and supplies.

Drop zones for paratroopers in the 82nd Airborne Division were located the farthest away from the beach itself. The original drop zone lay about fifteen miles inland and was located near a hill known as Hill 110, west of the town of Sainte-Mère-Église. The Division's goal was to begin to seal off the Cotentin Peninsula to prevent German reinforcements from reaching the port town of Cherbourg. It was charged with seizing bridges over the Merderet River and securing the west bank to prevent German troops from crossing.

This was an especially hazardous assignment. Since they were the farthest from the Utah beachhead, these paratroopers would be the most isolated—it would take longer for backup guns and reinforcements to reach them. The soldiers would have to fight with only the guns and ammunition they carried with them—or that the gliders delivered.

ON THE BEACHHEAD: 4TH INFANTRY DIVISION

The 4th Infantry Division consisted of three regiments comprised of about 3,100 soldiers each. At Utah Beach at 6:30 a.m., troops from the 8th Regiment were in the first wave. While the German defenses were not as robust as on Omaha, troops on the beachhead also braved heavy fire. Compared with Omaha, more of the beach obstacles on Utah Beach were cleared in advance by demolition experts; preinvasion bombing was more effective. The terrain on the beach also proved more favorable to an amphibious assault, since Utah did not have the high cliffs that made the German guns on Omaha so deadly.

Even so, soldiers on Utah Beach endured heavy artillery attacks, as well as machine-gun and sniper fire. As historian Joseph Balkoski notes, "No veteran of the Utah Beach invasion could ever declare that his accomplishments on June 6, 1944 were easy."

PART 4

UTAH

"There was not anything that prepared us for this."

DWAYNE T. BURNS, paratrooper

"If all World War II battles were to some extent chaotic, what transpired in the Cotentin Peninsula in the opening hours of the D-Day invasion can only be described as absolute bedlam. In the middle of the night, Troop Carrier pilots had just dropped more than 13,000 heavily armed and highly motivated paratroopers into Normandy, directly in the midst of two unsuspecting enemy divisions and a slumbering civilian population."

JOSEPH BALKOSKI, historian

"The hard and difficult thing about war for those at the front were the long days that went by when none of us could raise his eyes beyond the next foxhole or above the next rise of muddy ground."

FATHER FRANCIS L. SAMPSON,
Chaplain, 501st Parachute Infantry Regiment, 101st Airborne Division

Paratroopers [illegible] nding behind

VOICES FROM THE

The Chutes

"We loaded up our equipment and moved out to the planes just before dark. The chutes were laid out in rows beside the ships. Each of us selected a main and reserve. I carried my chutes to one side and looked them over very carefully. Once you pick and inspect your chutes, you don't want anybody

Aerial view of Utah Beach.

to mess with them or try to trade. It's your chute, and that's the one you want to jump. Maybe we were just a little bit superstitious."

DWAYNE T. BURNS,
508th Parachute Infantry Regiment, 82nd Airborne Division

The Jump

"Now here we sat, each man alone in the dark, with his own thoughts and fears. These men around me were the best friends I will ever know . . . Flak is getting heavy as we stand waiting for the green light . . . The roar of the engines, the flak hitting the wings and fuselage, and everyone is yelling, 'Let's go!' but still the green light does not come on . . .

"I landed in a long narrow field with two anti-glider poles in it, and I hit hard and rolled over on my back . . . Some of the troopers were not so lucky.

"Many landed in flooded rivers and drowned. One went through the roof of a greenhouse, another went down a well. Some landed in towns, with one landing on a church steeple. Others hit burning buildings. Some landed in trees. Some died in the air . . . Some jumped too late and landed on the beach-head while others landed in the English Channel."

DWAYNE T. BURNS,
508th Parachute Infantry Regiment, 82nd Airborne Division

Glider Landing

"It was now time to prepare for landing, or as the Glider Gang calls it, 'a controlled crash.' Fields of any good size in the area had been planted with the large poles known as 'Rommel's Asparagus.' The standard landing technique was to aim the nose between the poles, shear off the wings, pray, and hope for the best . . .

"We banged down hard in the middle of the field, and bounced into the hedgerow trees . . . I managed to crawl through what was left of the nose section and get on my feet.

Wrecked Allied glider.

"Of course, there were many bruises and contusions, plus a slight concussion that put me into a rather happy state of mind. I have been that way ever since."

EDGAR SCHROEDER,
320th Glider Field Artillery Battalion, 82nd Airborne Division

Paratrooper Surgeon

Challenging a cow

"I heard noises inside nearby hedgerows and went to investigate . . . I lashed out and up at the intruder. I hit nothing, and to this day, I believe I must have challenged a cow. If the cow had mooed then, I would have taken off like a rocket and still be circling Normandy."

Captured in a farmhouse while treating wounded

"I noticed some German solders coming down a nearby field towards us . . . I stuck my red cross painted helmet on a long pole and pushed it out the door. They stopped firing and came in to capture us. A medic and I put [wounded Lieutenant] Lehman on a litter and carried him over hill and dale to a German aid station where we medics were treated as friends by the German medical personnel.

"From there, we were transported to a field hospital . . . A steady stream of American casualties were brought in that day, leaving me no time to eat or rest . . . A Catholic priest who was a sergeant in the German army and in charge of scheduling in the surgical suite . . . proved to be a godsend in enabling us to rush a few American wounded in [for surgery] . . .

"We were rescued by the 47th Infantry, of the 9th Division, on the 16th of July."

BRIAND N. BEAUDIN,
Assistant Battalion Surgeon, 508th Parachute Infantry Regiment,
82nd Airborne Division

Recollections of a Jumping "Dogface"

Helmets

"In World War II, they [infantry soldiers] were known as 'Dogfaces' or 'Doggies' . . . Our unit was known as jumping 'Dogfaces' . . . The 'Dogface' cursed the steel helmet he had to wear. It was cold in the winter and hot in the summer, but it was one of the handiest things he possessed. He could drink out of it, shave in it, carry water in it, bathe in it, dig a hole with it if the dirt was not too hard, and probably most of all, he could carry his tobacco and cigarettes and other small things to keep them dry . . .

Hedgerows, Snipers, and Cows

"Snipers in Normandy were awful. If there was any place in Europe suitable for sniping it was Normandy with all those hedgerows. When the Germans retreated they left snipers behind everywhere. They would lie in the grass, in trees, buildings and most of all in those darned hedgerows . . .

"One 'Dogface' told me he and a buddy were dug in on one side of a hedgerow when he heard some heavy walking on the other side. He thought it could be a sniper changing positions. He thought the heavy walking was from the hob-nailed boots the Germans wore. He placed his bayonet and his rifle and waited until he heard the walking directly across the hedge from him. At this time he plunged the bayonet in flesh. A cow ran down the hedgerow bawling and in great pain."

KENNETH RUSSELL,
505th Parachute Infantry Regiment, 82nd Airborne Division

First Night

"The drop zone was like a scene from a dream. Guys appeared from the darkness and then disappeared back into it. There must have been some Germans there but they weren't wandering around like we were . . . None of us knew where we were . . . I guess all of us were beginning to suspect that this thing wasn't coming off as planned . . .

"Eventually, by pure chance, I stumbled onto my own company. I don't remember exactly what we did or where we did it but in retrospect it seemed that we marched all night and stayed awake all day."

LEN GRIFFING,
501st Parachute Infantry Regiment, 101st Airborne Division

CHAPTER 10

CRICKETS: NORMANDY BEFORE DAWN

"Each man knew he might never see the dawn," said twenty-year-old John E. Fitzgerald. Like fellow paratrooper David Kenyon Webster, John began his D-Day in a rumbling C-47 crossing the English Channel. And also like David, he'd trained in England for months in the 101st Airborne Division. But he'd never faced combat—until this moment.

They were over land, close to the drop zone. John saw Lieutenant Colonel Robert G. Cole go to the open door and lean out, searching for a landmark. Cole barked the order: " 'Stand up and hook up!' "

The men struggled to their feet. "The heavy equipment we carried added up to about 125 pounds to our weight," John said. "Some of the men stumbled and had to be helped up." The soldiers hooked their static lines to a cable running overhead, part of a safety system that would also open their parachutes automatically.

"My legs felt as if they would go out from under me. Over the roar of the engines and flak came Cole's next order: 'Check equipment!' "

They sounded off for their equipment check, starting at the rear and calling out each number in turn. Cole would jump first. By the time John heard him yell, "1-OK!" he knew the enemy's guns were trained right on them. "Tracer fire from below was beginning to find its mark. The bullets made a sound like corn popping as they passed through the plane's fuselage."

Cole stood in the door, looked back once more and barked the order: " 'Go!' "

John shuffled closer. He was third to jump. Then second. Then first. He felt a blast of cold air, took a breath, and leaped. "A blast of cool night air caught me . . . and hurdled me toward the earth . . . my chute popped open with a bone-breaking jolt."

The tracer bullets looked almost like fireworks, flashing in every color of the rainbow and lighting up eerie floating shapes around him as he drifted down. John stared up helplessly as bullets ripped through two panels of his chute. Nearby, a plane was on fire. The recommendation was a speed of 110 miles per hour, with paratroopers dropping at 700 feet. The pilots had been told not to take evasive action that might throw off hitting the drop zone precisely. Still, it seemed to John that some planes were flying so low paratroopers were nearly in the trees before their chutes opened.

Then John looked down and got a shock. He saw figures running in all directions. He had a moment of panic: "I'm going to land right in the middle of a bunch of Germans!" Then his chute floated into the branches of an apple tree and dumped him to the ground with a thud.

He froze, bracing for shots that never came. And then the moving shapes materialized into frightened cows. "I felt a strange surge of elation: I was alive!"

Gunfire sputtered nearby. John grabbed his switchblade from his jacket pocket, cut away the lines of his chute, and scrambled for cover behind a hedgerow. He didn't see a soul. Like so many of the paratroopers dropped behind Utah Beach that night, John had landed alone, separated from his unit.

Later John compared it to dropping a handful of peas onto an egg carton. "The peas would all land in different compartments, in ones and twos and threes, and that's exactly how we landed.

"Everyone had the feeling they were alone or almost alone."

The paratroopers had landed in the terrain called *bocage*—small squares of pastureland separated by ancient hedgerows. But these hedges were like nothing they'd ever seen before. Some were three or four feet thick, packed with rocks, trees, roots, and bushes. They could be five, ten, twenty feet high. Hazardous to gliders, the hedgerows could hide snipers. But they also offered cover to young soldiers making their first jump into combat.

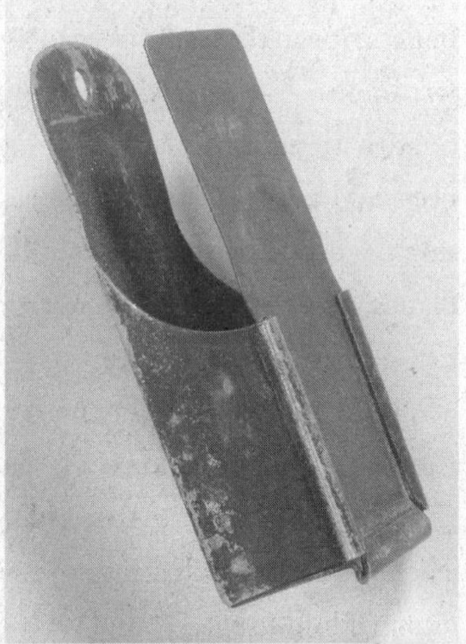

"Cricket" toy used as identification device by paratroopers.

Soldiers wandering at night in this confused landscape of flooded fields, hedgerows, and the narrow raised tracks called causeways had a hard time telling friend from foe. Paratroopers in the 82nd Airborne had been given a password: *Flash* with the answering countersign *Thunder*. Paratroopers in the 101st Airborne Division had been issued a toy to use first, the idea being it might be safer than speaking English in the darkness. It was a small clicker called a cricket.

"When you put it between your thumb and forefinger and squeezed the fingers together it clicked and it clicked again when you released the pressure on the fingers," explained paratrooper Len Griffing, a nineteen-year-old from Long Island. "The idea was that if one of us heard someone, he was to stop and go click, click. If it was one of our guys, he would have a clicker of his own and he would go click-click, click-click in reply."

But when John Fitzgerald needed his cricket, he couldn't find it. He'd tried to orient himself and found a road on the other side of a hedge. Then he realized he was no longer alone.

"I heard footsteps coming towards me. Crouching down, I began searching for my cricket to identify myself, but couldn't find it," said John. "It was on a string tied around my neck, and had worked itself behind my back."

The figures were coming closer. John decided to stay silent. He counted eight men. "The sound of their hob-nail boots told me they were Germans. My M-1 rifle was still in the carrying case used for jumping. It was broken into two parts. We were supposed to assemble it as soon as we hit the ground, but there was simply not enough time.

"The group marched past me, about three feet away. With a big sigh of relief, I decided it was time to get the hell out of there and look for some company."

David Kenyon Webster had landed not in an apple tree, but in three feet of water. Alone and disoriented, he wanted desperately to find his unit. First, he had to figure out where he was. He pulled his compass from his pocket: the needle was frozen, the compass filled with water. So much for that.

David thought of the landmarks he'd heard about in the briefings: an orchard, white lights to mark the drop zone. None of that matched his experience. And for a moment he feared the whole invasion might fail. Maybe there were Germans everywhere, ready to round up each paratrooper one by one.

In fact, the weather had caused some of the chaos. "Cloud banks forced the closely packed nighttime formations to disperse. As the planes neared their drop zones now marked by pathfinder parties, enemy flak scattered the formations still farther apart," said General Omar Bradley later.

Major General Matthew B. Ridgway was in charge of the entire 82nd Airborne Division. General James M. Gavin served as commander of Task Force A, a consolidation of three parachute regiments: the experienced 505th (for which he had been the first commander back in 1942), and new, untested soldiers in the 507th and the 508th.

"A night jump into combat is not as scary as it might seem," wrote Gavin, who flew as jumpmaster in the lead plane of the 508th Parachute Infantry. "When you hear the roar of the engines turning over and you move down the runway and become airborne, you realize at that moment there is no turning back."

Still, even the experienced Gavin began to worry as he faced challenging cloud conditions that night. "Suddenly we entered a dense cloudbank. It was so thick that I could not see the wing tips of our plane, and of course I could not see any other planes. Since we had been flying in close formation, it was quite dangerous."

Gavin's plane was now totally on its own. "I began to worry and to check our time. Every jumpmaster had been told to memorize his time from the moment of landfall, I knew that my plane had to jump eight and a half minutes after passing the French coast if we were to land on our drop zone, assuming that we were flying on a correct heading."

In the end, Gavin landed a few miles from the designated drop zone. And his plane wasn't the only one.

"More than 60 planeloads were dumped from eight to 20 miles beyond their drop zones. Others were scattered from Utah Beach through the lagoons. Nevertheless, remnants of the 101st struck smartly toward the causeways that led from Utah Beach while others headed south to seal off Carentan and block that path of enemy reinforcement," noted General Omar Bradley.

"Like the 101st, however, Ridgway's 82nd was badly scattered on landing, especially those elements scheduled to drop west of the Merderet [River]. As a consequence, much of the division's effort on that first day was wasted in the difficult task of assembling combat units.

"However the division did establish a base in Sainte Mère Église from among the paratroopers who landed near the tiny dairying town. And like the 101st, it panicked the enemy in most rear areas during those first critical hours of the assault."

Like other officers in the 82nd Airborne Division, General James M. Gavin spent the predawn hours of D-Day rounding up troops and trying to organize them. His mission was to seize a bridge over the Merderet. He had about a hundred soldiers.

"I should have been able to accomplish a lot. To my utter frustration, I found them completely disorganized . . . With the amount of German fire increasing and the troopers milling about and seeking the protection of the nearby hedgerows, it was impossible to get them organized in any rational way."

For paratroopers still wandering alone in this confusing landscape, the situation was even worse. David Kenyon Webster thought of all the maps, sand tables, and careful briefings. "For all the good they did, the army might as well have yanked us out of a pub and dumped us off helter-skelter to find our own way to the Germans.

"Instead of a regiment of over fifteen hundred men carefully assembled on a well-defined drop zone, D-Day was one man alone in an old swamp."

David was still in the water when he heard the drone of planes. Tracer bullets lit up the sky. More soldiers were about to jump. He could only watch helplessly as paratroopers drifted into danger.

And then it came. *Swish. Swish. Swish.*

Someone else was in the water. David got his rifle ready and sank low in the water, at the same time reaching for the cricket, which hung from a string around his neck.

He squeezed the cricket once. *Click-click*.

Silence. He waited, holding his breath, afraid to make a noise. If the wader came closer, he'd shoot. He'd have to shoot.

Click-click, click-click.

The young soldier was no longer alone.

David soon linked up with other soldiers from his 101st Airborne Division and fell into a column of men marching out. He wasn't sure where exactly they were headed, but it didn't matter.

He was just glad to be back with his outfit—an outfit he would stay with through a month in Normandy, being wounded in Holland, and through to the very end of the war.

"I was home again," David said.

Weeks later, back in England for a furlough, David Kenyon Webster's regiment held a memorial service one hot August day for those paratroopers who had died in the invasion. More than two hundred names were read out.

"In Normandy, the dead lay forever silent in the dappled-green parachutes that had carried them to earth," wrote David later.

His war, however, was not over. "We were ready to go again, because we could only go forward, never back . . . And so we went forward, one regiment, filled up with replacements, the dead as fine and strong a part of us as the living men, so fresh and new, who had come to take their place."

LOOK, LISTEN, REMEMBER: David Kenyon Webster returned home to become a writer and journalist. His memoir, *Parachute Infantry: An American Paratrooper's Memoir of D-Day and the Fall of the Third Reich*, was published by his widow, Barbara, after his tragic death in a boating accident in 1961 at age thirty-nine. He was the father of three. You can read excerpts from his books and World War II letters home online at http://www.davidkenyonwebster.com/.

David Kenyon Webster was featured in the HBO miniseries, *Band of Brothers*, based on the book by Stephen Ambrose, which followed members of E Company of the 506th Parachute Infantry, 101st Airborne Division. In his introduction to David's *Parachute Infantry*, Ambrose called it "an outstanding memoir of the war."

CHAPTER 11

SCENES FROM A CHAPLAIN'S D-DAY

Diving into a Dark Swamp

Chaplains jumped out of planes, too. Thirty-two-year-old Father Francis L. Sampson, the Roman Catholic priest and chaplain to the 501st Parachute Infantry Regiment, 101st Airborne Division, carried no rifle. He did, though, carry a knife and some bags, including one with everything he'd need to say Mass in the field.

The crossing over the English Channel was quiet at first. Father Sampson knew right when they'd begun to fly over land: He heard the *ack ack* of anti-aircraft fire from German guns below. "The plane was hit many times and one boy had a bullet go right through his leg. As we stood up and hooked up, the plane was rocking badly in a strong wind. The green light came on and the jump master pushed our equipment bundle out and we went out as fast as we could.

"The Germans were waiting for us and they sent such a barrage of bullets at us that it will always remain a mystery to me how any of us lived. The tracer bullets alone made it look like Fourth of July.

"I collapsed part of my chute to come down faster. From there on my guardian angel took over." Father Sampson landed in a stream so deep the water was over his head. Grabbing his knife, he managed to free himself by cutting away anything he could that was attached, including his Mass kit (the garments and objects needed to conduct the Catholic religious service).

"The canopy of my chute stayed open and the strong wind blew me down the stream about 100 yards and into shallow water. I lay there a few minutes exhausted and as securely pinned down by equipment as if I had been in a straitjacket.

"None of our men was near, and it took about twenty minutes to get out of my chute (it seemed a year) with German machine gun and mortar fire sweeping the area."

Crawling back along the bank, he managed to find the spot where he had landed. If it had been food or extra equipment, he might have left it behind. But what had disappeared into the dark water was priceless and necessary: his Mass kit. He began to dive down into the cold black water, determined to find it. "By pure luck I recovered it after the fifth or sixth dive."

Next, Father Sampson began to look for the lights that would mark the designated drop zone area where the soldiers were supposed to assemble. He saw nothing but dark swampy land. The pathfinders—dropped first to mark the zones—had not been successful here. He said, "I learned later that they were shot out as soon as they were turned on and the men in charge were mostly killed or wounded."

Father Sampson found his assistant nearby, still struggling to free himself from his parachute. The two quickly made for the nearest hedgerow for cover to decide what to do next. "We no sooner got there than a plane on fire came straight at us. The plane crashed about eighty yards in front of us and threw flaming pieces over our heads. We saw two more planes go down not far away."

The chaos of Father Sampson's D-Day had begun—and it wouldn't let up.

Helping the Wounded

Father Sampson spent most of the first twenty-four hours of D-Day in a farmhouse that had been turned into a makeshift aid station. It was a dangerous place to be. Once, when he saw

A medic bandages a soldier's hand, Utah Beach.

Germans setting up a machine gun in the yard, he ran out waving a white flag.

"A German jumped at me and stuck a gun in my stomach." Certain that he was about to be shot, Father Sampson began to mumble a quick prayer, an Act of Contrition. He was so frightened he found himself repeating the grace before meals instead!

Father Sampson was then marched off to see a German officer who spoke a little English. "I told him I was a Catholic priest and showed him my credentials. And to my real amazement he snapped to attention, saluted, made a slight bow, and showed me a [religious] medal pinned inside his uniform."

The Germans allowed Father Sampson to stay with wounded soldiers in the farmhouse, but they were by no means out of danger. Later in the day, three German shells hit the house, collapsing the ceiling in places and killing two wounded soldiers.

Later still, they came under friendly fire. "The house was riddled with rifle and machine gun fire. A tracer bullet ricocheted off the ceiling, grazed my leg and set my pants on fire.

"I saw an American lieutenant sneaking up on our building with hand grenades . . . I ran out and stopped him, yelling for all I was worth. He said he thought there were Germans in there."

The patients were evacuated to a large French château that had been set up as a hospital for two or three hundred wounded, both American and German, many in their teens.

Father Sampson moved among the men, saying prayers with soldiers of all faiths.

One incident stayed with him. Two gravely ill soldiers lay near each other. The American began to groan in pain; he'd lost a blanket cushioning his head. A German soldier with a heinous abdomen wound "crawled off his litter along the floor on his back to the side of the American, fixed the folded blanket under his head again, and crawled back to his own litter. The German boy died within the hour."

The next day, Father Sampson hitched a ride in a jeep to where the 501st Parachute Infantry Regiment was assembling. "A couple of boys from our demolition section dug a deep comfortable foxhole for me and bedded it down with a parachute."

Just as he was about to lie down, three bombs dropped into the nearby field. The Regimental staff came running out and dived into any foxhole they could find. "The bombs landed right in the middle of the field we were in, but the only casualties were three cows. If the whole German Luftwaffe came over, it couldn't have kept me from going to sleep.

"I slept twenty-four hours straight through."

CHAPTER 12

CRASH-LANDING INTO NORMANDY

"In the first hours of D-Day, a lot of small actions were fought by groups banding together to fight, only to become separated again," said paratrooper John E. Fitzgerald. "They may or may not have known each other."

Those words certainly reflected his own experience since landing in the dark, tangled branches of an apple tree. He couldn't find anyone from his regiment—or even his division. At one point, John linked up with a captain and private from the 82nd Airborne Division, which was also deployed behind Utah Beach. Suddenly, German anti-aircraft guns opened up near them, and they went into action. They got to within twenty-five yards of one gun by crawling on their hands and knees.

John fired at two Germans while the captain destroyed the machine gun with a grenade. "Perspiration broke out on my forehead, my hands were trembling," John recalled. "It was the first time I had ever fired at a living thing."

They tried to reach a second gun but were driven back by automatic machine-gun fire. In the retreat, John became separated again, and once again he found himself alone. It was beginning to dawn on him that he must have landed far from the intended drop zone. He wasn't the only one. "Of more than six thousand jumpers from the 101st Airborne, barely one thousand had landed on or near the H-hour objectives," wrote one historian.

John Fitzgerald had memorized his own unit's mission: Paratroopers in the 101st Airborne Division needed to wrest control of two of those critical causeways. So when he found some men who directed him to a command post, he was disappointed to find only men from the 82nd Airborne Division.

Nevertheless, he was still bent on trying to find his unit and get to the right place. "I asked if anyone knew the direction to the beaches. Our battalion objection was to secure a group of causeways leading inland from them. But none of the men were sure."

John felt torn. He knew his original mission was critically important. "I wanted very much to find Colonel [Robert] Cole, but it was becoming apparent that I had landed in an area assigned to the 82nd Airborne."

Unbeknownst to John Fitzgerald, Cole had also landed off target and spent the night making his way back to the beach over three miles of difficult terrain. As historian Joseph Balkoski observed, Cole was doing "what every bold airborne leader did that night: gathering stray paratroopers and leading them on to an objective, regardless of their unit affiliation." Cole reached his destination at sunrise, and soon had control of two causeways.

In response to John's question, a sergeant pointed to a

road, saying he'd spotted some men from the 101st Airborne Division on it. John set out. "I had only gone a short distance when I was fired on by a machine pistol that was quickly joined by another, firing from the opposite side of the road. The ferocity of the bursts sent me sheepishly back up the road to the CP [command post]."

There might be a rivalry between the two divisions, John figured, but there was also safety in numbers. And it was definitely time to improvise rather than risk a solo, and perhaps fatal, attempt to strike out across enemy territory by himself.

There was only one thing left for John to do. "I decided to join the 82nd."

John became part of a group of about fifty men. Their first goal was to protect a field for gliders that would be bringing in reinforcements and heavy equipment. Gliders usually flew when it was light, but about a hundred would be making the dangerous attempt in the predawn hours of D-Day.

The first landings were scheduled for about four in the morning. Their cargo was critical. The gliders carried equipment paratroopers couldn't: ammunition, jeeps, water, medical supplies, anti-tank guns, mines, and grenades.

The troopers overcame a small group of defenders and formed a perimeter defense around the field. Then they waited.

"It was a typical warm June night," said John. "The moon would appear every now and then between the clouds. I had a long drink of water from my canteen and wondered what I would be doing if I were at home now. For the first time that night, I realized I was tired."

Then he heard them: First, a drone of engines in the distance, followed by strange swishing noises. "Adding to the swelling crescendo of sounds were the tearing of branches and trees followed by loud crashes and intermittent screams.

"The gliders were coming in rapidly, one after the other, from all different directions. Many overshot the field and landed in the surrounding woods, while others crashed into nearby farmhouses and stone walls. The gliders had been loaded with heavy guns, radios, and other arms too large to drop by parachute," said John.

"In a moment, the field was complete chaos. Equipment broke away and catapulted as it hit the ground, plowing up huge mounds of dirt. Bodies and bundles were thrown all along the length of the field. Some of the glider troops were impaled by the splintering wood of the fragile machines."

While these gliders landed in the correct zone, many did not. Some gliders missed their designated area, scattering much-needed equipment in fields, marshes, and the flooded terrain of the Cotentin Peninsula. Historian Cornelius Ryan noted, "For the hard-pressed 82nd, the wide dispersion of the glider train was calamitous. It would take hours to salvage and collect the few guns and supplies that had arrived safely.

"In the meantime, troopers would have to fight on with the weapons they had carried with them."

Seattle-born Edgar A. Schroeder was a member of the 320th Glider Field Artillery Battalion, 82nd Airborne Division.

Gliders ferry supplies to U.S. troops.

The 320th took part in the last glider mission of June 6, scheduled not at dawn but on Tuesday evening. This group would bring "twelve 105mm howitzers, thirty-three tons of ammunition, twenty-eight jeeps, medical supplies, water, and twenty-three tons of additional matériel [military materials and equipment]."

The days leading up to D-Day were busy, as the glidermen, as they were called, worked to secure and chain down jeeps, large howitzer guns, and ammunition within the wooden planes. Ed's glider contained a jeep and a trailer full of ammunition for the 105mm howitzers, an accurate and powerful artillery weapon used for supporting infantry in the field.

The soldiers themselves were issued anti-gas clothing Ed didn't much like. "This stuff was like bacon grease," he recalled years later. "Stiff and dank when the weather was cool, and irritating to one's sweaty skin when it was warm. Soon after the landing, I cut a piece of nylon from a parachute to ease my badly chafed neck [and protect it from the clothing].

"I still have that scarf, and by now it's in better shape than the neck. We also got the little sleeve flags to sew on, in case we might forget what country we were from."

The landing was hard, and for a few minutes Ed thought he might have broken his leg, but he managed to crawl out of the plane. The copilot and one corporal were injured badly. They'd landed northeast of Sainte-Mère-Église, although their designated area was southwest of town. Ed was philosophical about it. He was in the correct province, or, as the American put it: "Oh, well, so at least it was the right county."

Ed also discovered disadvantages to landing later in the day. It wasn't, he reflected, "exactly a bed of roses. We didn't have the advantage of darkness and surprise. The reception party was ready and waiting . . . We landed right in the middle of a fierce enemy counter-attack."

His first goal was to unload the equipment through a large tail section that could be unbolted and pulled aside. "That, of course, was according to the book and under normal conditions. D-Day was not exactly a normal condition."

The crash landing had damaged the bolts. "After grunting and swearing for quite some time, and so mad and frustrated that I was even oblivious to enemy fire, I finally gave up, cocked my carbine, and joined in the defense of the area for the rest of the night.

"D-Day was not automatically shut down at midnight," Ed reflected. "Some of the bloodiest confrontations took place the following day, and for many days thereafter."

Ed was proud of the Distinguished Unit Citation his outfit received for their contributions that day. It read: " 'Before they touched the soil of Normandy on D-Day, the men of the 320th were menaced by a barrage of ack-ack machine-gun and mortar fire. On landing, they were immediately attacked by mobile Nazi anti-airborne landing groups.

" 'While other elements of the Division were assembling, the Battalion went into position, helped materially to push back the bitterly counter-attacking Nazis. All night superior

German artillery attacked. All night the 320th hung on protecting the advance of our seaborne assault forces, helping to keep the Nazis from crossing the Merderet River.' "

Ed never lost his sense of humor. When the veteran sent an oral history recording to historian Stephen Ambrose, he joked that he was always happy to talk about himself, his "favorite subject."

Yet at the end of the tape, he added, "I would like to dedicate this recording to the memory of my good friend and comrade-at-arms, Lt. Jesse Stewart . . . He was a little guy, but more than made up for his size in courage. He jumped in with the initial assault and survived, but was later deserted by Lady Luck, and buried in Normandy."

At the glider landing site earlier that morning, John Fitzgerald and other soldiers had rushed to help the wounded. A makeshift aid station was hastily set up to handle injuries. "Medics were working feverishly administering morphine, sulfa pills, and whatever bandages they had," he said. They couldn't linger long.

"Word was passed to us by an officer that time was running out and we would have to leave soon." Their next objective: to help capture and defend the crossroads town of Sainte-Mère-Église, not far away.

As they marched, John came upon some of the horrors of that night—paratroopers who had come down in the wrong place. One had landed on a church steeple, others, in the midst of a German command post. "Many of the troopers were killed before they hit the ground or shortly after they landed.

A glider that crash-landed into a Normandy hedgerow.

Some were still hanging in trees. They looked like rag dolls shot full of holes. Their blood was dripping on this place they came to free. Seeing these first American dead and the way they had died had a chilling effect on us."

When a short break was called, John leaned against a stone wall and instantly slipped into a deep sleep. When he awoke a short time later, it was almost light. "While looking for water to fill my canteen, I spotted a well at the rear of a nearby farmhouse. On my way to the well, the scene I came upon was one that has never left my memory."

He'd found a foxhole surrounded by the bodies of nine German soldiers, the closest only three feet from a soldier who had made that foxhole "his personal Alamo."

"He had fought alone, and like many others, he had died alone. I looked at his dog tags. The name read Martin V. Hersh. I wrote the name down in a small prayer book I carried, hoping someday I would meet someone who knew him. I never did."

★★★★ DISPATCH ★★★★

Hedgerows and American Ingenuity

The Allied soldiers and glider pilots on D-Day faced a challenge they hadn't fully prepared for: the hedgerows of Normandy. Bob Bearden, a paratrooper with the 507th Parachute Infantry Regiment, 82nd Airborne Division, didn't even recall hearing the word *hedgerow* in his preinvasion briefing.

Yet this distinguishing feature of the landscape soon became familiar territory to paratroopers and infantrymen. "Like many of my fellow troopers, I immediately encountered twenty-foot-high hedges, which were so impassable that not even tanks could penetrate them," said Bob. "Used to divide farming acreage, most often pasturage for cows, the hedgerows had often grown together to form a canopy over somewhat sunken, sand roadbeds, where no sunlight ever penetrated.

"These dark, covered settings prompted much fear, and we quickly came by fine-tuned ears able to detect the slightest sound—like the activation of a rifle bolt, or the click of a German MG-43, .30 caliber aluminum machine-gun belt being run through the metallic breech of a gun in preparation for firing."

General James M. Gavin agreed. He spent the first hours and days of the invasion rounding up troops, pushing through swamps and meadows, and trying to take villages, causeways, and bridges.

It had been, he concluded later, "surprisingly difficult. It was because of the hedgerows. Although there had been some talk in the United Kingdom before D-Day about the hedgerows, none of us had really appreciated how difficult they would turn out to be.

"All the *bocage* country of Normandy is cut up into small fields that have been handed down for centuries from family to family, and for centuries trees have grown up in the hedges between the fields . . . Rocks, old tree roots, and the roots of living trees and dirt entwined into an impenetrable mass. In each field a small opening occurred to permit a man, or, in some cases, a vehicle, to enter. These openings were invariably covered by machine-gun fire, and thus each field was a small fortress in itself."

But if Normandy's hedgerows slowed down the soldiers on D-Day, it wasn't long before American ingenuity found a way to conquer them. A sergeant named Curtis Grubb Culin III is credited with coming up with a device to enable tanks to cut through the terrain.

The idea apparently came during a brainstorming session about the problem, when a soldier from Tennessee had suggested that they put some saw teeth on the front of the tank and just cut through the hedges.

As with the invention of the Mulberry harbors, what at first started as a joke ended up inspiring an ingenious solution. Culin designed a plow device with four steel prongs using scrap metal salvaged from a German roadblock. Culin tried to give some credit to his comrade from Tennessee, but that was largely forgotten in the publicity about the device, which was brought to the attention of General Omar Bradley himself.

"The invention came on the eve of its greatest need," said Bradley. Several weeks after D-Day, he received a call in his Normandy headquarters from General Leonard Gerow, commander of the 29th Division, asking him to meet. "'We've got something that will knock your eyes out.'"

Bradley found Gerow and his staff gathered around a tank with four tusklike prongs protruding from the front, just as Sergeant Culin had designed. They watched a demonstration. "The tank backed off and ran head-on toward a hedgerow at ten miles an hour. Its tusks bored into the wall, pinned down the belly, the tank broke through under a canopy of dirt."

Immediately, they gave the order for round-the-clock production. As for where the metal came from—that was a no-brainer. Said Bradley, "Scrap metal for the tank tusks came from Rommel's underwater obstacles on the beaches."

Recycling—Overlord style.

CHAPTER 13

FIRST BATTLES

The residents of a quiet village in Normandy went to bed on Monday night with no inkling that nothing would ever be the same—for them or for the town of Sainte-Mère-Église, which boasted a lovely eleventh-century church. But it had something else much more critical to the invasion's success: roads.

It was, in fact, a crossroads town with six major roads running through it, which made it one of the first objectives of D-Day. Any German troops bent on driving back the invasion would need those roads. As historian Joseph Balkoski put it: "The Americans could accomplish nothing without Sainte Mère Église."

Although his original mission didn't include capturing the town, Lieutenant Colonel Edward "Cannonball" Krause of the experienced 505th Parachute Infantry Regiment had managed to gather about 200 paratroopers in the darkness. When he found out they were near Sainte-Mère-Église, Krause marched in anyway, leading this ragtag group. The soldiers initially met with little resistance. At five that morning, Krause radioed news of the capture and raised an American flag from a pole in front of the town hall.

It was an early, important victory. But everyone knew that once the Germans in the area were roused, they would launch a counterattack. The Americans had to be ready.

And one of those who would take part would be lost and wandering paratrooper John Fitzgerald. John was now part of a group of soldiers from the 82nd Airborne Division, which included members of the 505th Parachute Infantry Regiment, who, unlike John, had seen combat before. Squads were hastily organized, and soldiers sent to defend the town from counterattack—which wasn't long in coming.

It would be John's first experience of battle.

Soldiers from the 82nd Airborne enter Sainte-Mère-Église.

★

"We were given a position on a defense perimeter outside the town," John said. "The Germans held the high ground to our front. They were quickly gaining control of the entire area and were shelling it with artillery and chemical mortars. The mortars would announce themselves with an unholy scream that was spine-chilling. A few seconds later, they would land, spreading shovel-size fragments of shrapnel."

One of Germany's strengths was its powerful artillery guns. They had longer ranges and were often hidden from sight behind hedgerows. In this case, the Americans were coming under fire from a powerful 88mm gun that was tucked away, all but invisible, in a wooded area.

The fire was trained on the Americans' machine gun. To protect it, a sergeant moved it. There was only one problem—John and another soldier, also a "stray" from the 101st Airborne, were left in the gap where it had been.

There he endured a harrowing half hour under fire—his indoctrination to battle.

"Rounds were coming in, one after the other, most landed within feet of us. The impact of the shells threw up mounds of dirt and mud. The ground trembled and my eardrums felt as if they would burst," he said. "Dirt was filling my shirt, and was beginning to get into my eyes and mouth. The tales the Americans would later tell about this 88mm gun would make it a legend. It could be fired from a great distance to a target, and some said it had the accuracy of a rifle."

By midafternoon, the Americans were still holding on. “There was talk of tanks coming up from the beaches to help us,” said John. When he finally ventured out of his foxhole, his ears were still ringing. “I could not hold a razor steady enough to shave for the next few days.

“My friend said he had had enough and was going south to find his own unit,” John recalled. He asked John to go with him. “I thought it over for a while, and then suddenly realized the importance of the decision. Somehow, I knew that whatever I decided would affect all my future decisions. I remembered the glider field, the paratroopers hanging from the trees, and the lone trooper at his Alamo. And I knew there were more reasons to stay than to go.”

The quiet was broken again by another attack. “The Germans were recovering from their initial shock and seemed much better organized. We could see several squads of the enemy working forward to our left. They were being supported by two tanks firing from about 100 yards to their rear.

“Several machine guns were covering the advance and mortar rounds began to land amongst us. It was difficult to return fire. Anyone with an ounce of brains was hugging the ground as closely as he could. I heard a lieutenant nearby yelling for a runner, but he could not find one.

“Up until now, I had been mentally on the defensive. My indoctrination to combat had been a shocker, but it was beginning to wear off.”

Now John realized he felt anger: “at the Germans, the dirt, the noise, and the idea of being pushed back. I ran over to the lieutenant and blurted out, 'I'm a runner, sir! I worked for a battalion commander for over a year!'

" 'Good.' "

The officer pointed about a hundred yards away in an orchard. John was instructed to give firing directions to soldiers manning a mortar gun to adjust their aim.

"I zigzagged through fields and ditches. The German tanks began to zero in on the farmhouse I was headed for. I had to crawl on my stomach for the last 25 yards. Machine gun fire was following me. My canteen had received two hits and water was running down my leg. For a moment, I thought I was hit."

John got the message through to the sergeant in charge. The mortar rounds began hitting their targets and the German infantry, confused, drew back.

"With the last light of day, the attack came to a halt. With the darkness came the first quiet period we had since landing," said John. He picked up another canteen from a dead paratrooper and used the water to wipe the grime off his face, and the rest to make coffee.

"Hot biscuits and ham from my dinner rations rounded out the menu. I drifted off to sleep listening to the sound of naval shells landing into the area that the Germans had just moved into," he recalled.

"The large shells passing overhead made a strange noise that sounded like a freight train passing through a station at very high speed. We could hear tremendous explosions in the distance, followed by tremors moving the ground that would loosen the dirt on the sides of our foxholes."

When he was awakened at three in the morning on June 7 with the order to move out, it took John a few minutes to even remember where he was. Six tanks which had come up from the beach in the night had joined the unit. "They were a welcome sight, and the first confirmation for us that the landings had succeeded . . . Now that reinforcements were arriving, we were starting to meet the Germans on our own terms."

John Fitzgerald stayed with the 82nd Division as the soldiers began to push north toward the port of Cherbourg. From a new recruit, he was becoming a tried combat veteran. But, he found, his emotions ran the gamut. "One night, I found myself leading a charge up a hill and had to be restrained by a sergeant. I had experienced that moment in combat when you become completely oblivious to any fear or danger. On another occasion, that same sergeant gave me a boot in the ass when I started to fall behind during an artillery barrage. Fear would come suddenly, at unexpected times for reasons unknown, and then would wear off."

John gauged his acceptance by the quality of food he received from his fellow soldiers. One morning he got a K-ration breakfast with eggs—a special treat. "I was becoming a member of F Company, 2nd Battalion, 505 Parachute Infantry, 82nd Airborne Division."

It would be more than a week before John returned to his original company. He and about fifty other "lost" troopers were gathered together. A major thanked them for the help they'd given under challenging conditions. Then they were taken by a small convoy of trucks to their own units. "The beaches were now secure, and the initial phase of the invasion was winding down. It was good to be home," John said. "The 101st was my outfit, first, last, and always."

John learned that his fellow paratroopers in his home regiment had been engaged in heavy fighting themselves: One of his closest friends had been wounded and another killed. Others were still missing in action or had been sent back to hospitals in England.

"A lot of the guys greeted me with, 'We thought you were dead!' " John said. He'd been listed as missing in action because someone had reported seeing his body.

U.S. mortar crew just before firing into Nazi position.

"As soon as I could, I reported to Colonel [Robert] Cole. He looked me right in the eye and said, 'Fitzgerald, if I wasn't so damn glad to see you, I'd shoot you.' "

The reason? Before they jumped, Cole had asked him to put some tape on his .45 holster so he wouldn't lose the gun out of it during the jump. "Evidently I became carried away with my task. Shortly after he landed, he had to drop on a couple of Germans."

But when Cole reached for his gun, it took him several minutes to unwind the tape! In the meantime, the Germans escaped.

John Fitzgerald was decorated for his service in Normandy—in two different divisions. He received a Bronze Star for actions with the 82nd Airborne Division, as well as one for service as a runner with Lieutenant Colonel Robert Cole with the 101st Airborne Division.

John Fitzgerald had been assigned as a runner to Cole in the fall of 1942. He stayed with Cole in battles throughout the summer. And John was still serving with him when Cole was killed in action on September 17, 1944, during Operation Market Garden in Holland. Cole was awarded the Medal of Honor posthumously for his actions in Normandy.

LOOK, LISTEN, REMEMBER: Read more about the history of the 502nd Parachute Infantry, 101st Airborne Division at http://www.ww2-airborne.us/units/502/502.html.

You can find Lieutenant Robert G. Cole's Medal of Honor Citation at http://www.cmohs.org/recipient-detail/2685/cole-robert-g.php and read more about his life and death in the Market Garden operation here: http://www.ww2marketgarden.com/ltcolrobertgcole.html.

To read more about Sainte-Mère-Église today, visit the website of its Airborne Museum http://www.airborne-museum.org/en/.

CHAPTER 14

APPROACH FROM THE SEA: VOICES FROM THE BEACHHEAD

The assault on the Cotentin Peninsula had begun in darkness, when paratroopers like David Kenyon Webster and John Fitzgerald jumped inland from the beach itself.

But the invasion plan for Utah Beach also included an amphibious aspect. The entire 4th Infantry Division along with many specialized units made their way through rough seas to land on the shore beginning at 6:30 a.m. On the following pages are the voices of soldiers who arrived on the Cotentin Peninsula not from the air, but from the sea.

"Fire in the Hole": Demolishing the Beach Obstacles

"Everything lit up. Bombers went in, and so many shells exploded from ships' gunfire that it looked like the biggest Fourth of July anyone could make," said demolition expert Orval B. Wakefield. "I told the chief petty officer in our unit that no one could survive a bombardment like that.

"He said, 'You can bet there will be someone waiting when we get there.' He was right."

Orval remembered the scene. "The big guns of the battleships were booming behind us. They were so loud that they seemed to shake the boat. The surf was so rough that I was feeling seasick. By the time we hit the shore and put our feet on solid ground, we were just glad to be there.

"That sense of relief was especially true in my case," Orval added. "I am only five feet, six inches tall, so when I got off the landing craft, I was in water up to my chin."

Orval carried two sacks, the kind newspaper boys slung over their shoulders. Only his were full of explosives wrapped in old socks. "When I got out of the landing craft and found that my legs would hardly hold me up, I thought maybe I was a coward. Then I realized that the problem came from those two heavy seabags; the load of water and explosives in them probably came to more than one hundred pounds."

Orval used his knife to cut holes in the bags to drain the water, and then moved up onto Utah Beach. The beach obstacles, about five feet tall, reminded him of children's jacks—only, these were made for the children of giants. They were designed to rip the bottoms out of landing craft.

The job of the demolition unit was to destroy them as soon as possible. "Soldiers of the first wave were already coming in as well, dodging around us, and sometimes taking cover behind these giant metal pretzels because machine-gun bullets and mortar rounds were arriving on the beach in large numbers," said Orval. "We had to keep chasing the GIs away because they didn't realize how hazardous those obstacles had become."

After they set the explosives, the soldiers took cover nearby. "Someone shouted the usual warning, 'Fire in the hole,' and soon pieces of steel were flying into the air and then raining down. We had been successful," said Orval.

vision move tow
ng enemy aircra

"I don't think anything could have gotten by those obstacles because they were too solidly made. Of course, there was much more ahead for the soldiers who had to fight their way inland," reflected Orval. "The GIs gathered at the seawall, sort of working up their courage to charge ahead. The officers would say, 'Go,' and finally one brave man went up and over, then a second, and finally the rest. They looked like ants when they all went over that wall."

"When we first got ashore, there had been nothing but obstacles—then men running, turning, and dodging. With the obstacles blown apart, the beach was transformed into a beehive," said Orval.

"Even though the tide was rising higher and higher on the beach, both landing craft and amphibian vehicles were now able to move ashore safely. By evening there was a rush of vehicles. It was as busy as you could possibly believe . . . as far as I could see, the beach had been opened."

Catching It in the Face: Landing the Soldiers in an LCVP

Marvin J. Perrett was a coxswain for a Higgins landing craft, and like Andrew Higgins himself, lived in New Orleans. Just after his eighteenth birthday in September 1943, Marvin signed up for the Coast Guard and was soon on his way to boot camp in Florida.

That's where Marvin first heard about Landing Barge School. "Of course a lot of the kids didn't really know what that was but having been born and reared in New Orleans I had seen Mr. Higgins' crew building these landing craft."

Aerial view of Utah Beach.

CHAPTER 14

At Landing Barge School at Camp Lejeune, in North Carolina, Marvin learned how to operate a Higgins boat, which featured a droppable front ramp that enabled heavily equipped soldiers to exit straight out instead of having to struggle to climb over the sides.

As the new recruits practiced, instructors took notes and made assignments. Marvin was chosen to be a boat operator, a coxswain. He practiced bringing the boat into a target area from twelve miles out to sea, using a magnetic compass. It was a bit, he said, "like driving a bulldozer in water."

Marvin's LCVP (Landing Craft, Vehicle/Personnel) was approximately thirty-six feet long and ten feet wide and could hold about thirty-six fully equipped soldiers. Marvin explained, "Every one of these fellows had backpacks on with like 80 or 90 pounds of gear. Everything they owned was on their person because they didn't know whether it would be the next day or a month from now" before they could get more supplies.

Although Marvin was confident of his skills at the helm, there was another, more serious problem he faced: being seasick. "Here I am a coxswain in a foreign invasion but at that point in time I really thought that maybe they might have to put me off the ship because I was bordering on what might be termed as a 'Chronic Seasick Person,' which of course could get you into another area of duties. But what happened, for seven straight days, man, I was throwing up green because I had nothing in my stomach."

One doctor suggested he stuff his stomach with soda

crackers and go up on deck by the bow and breathe the fresh air as vigorously as he could. It worked!

The early hours of D-Day found Marvin on the attack transport ship, USS *Bayfield* (APA-33), anchored eleven or twelve miles offshore as part of Force U, destined for Utah Beach. (Also on board was a gunner's mate named Yogi Berra, who would go on to become a famous major league baseball Hall-of-Famer.)

On his first trip, Marvin struggled to keep his landing craft in line with about twelve others as they approached the beach. It was important to stay close to the other boats so that the soldiers would be with their own units once they landed. Ahead, he could see machine-gun bullets raining into the water. Anyone in their right mind would want to stop. Marvin said, "But you can't do that. You can't stop."

The thirty-six soldiers in his boat were quiet as they approached the beach. Marvin could feel the men staring at him. Finally, one said, " 'Look Cox, we landed at Sicily and Salerno a few months ago and the coxswain there put us off in about three or four feet of water, and we're telling you, you better not do that today.' "

Marvin assured the soldier he'd do his best to bring them in right to the sand. But Marvin ended up with an unexpected problem. A chaplain in the boat became violently seasick.

"He just stuck his head out over the side of the boat, up to the wind, and of course as you might imagine it was the windward side and I caught it all in the face," said Marvin. He couldn't see a thing.

"My trusty Motor Mac [motor machinist mate, in charge of the engine], seeing my dilemma he reached over and got a bucket of seawater and said, 'Close your eyes, Boats.' "

Marvin replied, " 'They're already closed. Man, hit me!' "

After two buckets of seawater, Marvin could see again. Around him, the soldiers burst out laughing. And he got them in to shore safely.

Marvin took his landing craft back to the *Bayfield,* where, to his surprise, he was asked to take just one person to shore: "the boss."

The man reminded Marvin a bit of the movie star Clark Gable, complete with a moustache. He was Major General Raymond "Tubby" Barton, commander of the 4th Infantry Division. "I'm proud to tell you that Marvin Perrett, U.S. Coast Guard, brought him ashore safely on D-Day in my New Orleans[–]made Higgins landing craft."

BRIEFING

Higgins Boats

Supreme Commander Dwight D. Eisenhower fretted about landing craft throughout World War II. His aide, Harry Butcher, once noted, "Ike says that when he is buried, his coffin should be in the shape of a landing craft, as they are practically killing him with worry." No wonder Ike is credited with calling Andrew Jackson Higgins "the man who won the war": The boats he designed helped to revolutionize amphibious landings.

Originally from Nebraska, Andrew Jackson Higgins (1886–1952) became a businessman and boat designer in New Orleans. In 1930, he incorporated Higgins Industries. Higgins built boats that could navigate shallow waters and marshes of the Gulf Coast for oil and gas exploration. This led to government contracts designing landing craft. Higgins Industries became one of the largest manufacturers of naval combat boats during World War II.

The first boats were designed without ramps, which meant troops had to jump over the side to disembark. This wasn't practical in combat conditions, which led to the innovative front ramp design, which was so integral to the D-Day landings.

Higgins Industries became an innovator in another way. According to the National World War II Museum, the company was employing over 25,000 people by the end of 1943 and was the first workforce in New Orleans to be racially integrated. "His employees included undrafted white males, women, African

Americans, the elderly and handicapped persons. All were paid equal wages according to their job rating. They responded by shattering production records, turning out more than 20,000 boats by the end of the war."

LOOK, LISTEN, REMEMBER: Find out more about the Higgins boats at the National World War II Museum: https://www.nationalww2museum.org/sites/default/files/2017-07/higgins-in-new-orleans-fact.pdf.

CHAPTER 15

ON UTAH BEACH: STARTING THE WAR FROM HERE

Major General Raymond "Tubby" Barton didn't actually expect to see Theodore Roosevelt Jr. alive again.

Ted Roosevelt was in poor health. He walked with a cane and had a heart condition he kept hidden. But when Barton went ashore on Utah Beach on the morning of June 6 (in Marvin Perrett's boat, no less), the eldest son of former president Theodore Roosevelt was there to greet him.

At fifty-six, Brigadier General Ted Roosevelt was the oldest man and highest-ranking officer to land at D-Day. He had convinced Barton to let him command the first wave of troops at Utah Beach, believing that it would help settle nervous young soldiers to know he was there.

General Omar Bradley said of him, "A brave, gamy, undersized man who trudged about the front with a walking stick, Roosevelt helped hold the division together by personal charm."

One night by the side of the road in Sicily, Roosevelt told Bradley that he'd talked to every man in the 1st Division and he'd bet the soldiers could recognize his voice even in the darkness.

Roosevelt proceeded to call out, " 'Hey, what outfit is that?'

Moving in to the beach.

" 'Company C of the 18th Infantry, General Roosevelt,' a hearty voice called back."

Not only was Roosevelt on the beach, his rallying cry there has become part of D-Day unforgettable lore. The first wave of men in about twenty boats had been put on the beach farther south than the destination. None of the landmarks they'd been briefed to look for were visible.

Realizing the error, Theodore Roosevelt gave a now-famous exhortation, " 'We're going to start the war from here.' "

Moving over the seawall at Utah Beach.

"Because the 4th Division was green to fire, it was difficult to anticipate how it might act on the assault," observed General Omar Bradley later. If Roosevelt went in with the leading wave, he could steady it as no other man could. "For Ted was immune to fear, he would stroll casually about under fire while troops about him scrambled for cover and he would banter with them and urge them forward."

With that in mind, Bradley wrote to Roosevelt and asked him to serve as a "spare" brigadier general with the 4th Infantry Division, and to help lead green troops in battle. Bradley had warned Roosevelt that he might get killed under fire. He never got a reply to his letter. Instead, Roosevelt showed up in person in London.

"He broke out of the hospital in Italy where he had been stricken with pneumonia and reported to me in London a few days later with a raging fever."

After the D-Day invasion, on July 13, Bradley was about to give Roosevelt another assignment—to help out a struggling division in Normandy. He telephoned Eisenhower's headquarters at almost midnight and got an approval from the Supreme Commander the next morning.

It was too late. Overnight, Roosevelt passed away unexpectedly of a heart attack. "Ted died as no one could have believed he would," said Bradley, "in the quiet of his tent."

Ted Roosevelt Jr. did more than inspire the first troops to land at Utah Beach. According to General Omar Bradley, Roosevelt helped turn what might have been a disaster into a success by day's end.

"With the skill and instinct of a veteran campaigner, he quickly improvised an attack to secure an exit across the lagoon that had caused us such anxiety in planning. As the lead regiment pushed across this marshland toward the lateral road three miles inland, it radioed reassuring reports to the 4th Division on the *Bayfield*," said Bradley.

Theodore Roosevelt Jr. received A Medal of Honor, the nation's highest military award, for his actions at D-Day. His Medal of Honor Citation reads, in part: "His valor, courage, and presence in the very front of the attack and his complete unconcern at being under heavy fire inspired the troops to heights of enthusiasm and self-sacrifice . . . Under his seasoned, precise, calm, and unfaltering leadership, assault troops reduced beach strong points and rapidly moved inland with minimum casualties.

"He thus contributed substantially to the successful establishment of the beachhead in France."

And Utah could be counted a success, despite the nighttime chaos and dispersed troops, the tragic loss of paratroopers, the machine-gun and sniper fire. On the beach, the bombs dropped prior to H-Hour had hit their targets. Demolition experts cleared the beaches before high tide, and German reinforcements were effectively hampered.

"By evening 22,000 men and 1,800 vehicles" had come ashore, noted historian Cornelius Ryan. "With the paratroopers, the 4th Division had secured the first major American beachhead in France."

As General James M. Gavin had discovered, the drops for

U.S. troops land reinforcements on Utah Beach.

the paratroopers of the 82nd Airborne Division were the most scattered; the Americans met with stiff German resistance from German troops in the area. That meant that for most of June 6, paratroopers were forced to group together into impromptu units and hold whatever ground they could until infantry reinforcements pushed inland from the beach.

Despite these challenges, Gavin could also report success. "By daylight, D+1, June 7, the 82nd Airborne Division occupied an area roughly triangular in shape, five or six miles on a side, on the English Channel side of the Merderet River.

Soldiers of the 8th Infantry Regiment, 4th Infantry Division, move inland.

"To the east it occupied the town of Sainte Mère Église. A number of the troopers had jumped into the town and had been killed by the German occupying forces. One trooper had dangled from one of the spires on the church and saved himself by feigning death."

But the town was in Allied hands and able to withstand counterattacks until reinforcements from the beach arrived. In part, that was thanks to a group of forty-three soldiers under the leadership of Lieutenant Turner Turnbull of the 505th Parachute Infantry Regiment.

Turnbull's men encountered a German regiment at Neuville to the north. Even though the Americans were outnumbered, they managed to keep the enemy from moving south into Sainte-Mère-Église for hours, enabling the Americans to solidify their hold on the town. With twenty-seven wounded or dead, only sixteen soldiers of Turnbull's band were able to withdraw. Some of the wounded were captured but later freed.

Thousands of soldiers took part in D-Day. The stand at Neuville by less than fifty members of one reinforced platoon became one of the most strategically important actions of the day. It came with a high cost. Turner Turnbull was killed the next day. He was posthumously awarded a Silver Star for his bravery.

Wrap-Up: Utah Beach and the Cotentin Peninsula

Very little went as planned in the assault on the Cotentin Peninsula. Thick cloud banks made it hard for the C-47 pilots flying in tight formations, as they worried about crashing into each other. Pilots carrying the paratroopers had been ordered not to take evasive action so as not to get off course, but in thick anti-aircraft fire, some did anyway. Soldiers were often stranded without extra ammunition or supplies as bundles of equipment sank out of sight in flooded fields. And while paratroopers like John Fitzgerald in the 101st Airborne Division missed their drop zones, the situation for those in the 82nd Airborne Division was, if anything, worse, with some soldiers landing miles outside the target area.

U.S. medics attend wounded soldier in first wave of D-Day landings on Utah Beach.

★

Not everything went according to plan at Utah. Paratroopers landed in a scattered fashion and sometimes far from their original drop zones. It took officers hours—sometimes days—to find the men in their unit. Strong currents meant that landing craft deposited soldiers of the 4th Infantry Division far from their target sites. Despite these setbacks and the challenging terrain, the soldiers persevered.

Omaha Beach would be more difficult—and even more deadly.

DISPATCH

The Spymaster Forgets His Cyanide

William J. "Wild Bill" Donovan was another old soldier who, like Ted Roosevelt, wasn't about to miss D-Day, even though the Secretary of the Navy had forbidden him to take part because of his position: Donovan was head of the Office of Strategic Services (OSS) America's first spy agency, and the precursor of today's Central Intelligence Agency (CIA).

Soon after Pearl Harbor, President Franklin D. Roosevelt had tapped the well-known attorney and colorful World War I hero to lead the new organization. The highly decorated Donovan (he received the Medal of Honor, Distinguished Service Cross, Silver Star, and other medals during World War I) was then in his fifties. Donovan was returned to active duty and promoted to general.

In May 1944, Donovan left Washington, D.C., for London to check on preinvasion efforts organized by Colonel David Bruce, chief of OSS activities in Europe. Donovan sat in on meetings and briefings, and never hesitated to weigh in. For instance, at one meeting, he said, "'Gentlemen, I find that here in London you have been doing too much planning. Plans are no good on the day of battle.'"

That would certainly turn out to be the case on D-Day.

★

Somehow, the old soldier managed to get himself onto a ship, and then into Normandy, arriving in the area behind Utah Beach.

Spying three French villagers in a nearby field, Donovan announced his intention of talking to them to see if they were members of the French Resistance. Warned by an American captain of the dangers, he nevertheless forged ahead, dragging his second-in-command behind him. The Frenchmen disappeared, leaving the two OSS leaders crouching behind a hedgerow as German machine-gun fire broke out.

"'David, we mustn't be captured, we know too much,'" the general declared. David Bruce agreed and then asked his boss if he'd brought his cyanide pill with him. Donovan said that yes, he had indeed brought along two suicide pills.

"Thereupon, still lying prone, he disgorged the contents of all his pockets," Bruce said later. "There were a number of hotel keys, a passport, currency of several nationalities, photographs of grandchildren, travel orders, newspaper clips, and heaven knows what else, but no pills.

"'Never mind,' said Donovan, 'we can do without them, but if we get out of here you must send a message to Gibbs, the Hall Porter at Claridges [Hotel] in London, telling him on no account to allow the servants in the hotel to touch some dangerous medicines in my bathroom.'"

After that pronouncement designed to protect the welfare of any nosy hotel maids back in London, Donovan whispered, "'I must shoot first.'"

"'But can we do much against machine guns with our pistols?'" wondered Bruce.

"'Oh, you don't understand,'" he said. "'I mean if we are about to be captured I'll shoot you first. After all, I am your Commanding Officer.'"

Luckily, it didn't come to that. Both men escaped unharmed—except for a bad cut on Donovan's throat after David Bruce fell on him to avoid fire and Bruce's steel helmet nicked him.

It's not clear if Donovan ended up with a scar. But David Bruce left Utah Beach that day with a story he would tell for many years.

READER'S INVASION BRIEFING

Omaha

And now we come to Omaha: Hell's Beach, Bloody Omaha; unforgettable and terrible.

"For this great seaborne assault which the free world had toiled so hard to mount, only about three thousand men were leading the attack," wrote the great D-Day historian Cornelius Ryan.

"The build-up was so carefully timed that heavy equipment like artillery was expected to be landed on Omaha Beach within an hour and a half, and even cranes, half-tracks and tank recovery vehicles were scheduled to come in by 10:30 a.m. It was an involved, elaborate timetable which looked as if it could not possibly hold up."

The timetable did not hold up—far from it.

★

The six-mile stretch called Omaha Beach was the longest of D-Day's five landing areas. It lay second from the west, between Utah Beach and Gold Beach. Its high sandstone bluffs offered excellent opportunities for the Germans to build defense fortifications—and they had. The cliffs themselves were too steep for tanks or vehicles. But there were five exits, or draws, off the beach leading inland.

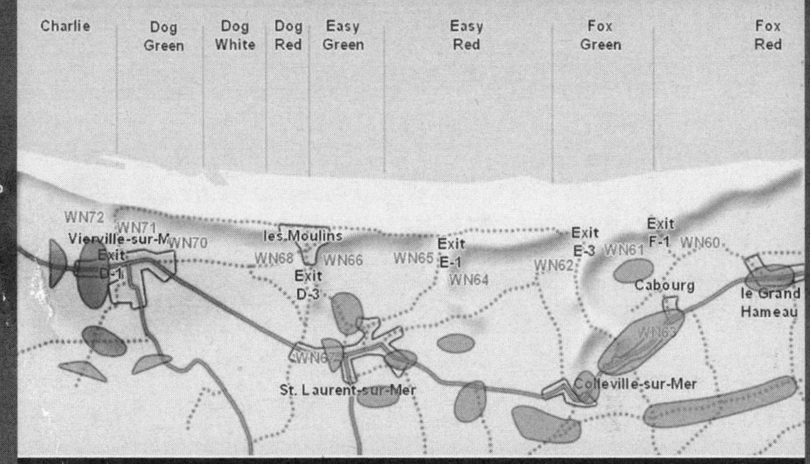

Map of Omaha Beach.

While the plans were far more detailed than presented here, it's helpful to think of Omaha as divided into two, since each part was assaulted by a separate army division.

Eastern Part of Omaha—The 16th Regiment of the 1st Division was deployed on the eastern part of Omaha. The eastern part was subdivided further into smaller sections codenamed, from east to west, Fox Red, Fox Green, and Easy Red.

Western Part of Omaha—Soldiers of the 116th Regiment of the 29th Division landed on the western part of the beach, which had also been subdivided. From east to west these sections were called Easy Green, Dog Red, Dog White, and Dog Green. The final, westernmost area was called Charlie, the target area for Army Rangers who would also assault a cliff called Pointe du Hoc. (More on that later.)

German Defenses—The Germans had mounted a series of defense strongholds, or gun nests, on the bluffs overlooking the entire beach. These were called *Widerstandsnest* (abbreviation:

WN). Well-protected and camouflaged, they contained powerful cannon-like guns trained directly on the beach and on the draws.

Some of the defense bunkers in this area were new and had only been completed in April and May. By then there were fifteen WN strongpoints along the beach. The bunkers, often encased in thick concrete, were manned by German troops and officers. They contained a variety of large guns and mortars, as well as ammunition storage rooms. The strongholds allowed the Germans a clear view of the beach—and the soldiers in the landing craft struggling in the water.

The Draws—Another important aspect of the Omaha Beach landing area was its exits, also called draws. Once soldiers landed, they needed to advance inland as quickly as possible with their equipment and vehicles to prevent being thrown back into the sea.

Omaha Beach had five such exits. Four of these were mostly rough tracks or ravines between the bluffs. But one, on the western part of the beach near Dog Green and Charlie, was a paved road. It was called the Vierville draw since it led inland to a village by that name. It also led to a coastal road. All these things combined to make the Vierville draw one of the most strategically important points on the beach.

Of course, what was obvious to the Allies was also clear to the enemy. The Germans had erected a defense stronghold, named WN72, right next to the Vierville draw. It had only recently been completed in May 1944. Another gun nearby helped to protect the road itself. The Germans were in the process of adding guns to other bunkers as well. In other words, the crucial

Vierville draw was the most heavily defended point on Omaha Beach.

★

What Went Wrong—The goals for the assault troops at Omaha included capturing inland villages and controlling coastal roads, linking up with British forces from Gold Beach, and capturing the guns at a high promontory called Pointe du Hoc between Omaha and Utah Beach.

Many things went wrong at Omaha. The tide in Normandy is ferociously fast and extreme. The difference between high and low tide is more than twenty feet, and the tide rises at a rate of one foot every eight minutes. Strong currents and winds pushed landing craft consistently eastward, away from their precise targets. This resulted in separated units and stranded, seasick, waterlogged, and lost soldiers. Just as on Utah, many of the protruding beach obstacles were mined, but on Omaha they weren't demolished before the landing craft arrived.

Another critical factor was the failure of the preassault bombings by Allied planes and ships to destroy German defensive positions. The enemy's powerful guns remained intact. The Allies also faced more troops than expected: Word that elements from experienced German troops of the 352nd Division had been moved into the area came too late to impact the plan.

Taken together, all these factors made Omaha Beach the deadliest landing site. On D-Day, it was the selfless, courageous acts of individuals against extraordinary odds that made the difference. Only a few of their stories are told here.

PART 5

OMAHA

"Then we saw the coast of France and suddenly we were in the midst of the armada of the invasion. People will be writing about this sight for a hundred years and whoever saw it will never forget it . . . there could not be so many ships in the world . . ."

MARTHA GELLHORN, war correspondent

"The thought came that the crusade in Europe had been called off as a bad job, and that we waterlogged few were left to struggle alone in the great, dark seascape. The first assault wave, already on the beach, did not resemble a battle line as much as it did heaps of refuse, deposited there to burn and smolder unattended."

CHARLES R. CAWTHON,
116th "Stonewall" Regiment, 29th Infantry Division

USS *AUGUSTA* 3:35 A.M., OFF THE NORMANDY COAST

"It was 3:35 a.m. when the clanking bell outside my cabin called the crew to battle stations," said General Omar Bradley. He grabbed his helmet and hurried to the bridge. "The moon hung misted in an overcast sky and the wind still lashed the

USS *Augusta* off coast while landing craft head for shore.

Channel . . . Off in the Cotentin Peninsula, almost 30 miles to the west, both airborne divisions had already been dropped."

H-Hour for the beaches would be next. Truman "Tubby" Thorson ("Tubby" was, it seems, a popular nickname for high-ranking officers), a top general on Bradley's staff, shook his head at the heaving black waves. " 'I don't like it, General. The DDs [duplex drive amphibious tanks] are going to have one helluva time in getting through this sea.'

" 'Yes, Tubby, I'm afraid you're right. But at this point there's nothing we can do.' " As Bradley knew all too well, final decisions or last-minute changes about the tanks—and most everything else—now rested with commanders on the front lines of combat.

"By now Overlord had run beyond the reach of its admirals and generals," he reflected. "For the next few tortured hours we could do little but pace our decks and trust in the men to whom The Plan had been given for execution."

As the *Augusta* moved into position for firing its guns, Bradley plugged his ears with cotton. The ship was mounted with eight-inch turret guns that were now trained on German machine nests and concrete bunkers high on the bluffs overlooking Omaha Beach.

Omaha's formidable defensive fortifications covered not only the beach but the draws, the exit routes inland. One bunker, located on the eastern part of Omaha, was manned by thirty-nine troops. It contained "no fewer than seven machine guns, two mortars, two antitank guns, and two field guns."

Built directly into cliffs and the crests of hills, these fortifications were well camouflaged. Even so, many had been identified in advance by Allied intelligence. But there were more guns than the Americans realized—and the time allotted for naval bombardment was short.

In the spring of 1944, the Germans had added more firepower to the beach defenses, meaning that some artillery batteries at Omaha escaped detection and were not targeted. Military historian Steven Zaloga, who has written extensively about the German defense of Omaha, notes that "One reason that the U.S. Army was so unprepared for the scale of defenses on Omaha Beach was their relatively late appearance." In other words, much of the naval gunfire was ineffective.

Later, a German soldier in one of the Omaha defensive strongholds commented on the rockets launched from one aspect of the preinvasion naval bombardment—rockets from Allied LCT(R) rocket ships offshore: "'All the rockets landed in front of us. Some hit the beach but most landed harmlessly in the water.'"

On the *Augusta*, naval officer John Mason Brown described the first salvos from the ship. "At 6:10 we prepare to fire. In the Pilot House we see our guns pause ominously; pause and point . . . Then we wait . . . We wait. And just when we are holding our twice-inhaled breath, the *Augusta* quivers beneath us. The sound invades our ears. Even the cotton cannot hold it back.

"It roars at well-timed intervals, like a volcano trained to choral action. Each time the roar comes fore or aft, the *Augusta* lurches slightly, as from a ground swell of noise . . . The smoke ahead of us is heavy whenever the forward turrets have their say. Thereafter this smoke vanishes, like the flames which beckoned it into wide rings, even as the smoke evaporates, screening a conjurer's trick."

Fog and clouds of smoke obscured the coastline. The bombers of the Eighth Air Force could be heard overhead, roaring toward the shore to destroy these guns of Hitler's Atlantic Wall. But at Omaha, they didn't succeed. "Not until later did we learn that most of the 13,000 bombs dropped by these heavies had cascaded harmlessly into the hedgerows three miles behind the coast," Bradley said.

And that meant that many of these deadly German guns—more than the Allies even knew—were aimed and ready to stop anyone and anything emerging from the sea.

H-Hour was 6:30 a.m. In the minutes and hours that followed, John Mason Brown felt removed from the action on shore. "Seen through binoculars on the large ships, the shore is an anthill in turmoil. The death cries do not reach us," said Brown. "The falling bodies we do not see. The first desperate dash through the water is beyond our vision.

"The first contacts with the barriers and obstacles we can only guess at. The first, and all-important, hand-to-hand test of arms we do not see. We do not even hear the sulphurous stammering of the machine guns.

"The initial confusion is not ours. We know only this unholy and disquieting calm."

For the soldiers at Omaha nothing was calm—not in the wave-tossed boats, not in the cold, rough sea, and not on the deadly sand.

VOICES FROM

What We Carried

"About 2:00 a.m., we were called out to get ready. Instead of our regular back packs, we had been issued an assault jacket, a sort of vest like garment with many pockets and pull strap fasteners to yank off in a hurry.

"In the various pockets we stored K-rations, a quarter pound of TNT with fuses, hand grenades, a smoke grenade and a medical kit with a syringe and morphine. Besides our regular M-1 clips, we had two slings of ammo belts across our shoulders. On our backs, we carried an entrenching tool, a bayonet, and a poncho and whatever else we could stuff in . . .

"Our rifles were wrapped in a protective cellophane wrapper with an inflated life preserver tube strapped to it to keep it afloat. Altogether our equipment weighed about 70 pounds. It was an awkward assortment around which we buckled a rubber life belt which was to be inflated by squeezing a C0/2 tube."

JOHN J. BARNES,
116th Regiment, 29th Infantry Division

"Here is a list of what I had on me. First we started with the invasion vest, and the helmet of course, four bandoliers across my chest, full of cartridges . . . two hand grenades, one smoke grenade, one M-1 rifle and cartridge belt, one full canteen . . . one invasion gas mask . . . one bayonet rifle, one pole charge [explosive device] with 30 lbs. of TNT, that's about six foot tall. In my vest pockets I carried two pairs of socks and underwear, three days of C-rations, two and a half cartons of cigarettes, old letters and pictures, one raincoat and one apple from breakfast . . . I figured I must have had about 75 lbs. altogether extra weight. I also had a small folding shovel."

CHARLES "CHUCK" H. THOMAS,
16th Infantry Regiment, 1st Division

In the Boats

"In my boat, there was no conversation. Talk would have been difficult in any event above the roar of the engine, the wind, slamming of the waves against the ramp, and the laboring of the bilge pump that just managed to keep up with the water washing in over bow and sides. We simply stood packed together, encased in equipment, inarticulate with the noise and with the enormity toward which we were laboring."

CHARLES CAWTHON,
116th Regiment, 29th Infantry Division

"The towering gray-black waves smashed against our small boat, attempting to swallow it up. All the boats were tossed

around like matchsticks. We were immediately soaked by the icy English Channel's ten-to-fifteen-foot waves. The bilge pumps were not capable of handling all the water in the boat, so we had to bail out the water with our helmets.

"There was not only water in the boat, but also floating vomit. Unlike so many others, I was not afflicted by the vomiting caused by seasickness. My theory for not vomiting was to chew gum, suck on candy, and keep swallowing."

HAROLD BAUMGARTEN,
116th Infantry Regiment, 29th Infantry Division

"In my own boat and many others I discovered we had to rip up the floor boards and use our helmets to bail out the water and on top of that some of the fellows were vomiting and a little later on while being shot at you can imagine the situation there with the bailing water with your helmet dodging bullets and vomiting all at the same time, not much fun I can assure you."

JAMES W. EIKNER,
2nd Ranger Battalion

"Gradually, we began to see shapes of other boats, many small ones, many larger hulks, we heard the noise of planes droning overhead, flying off toward the coast. Now we could see the anti-aircraft fire lighting up the sky, tracing arcing the night. The seasickness seemed to end as more men stood up and watched the growing sight . . .

"Then a flash, followed by a mighty roar came from one of the black hulks we had just passed. It was a gun of the big battleship whose great shadow loomed behind us. The bright flash, the loud roar and the reverberation that followed was overwhelming.

"Dawn lightened, and we could see more and more ships and more planes in the sky. We were entranced at this huge scene. Someone shouted, 'Take a good look! This is something you will tell your grandchildren!' No one muttered the question, 'What if we don't live?' "

JOHN J. BARNES,
116th Regiment, 29th Infantry Division

In the Water

"Suddenly, a swirl of water wrapped around my ankles, and the front of the craft dipped down. The water quickly reached my knees . . . Quickly, the boat fell away from me, and I squeezed the CO tubes in my life belt. Just as I did, it popped away. The buckle had broken. I was going under . . . I was unable to keep my head above the surface, I tried to pull the release straps on my jacket, but I couldn't free them . . . Lieutenant [Edward] Gearing grabbed my jacket, and, using his bayonet, he cut the straps and others helped release me from the weight. I was all right now. I could swim."

JOHN J. BARNES,
116th Regiment, 29th Infantry Division

"There was a strong undercurrent carrying us to the left . . . Sergeant [Philip] Streczyk [who later received the Distinguished Service Cross for his actions on D-Day] and the medic . . .

were carrying an eighteen-foot ladder, which was to be used for crossing the anti-tank ditch or any other purpose which might arise. They were struggling with it in the water just about the time that I was having my worst trouble staying afloat.

"As the ladder came by, I grabbed it. Streczyk yelled and said, 'Lieutenant, we don't need any help.'

"But hell, I was busy trying to get help, not give it."

JOHN SPALDING [sometimes spelled Spaulding],
16th Regiment, 1st Infantry Division

Bringing in Six Tanks on Landing Craft Tank 1171

"We were due at 8:30 to land our first tanks . . . There were ships everywhere and merchant ships everywhere and balloons flying and God knows what, and it was rough . . . Couldn't get in anywhere. It was all cluttered up with junk . . . broken down landing craft, assault craft, broken down tanks—we couldn't get in . . . So we were told to push off down the beach and see if we could find somewhere to beach. And we eventually went in . . .

"The beach itself was chaos. I mean it was just a mass of moving things and then we were being shelled from a bunker. We were being shelled from both ends . . . We were under these heavy guns being blasted by the Yankee battleships. Every time they fired, I think, we lifted out of the water. You weren't scared because you were so busy but we watched our tanks go off towards the gully they were trying to get up, and they were all shot up before they got off the beach—all the tanks we landed. We saw them all shot up."

AUSTIN PROSSER,
Royal Naval Reserve

If I'm Going to Die

"We were all wearing the new sleeveless combat jackets, with all kinds of pockets. Everything was impregnated against the eventuality of a gas attack. This included long johns. I did not wear mine that morning. I figured if I'm going to die, I'm not going to go scratching myself. I was a rifleman—demolition man. I estimated that I had approximately 85 lbs. on my person.

"When the ramp went down, I inflated my Mae West [life vest] and I went down. It [the water] was up to my neck . . . The beach was mined at low tide with those jumping mines that detonated when you stepped on them. There were mines floating on the surface too. They were setting these off with automatic weapon fire and shelling from 88s [a powerful German gun] and mortars. There were many yards of water to get out of. Many were hit in the water and many drowned as a result.

"At one point, I found myself trying to take cover behind one of those fence post type obstacles. I must have looked like an ostrich hiding. But believe me, at the time it looked like a wall. I was seasick and exhausted and scared to death . . . I was wounded three times at very short intervals . . . I lost all my fear and knew I was about to die, made peace with my Maker and was just waiting.

"I could not move. Confusion all around . . . After what seemed like an eternity, I was seen by two of my buddies . . . They did a very brave thing. They exposed themselves under fire, came down and dragged me up to the wall . . . Between all my wounds, loss of blood and all the pieces of shrapnel, my whole body was affected. I thought I was dead. It still feels like yesterday in my mind."

JOHN H. MACPHEE,
16th Regiment, 1st Infantry Division

Things Going Badly

"Signs that things were going amiss abounded, had I been battle-wise enough to read them: those silent guns of the battleship, indicating that it was out of touch with the assault and fearful of firing into it; a trickle, instead of stream, of return traffic from the landing of the first wave, which told of craft either destroyed or landing badly off target. Still another was the vacant sky where we had expected to see fighter-bombers diving and strafing the beach."

CHARLES CAWTHON,
116th Regiment, 29th Infantry Division

CHAPTER 16

SOME KIND OF PRAYER

On the eastern part of Omaha Beach

Breakfast that morning was at 3:00 a.m. on board the U.S. Coast Guard troop transport USS *Samuel Chase*. Along with the soldiers, photographer Robert Capa was served hot cakes, eggs, sausages, and, of course, coffee. And like many others, he found it hard to eat.

An hour later, the soldiers from the "Fighting First" division assembled on the open deck, watching as the landing boats swung from cranes, about to be lowered and loaded for the eastern part of the beach. Capa stood with them. "Waiting for the first ray of light, the two thousand men stood in perfect silence; whatever they were thinking, it was some kind of prayer."

The photographer was silent, too. He found his thoughts wandering to pleasant memories of the past—visions of green fields; pink clouds; peaceful, grazing sheep. "None of us was at all impatient, and we wouldn't have minded standing in the darkness for a very long time."

Capa was also thinking of what lay ahead, of the photos he would take when the sun came up. And it would come up, he knew. "The sun had no way of knowing that this day was different from all others, and rose on its usual schedule."

The seas were rough. Instantly the men got soaked. Even those who hadn't eaten breakfast got sick. Puke bags had been provided, but they weren't enough, since everyone was puking. "The coast of Normandy was still miles away when the first unmistakable popping reached our listening ears. We ducked down in the puky water in the bottom of the barge."

An African American boatswain, returning from the shore with an empty boat, flashed an encouraging "V for victory" sign. It was light enough now, and Capa took his first camera from its waterproof wrap. He had two cameras, both loaded with film. (These were the days before digital.) The bottom of the Higgins boat hit the sand in waist-deep water about a hundred yards from shore. Around him, the men began to wade out onto the Easy Red sector of Omaha Beach. Capa's photographs help us see, though we can never really know, what it was like.

As he paused to take his first picture, Capa suddenly felt a kick from behind. The boatswain had assumed Capa stopped because he was frozen with fear. Capa moved off. "The bullets tore holes in the water around me, and I made for the nearest steel obstacle."

Capa snapped a few photos. The tide was coming in; the sea was cold and rose to his chest. He wanted to keep moving forward. "The bullets chased me back every time." He saw a DD tank ahead, half-burned, sticking out of the water and

decided to try to make for its cover. He had to wade past floating bodies.

Behind the tank, Capa got pinned again by heavy fire. He snapped more photos, then gathered his courage to make a final push toward the sand. There seemed to be no letup in the fire. The tide kept coming in, higher and higher. It reached the farewell letter he'd tucked into a breast pocket. At last he waded in behind two soldiers, staggered to the sand, and threw himself down.

The beach here sloped a bit, affording a little protection if he pressed himself flat. Capa changed cameras and began to shoot again, frantically, one picture after another, barely raising his head. "Above the boots and faces, my picture frames

were filled with shrapnel smoke; burnt tanks and sinking barges formed my background."

Now both cameras were empty. Capa reached into his bag for a new roll of film. But his wet, shaking hands ruined the film.

"I paused for a moment . . . and then I had it bad.

"The empty camera trembled in my hands. It was a new kind of fear shaking my body from toe to hair, and twisting

my face. I unhooked my shovel and tried to dig a hole. The shovel hit stone under the sand and I hurled it away. The men around me lay motionless. Only the dead on the waterline rolled with the waves."

In the water, an LCI [Landing Craft Infantry, probably large] came close, and medics poured off it. Capa wrote later, "I did not think and I didn't decide it. I just stood up and ran toward the boat. I stepped into the sea between two bodies and the water reached to my neck. The rip tide hit my body and every wave slapped my face under my helmet.

"I held my cameras high above my head, and suddenly I knew that I was running away. I tried to turn but couldn't face the beach, and told myself, 'I am just going to dry my hands on that boat.' "

He climbed up on deck. And in the next few minutes everything seemed to happen all at once. He felt a hard shock—and then all at once something was flying through the air. He thought it was feathers. But it was kapok—it had been stuffed inside the jackets of men, and those men had just been blown apart by a mine explosion that had ripped away part of the boat. The skipper of the boat was crying. His assistant, right near him, had been killed.

Capa went down to the engine room. He managed to dry his hands and load his cameras again. He went back on deck and took a picture of the beach. A boat came by and picked up the survivors off the LCI, now sinking fast. He looked again at the beach, but he didn't get into the water.

Capa ended up back where he'd started, on the USS *Samuel*

Chase. The last wave of soldiers was being lowered into landing craft. But the decks weren't empty; they were already full with wounded and the dead. He put down his cameras and spent the rest of D-Day helping with stretchers.

Later, he started taking pictures again. "Then things got confused . . .

"I woke up in a bunk. My naked body was covered with a rough blanket. On my neck, a piece of paper read, 'Exhaustion case. No dog tags [i.e., a soldier's identification tags]. My camera bag was on the table, and I remembered who I was."

Robert Capa was next to another man, the only survivor from an amphibious tank crew. The soldier said he should have stayed on the beach. "I told him that I should have stayed on the beach myself."

Back in England, Capa was offered the chance to go to London to give a broadcast. He said people wanted to treat him like a hero. He turned down the offer. Instead, he went back to the beachhead in the first available boat.

A week later, he got word that his pictures were the best of the invasion. However, he was also told that an overexcited darkroom assistant had turned on too much heat at the end of the process, ruining all but eight of one hundred and six pictures.

Those that survived were slightly out of focus. When they were first printed, Robert Capa noted ruefully, "The captions under the heat-blurred pictures read that Capa's hands were badly shaking."

But they weren't. Not then, they weren't.

LOOK, LISTEN, REMEMBER: Robert Capa's few surviving photographs have become the most famous pictures taken of D-Day. The pictures epitomize the courage of the men who braved chaos, confusion, and death on Omaha Beach on D-Day. Capa later gave his World War II memoir the title *Slightly Out of Focus*.

To learn more about the Hungarian-born American photographer, visit the International Center of Photography at https://www.icp.org/browse/archive/constituents/robert-capa?all/all/all/all/1.

CHAPTER 17

A SCENE OF HAVOC AND DESTRUCTION

On the eastern part of Omaha Beach

Albert Mominee, 16th Regiment, 1st Infantry Division— on Fox Green, eastern part of Omaha Beach

Packed tightly onto a fully loaded landing craft, Corporal Albert Mominee carried not a camera, but a rifle and two boxes of machine-gun ammunition. He and thirty-four other infantry soldiers from the 16th Regiment, 1st Infantry Division were headed for Fox Green, on the eastern part of Omaha Beach. The 16th Regiment would lead the assault wave with four companies, about 750 men each, carried in on twenty-four landing craft.

Many of the men, including Albert, had combat experience in the Mediterranean. It would help them achieve their D-Day mission: to land and push inward along two exits, called the St. Laurent and Colleville draws. They expected to encounter some resistance from German defenses that hadn't been destroyed in the preinvasion bombings. Although they didn't yet know it, that resistance would be much fiercer than anticipated.

Approaching the beach.

Just getting to the beach turned out to be more difficult than he expected. "The rough sea with spray from the waves coming over the bow made it difficult for the coxswain to maneuver the craft," said Albert. "So right from the beginning we were in trouble. It seemed to me we were going in circles."

Once, they almost drew close enough for the soldiers to disembark. But they backed away again under heavy machine-gun fire. Trying to maneuver and correct their position took up precious minutes—and then more minutes. Albert's boat had been scheduled for landing at 6:40 a.m. Now they were more than an hour late, the tide was coming in, covering the obstacles that were laced with deadly mines.

And then they hit one. "About 400 yards from shore, the craft gave a sudden lurch as it hit an obstacle and in an instant an explosion erupted followed by a blinding flash of fire . . . Flames raced around and over us . . .

"It happened so quickly, so fast," said Albert. "I remember my first impulse was to get out of the craft . . . Not all could, or did, especially the men who had the flame thrower strapped to their backs. They never had a chance.

"Before I knew it I was in the water."

Engulfed by fire, Albert's stricken landing craft had come to rest partially out of the water, stuck on some underwater obstacle. Instinctively, he jumped clear of the flames.

"The first thing I remember doing was to pull the [emergency release] straps on my combat jacket and let it slip into the water," he said, knowing the heavy jacket would drag him down. Then he inflated his life vest.

A veteran of campaigns in North Africa and Sicily, Albert knew to keep moving. A few other survivors clung without moving to the sides of the remains of the boat, making them easy targets for German machine gunners onshore. Albert said, "It was because they panicked . . . it was their first time in action."

Albert kept propelling himself toward the shore. At five feet one inch, he was just tall enough to meet the army's height requirements. It seemed to take a long time until the sea became shallow enough that he could wade. "I was exhausted and in shock. A few times I stumbled, picked myself up and struggled, trying to force myself to continue on.

"Thirty yards to go and then twenty, I started to catch my breath, when I heard a voice shouting, 'Come on, Little One! Come on! You can make it!' "

It was his lieutenant, urging him on. And it worked. "It seemed like someone had awakened me from a dream. I looked ahead and saw him at the water's edge. I lunged towards him and as I reached him, he grabbed my hand and pulled me out of the water, then practically dragged me to the cover of the overhanging cliff, which gave us ample protection from the enemy fire."

Albert's eyebrows and hair were singed from the explosion. He was lucky: Only six of the thirty-five soldiers on board escaped unharmed. "As I sat underneath the safety of the cliff with the men of I Company, some wounded, others badly burnt, the suddenness of all that happened and the nearness I'd come to death . . . gradually wore off."

Albert took in the abandoned tanks and vehicles, medics tending the wounded, equipment littering the sand. "All I could see was a scene of havoc and destruction."

Albert and others stayed on the beach, disoriented, separated from their units, and exhausted. It wouldn't be until the next morning when Albert was able to find his unit again and return to "the Fighting Fronts."

Charles "Chuck" H. Thomas, 16th Regiment, 1st Infantry Division—on Easy Red, eastern part of Omaha

Easy Red belied its name. It was not an easy place to be that morning. But that's where twenty-year-old Chuck Thomas was headed on his first day of combat as a member of Company C, a rifle unit of the 16th Regiment, 1st Infantry Division.

Others in the division nicknamed the "Fighting Fronts" were combat-hardened veterans of amphibious assaults in North Africa and Sicily. Chuck, however, was a new replacement. He'd trained on anti-tank guns, but when he arrived in England in the fall of 1943, his new commanding officer told him with a laugh, "'You're a rifleman now. We don't lose many anti-tank men.'"

As they crossed the English Channel on board the *Samuel Chase*, Chuck had tried to memorize landmarks on the briefing map: "trees, farm houses, hills and hedgerows, and the beaches we were to land on, everything in detail." Like many

U.S. soldier rests at cliff on Omaha Beach.

An LCVP landing craft from the *Samuel Chase* approaches Omaha Beach. The boat is smoking from a fire that resulted when a German machine-gun bullet hit a hand grenade on board.

others, he got little sleep. Like many others, he took seasickness pills that didn't work.

And, like many others, his journey to shore was a nightmare. "The planes bombed the beach, the warships shelled, we got in Higgins boats on deck so we didn't have to climb down rope ladders like some other boats. The water was very rough. I would say the waves were about four or five feet . . . While I'm not sure exactly where we tried to land, it was supposed to be Easy Red."

On their approach, the coxswain was killed trying to open the ramp on their Higgins boat. The lieutenant tried next and was wounded in the arm. "They finally got it open and then I was last off the boat because I had a pole charge [a six-foot pole with 30 lbs. of TNT attached to it; Chuck had also tied a life belt on it so the pole would float]. I was in the corner. I . . . stopped to pick up a smoke grenade. Someone dropped it, as if I didn't have enough to carry. Anyway, the guy running the boat yelled to me to get off. I yelled back that I wasn't in any hurry!"

The water was deep, over Chuck's head. "Although I knew how to swim, I was scared because there were bullets landing all around . . . and I had 30 lbs. of TNT to worry about [which could explode if struck]. I had my helmet strapped around my neck, and I was dragging my rifle by the sling with one arm underwater and I couldn't reach the bottom . . .

"Then besides all that, a sergeant bobbed up next to me, yelling he can't swim," Chuck went on. "So I pushed my pole charge into him. I told him to hang on and I left him floating. He did make it in."

It felt like an hour before he touched the beach, though later Chuck guessed it was only about fifteen minutes. "When I finally got to shore, there were a lot of wounded and dead. But you couldn't tell who was who, and we had orders when we reached the beach to get as far in as we could and don't stop to help any wounded because the medics would take care of them. And we could get shot ourselves if we waited too long.

"So I reached the first layer of shale, or rocks, or whatever they were, shingles, I guess they called them. And I stayed there, because the next layer was crowded with men being killed and wounded. Some were trying to dig in with their bare hands. There were mortar and artillery shells landing all over the place . . .

"Then as I crawled up to the second layer of shale, and fired my rifle at the smoke filled hill, you couldn't see the enemy, but he could sure see us. One guy next to me had a slug through his helmet. It went through a pair of socks he had carried inside his helmet, but didn't hit his head, so he was lucky."

After resting, Chuck crawled back down to the water line to try to drag in some ammunition carts and short-barreled mortar guns. He also saw three tanks; two had been knocked out by German guns. Men were also trying to get the third operational. "Colonel [George A.] Taylor was there directing fire.

"They fired one tank that was left and yelling that we were being killed on the beach, let's go inland, and get off the beach."

Get off the beach. That wouldn't be easy, either. Chuck found a path going up a hill. A sergeant from his squad yelled to watch out for mines—they were everywhere.

"I made the top after an engineer with a mine detector put tape down [to show where the mines were]." By now it was close to eleven in the morning.

"When we got to the top, I could see the whole beach. What a mess! And the LCTs and LCIs were trying to get nearer to land . . . there were only about twenty-five or maybe thirty guys after we met at the top of the hill. So we divided up and

U.S. medic treats a wounded German on Omaha Beach.

went down both sides of the fields along the hedgerows. We had no radio or communications to anyone.

"As far as I could see the Germans could have swept us off with brooms if they knew we were there with so few men," Chuck said. "My best buddy from Chicago, named David, put on his glasses and said, 'Now I can see!' Ten minutes later he was killed going into a barnyard. I felt sick about it."

That afternoon, they ran into German machine-gun and artillery fire as they made their way inland. Chuck spent the night of June 6 dozing in a ditch. And somehow he had managed to keep a snack. "It calmed down a little and I ate my apple left over from breakfast."

June 6 was the first of many days of combat for Chuck Thomas, who fought through the summer and into the fall, battling all the way into Germany, where he was wounded. He was discharged and returned home in December 1945.

Once, before a night patrol, a soldier named Jake, who was also from Chicago, borrowed Chuck's watch, which had a luminous dial. He was killed on that patrol. After the war, at a memorial service in Chicago, Chuck asked Jake's mother if a watch had been sent home with his belongings. Yes, she told him, there had been a watch.

"It was a gift from my brother before I went overseas," said Chuck. "But I didn't tell her it was my watch. I thought it best that way."

CHAPTER 18

A THIN, WET LINE OF KHAKI

On the western part of Omaha Beach

Charles Cawthon, 116th Regiment, 29th Infantry Division—on Dog Red, western part of Omaha Beach

Farther west, the craft carrying Captain Charles Cawthon and other members of the 116th Regiment, 29th Infantry Division, was headed for Dog Red, near the middle of Omaha Beach.

"We were in among the beach obstacles: big, ugly structures of iron or logs partially covered by the rising tide." The Tennessee native saw no evidence that demolition experts had been able to clear paths through this deadly minefield.

Their boat jolted to a sudden stop. They were stuck on a sandbar two hundred yards from shore, but at least they were in one piece. The coxswain lowered the ramp; the men stumbled out into cold, shoulder-deep water.

As his life belt lifted him up on the crest of a wave, Charles saw a line of dark objects in the distance. "Some of the larger ones, recognizable as tanks and landing craft, were erupting black smoke. Higher up the beach were a line of smaller dots, straight as though drawn with a ruler, for they were aligned along a sea wall. Scattered black specks were detaching themselves from the surf and laboring toward this line."

And now he was one of those black specks. Charles spied a house set back from the beach—a landmark familiar from his preinvasion briefing. That was good news: They seemed to have landed in the right place.

In fact, the currents and winds wreaked havoc that morning, taking many boats off course. Some soldiers found themselves on unrecognizable stretches of sand, their memorized briefings rendered meaningless. One confused company of the 116th Regiment put to shore two miles from their target site. A company of the 16th Regiment fared even worse, landing so far to the east they were virtually isolated on a narrow stretch of beach directly in front of a German defense stronghold.

Charles fell into a pattern, riding the waves ever closer to the chaos ahead. As each wave receded, he was able to touch bottom. Then he was lifted again on the next wave. Like it or not, he was being pulled to Normandy on the rising tide.

The up-and-down motion gave him quick, snapshot-like glimpses of what lay ahead. "From the crests, the beach was visible, and then, in the troughs, only the green-black water."

And as he drew closer to Omaha Beach, Charles could see something else: "its exploding horror."

Charles crouched, trying to stay below the surface of the water as much as possible. He thought it was now about 7:30 a.m. He'd already seen enough to guess that the promised

28

naval and air attacks hadn't been very effective in destroying the German guns. "The havoc they had wrought was all around in an incredible chaos—bodies, weapons, boxes of demolitions, flame throwers, reels of telephone wire, and personal equipment from socks to toilet articles.

"Hundreds of the brown life belts were washing to and fro, writhing and twisting like brown sea slugs. The waves broke around the disabled tanks, bulldozers, and beached landing craft that were thick here in front of the heavily defended exit road."

The incoming tide was narrowing a wide stretch of sand. Beyond that was a bank of stones ending at a sea wall. "Against the wall were soldiers of the first assault teams. Some were scooping out shelters; a number were stretched out in the loose attitude of the wounded; others had the ultimate stillness of death; but most were just sitting with backs against the wall."

Charles tried to get his bearings. "While I was straining to see above the debris and still stay in the dubious protection of the water, one of the explosions that was still rippling up and down the beach erupted close by; there was a jar to the side of my face and blood started streaming off my chin." He realized that "this killing zone was no place to linger."

He tried to rise. But his new combat assault jacket, with its many pockets, had become so waterlogged he felt as if he carried the weight of the entire English Channel. "My overriding doubt on the edge of Omaha Beach was not about success of the invasion, but over whether I would ever make it up the steep rise for twenty to thirty yards with my burden.

"I had long preached the army's hopeful maxim that a good soldier never abandons his equipment, but, without a second thought, I jettisoned the assault jacket into the litter in the surf, and, free of its weight, went lumbering up the beach, streaming water at every step."

Charles reached the wall, gasping for air. He began to retch up all the salt water he'd swallowed. Minutes later, a colonel appeared beside him and said it was time to get the assault moving inland. "Gradually, my lungs and stomach stopped heaving, and taking thought that this was, after all, a battle in which I had responsibilities, I took my pistol from its holster and from the plastic bag that was to have protected it from water."

He discovered it was useless—gritty with sand and totally unusable. Charles noticed other discarded firearms littering the sand around him. If the Germans had been smart, he thought, the enemy soldiers would have left their gun emplacements and come down to sweep up every exhausted, wet American.

Charles was still sitting there when Major Sidney Bingham, who commanded Charles's battalion, the 2nd, appeared and announced, " 'This is a debacle.' "

Charles had to agree the word suited the scene. Most of the men in Bingham's unit had landed on an exceptionally well-fortified stretch of beach, near one of the draws, or exits. Historian Joseph Balkoski notes that "In the invasion's first hour, enemy troops occupying these strongpoints had inflicted dreadful casualties on Bingham's men, leaving most of the survivors paralyzed behind the shingle."

Bingham ordered Charles to get moving. Charles's original job had been to set up a battalion command post with field telephones and radios. In the piles of debris, he began to look for wire, a telephone, and other communications equipment. He spied a reel of telephone wire, coated with sand, but no telephone.

As Charles poked around in the debris, dashing and dodging behind anything that might shield him from fire, he was hit again—this time on the other cheek. Realizing that any attempt to set up communications was fruitless, he decided to follow the major, who had set out up the bluff.

Charles eventually found a path, though it didn't seem to be the one he remembered from his preinvasion briefing. But, he realized, so many things about that original plan hadn't come to pass. "The foot soldier who survives in combat long enough—that is to say, a few hours—learns that plans and circumstances seldom coincide.

"Our plan did not provide for four-to-five foot waves, winds up to eighteen knots, or for an additional German division in the defenses.

"The results of these unforeseen factors were shock, inertia, and disorder," said Charles, who would later recall the afternoon and night of D-Day as a time of confused scenes that sometimes faded or ran together, his memories concealed by the fog of battle.

"The only salvation of the day was the initiative and enterprise of a relative few who rose above the wreckage of the plan."

The wreckage of the plan: From the deck of the USS *Augusta*, General Omar Bradley continued to train binoculars on the hazy shore, trying to assess what was happening to the tightly orchestrated invasion schedule.

He was getting only fragmentary reports by radio. As Charles Cawthon was experiencing, establishing field communications wasn't feasible in these battle conditions. Bradley recalled that "As the morning lengthened, my worries deepened over the

U.S. troops rest at a chalk cliff, Omaha Beach.

alarming and fragmentary reports we picked up . . . From these messages we could piece together only an incoherent account of sinkings, swampings, heavy enemy fire, and chaos on the beaches."

The enemy fire was indeed extremely heavy. When the bombers and the naval ships failed to hit their target, the German defenses on the cliffs of Omaha, already more robust than any other beach, were left largely intact. Soldiers struggling off landing craft found themselves assaulted by fire from eighty-five machine-gun nests, thirty-five pillboxes containing machine guns, thirty-five rocket launchers, six mortar pits, and eight large concrete gun bunkers.

"By 8:30 the two assault regiments on Omaha had expected to break through the water's-edge defenses and force their way inland to where a road paralleled the coast line a mile behind the beaches," said Bradley.

But when 8:30 a.m. came, the general hadn't even received confirmation of the landing. And then, around ten in the morning, he got a dismal report confirming his fears: Some of the DD tanks had been swamped and never made it to shore.

Two tank divisions comprised of thirty-two DD tanks had been scheduled to land on Omaha. Thirty-two tanks of the 741st Tank Division, designated for the eastern half of the beach to support the 16th Regiment at Easy Red, Fox Green, and Fox Red, were launched according to the original plan—about 6,000 yards or three miles from shore. This proved disastrous. Twenty-seven of the thirty-three-ton vehicles foundered in the heavy seas, leaving soldiers without armored support as they emerged from the water and tried to cross the beach.

The tanks of the 743rd Division, scheduled to support soldiers in the 116th Regiment on the western half of Omaha, fared better. After seeing the treacherous waves, two officers ordered the LCTs (Landing Craft Tank) to come as close as possible and put the tanks down as near to the shore as they could. It was a decision that helped to save not only the lives of the men in the tanks, but those onshore.

While General Bradley was increasingly worried about the fate of the army assault troops, Admiral Alan Kirk, also on the *Augusta*, was concerned about the naval landing craft. A small boat was deployed to get close to shore for a better look at conditions.

The scouts returned with discouraging news. Soldiers were pinned against the sea wall, unable to advance; German machine guns were sweeping the beach, while the enemy's longer range artillery fire was continuing to harass the landing craft.

Boats were having a hard time getting safely in to shore for another reason, too. "Much of the difficulty had been caused by the underwater obstructions. Not only had the demolition teams suffered paralyzing casualties, but much of their equipment had been swept away," said Bradley.

Bradley knew the situation was dire—not only for troops already on the beach, but for the carefully laid plans to bring in reinforcements. "There was due to arrive at noon in the transport area off Omaha Beach a force of 25,000 troops and 4,400 more vehicles to be landed on the second tide. However, only a portion of the [initial] assault force of 34,000 troops and 3,300 vehicles had as yet gotten ashore."

Those additional troops were essential. Without them, the Allies might not be able to weather a strong counterattack should one materialize. The situation was so critical Bradley began to wonder if the follow-up troops should be diverted to Utah and the British beaches.

Still, he held off a little longer before making a decision, hoping for better news.

In the meantime, "The battle belonged that morning to the thin, wet line of khaki that dragged itself ashore on the Channel coast of France."

CHAPTER 19

"29, LET'S GO!"

On the western part of Omaha Beach

Harold Baumgarten, 116th Regiment, 29th Infantry Division—on Dog Green, western part of Omaha Beach

"It was 6:15 a.m. on my watch, and we heard the frightening sights and sounds of thousands of five-inch rockets headed toward the beach. It is too bad that they did no damage to the fortification and obstacles, or injury to the awaiting defenders," said Harold "Hal" Baumgarten.

"The white steeple of the Vierville-sur-Mer church could now be seen to our left, on the top of the bluff. This was our guide for finding Dog Green. I could still see the obstacles, with their mines attached, on the beach. Looking down at my watch, it was 6:30 a.m., and some of my buddies from Company A were directly in front of us.

"They were getting ready to land on the shores of immortality."

Hal Baumgarten was in one of six boats bringing the initial assault team of Company A of the 116th Regiment to the beach. Dog Green was the narrowest sector, and also the most heavily fortified—for good reason. It was near the Vierville draw—the paved road that connected to a coastal highway, which made it the most useful, and, therefore, strategically important, passage inland.

The significance of invaders gaining access to a road suitable for tanks and other vehicles wasn't lost on the Germans. They had erected a strongpoint on the bluff consisting of four defense nests, three of which were relatively near the draw itself: WN71, WN72, and WN73.

"WN72 was the smallest, but most important of the defense nests in this strongpoint. It was designed to physically block the entrance to the Vierville draw, thereby cutting off access to the main paved road off the beach," explains military historian Steven Zaloga.

The nest contained a bunker with a powerful, dangerous 88mm gun. It was also new, not having been completed until late May. The bunker itself was made of steel-reinforced concrete, six and a half feet thick, which protected it from artillery fire. These factors combined to make Dog Green the deadliest spot on D-Day.

But as the first assault landing craft of the 116th Regiment fought through the seas to the shore, no one yet knew this—certainly not Captain Taylor Fellers, Company A's leader, who like almost three dozen of the company's 210 men, hailed from Bedford, Virginia, where the company had its roots in a historic Virginia National Guard unit.

Fellers was proud of his men, writing home that "'I am beginning to think it is hard to beat a Bedford boy for a soldier . . . I am truly proud to be commanding my old hometown outfit, and just hope I can carry them right on through and bring all of them home.' "

It was not to be.

Nineteen-year-old John Barnes, like Hal Baumgarten, was a new member of Company A, assigned to the unit after arriving in England following his basic training. John recalled Captain Fellers addressing the replacement soldiers for the first time.

" 'My name is Captain Taylor Fellers,' he drawled in a strong voice. 'This company will be in the leading wave of infantry in the invasion of Europe. You men will be part of a great force to the end the war. Good luck!' "

Now that day had come. Company A gathered early. "It was dark up on deck that morning as we lined up by boat teams. Everyone checked each other's equipment," said John. "I don't remember any famous last words but guys shouted out to their friends in other boats. I didn't. I still felt like an outsider, not knowing most of them more than four months."

As John's landing craft approached the shore, it had become light enough to make out the single spire of the village church. "It was Vierville! We knew it from the photographs we had been shown in our briefings. We were right on target. The LCA [landing craft, assault, carrying about thirty-five men] roared ahead, buffeting the waves."

And that's when their boat began to sink, from an undetected leak or striking an obstacle. "I had heard no noise nor felt any impact," said John.

In just a few minutes, Company A was short one boat, its soldiers spilled into the water, trying to stay afloat. One man would go under and not come up. The rest would survive and be taken back to their British troop ship, the SS *Empire Javelin*, which they had left at four that morning. By the time they had returned, they had been gone for nine hours.

Their lieutenant went back to the beach on another boat but left the shaken soldiers behind to return to England to be rearmed and reequipped. He left Sergeant Roy Stevens, a Bedford, Virginia, man, in charge. Roy's twin brother, Ray, was also in Company A.

"There was no doubt that Stevens would get us back since he was concerned about his brother, Ray," remembered John.

"We had no weapons, no equipment whatsoever, no helmets, nothing but wet clothing." But unlike most of the men in Company A, John and the others in his boat were still alive.

Hal Baumgarten's boat had come close enough to shore to scrape sand. The front ramp of the Higgins boat came down. "The lowering of the ramp was like a signal for every German machine gun to open up on the exit from our boat."

Company A would be decimated in minutes by the attack. Hal made a split-second decision to run toward the beach. "The sound of the German machine guns was frightening due to their speed of fire. We were now running with our rifles across our chests . . . While running, we witnessed horrible sights, which would become horrible memories for a nineteen

Soldiers he

year old to harbor . . . Another instantaneous thud sounded behind me to the left, and that soldier was gone . . ."

Hal took cover behind a beach obstacle. Soldiers around him were being hit—or were already dead. He got off one shot, but his rifle had been hit by fire. It was useless. "Now I was weaponless, surrounded by dead buddies, and the pillbox on the right was shooting up the sand around me . . . At that moment, an 88mm shell went off right in front of me. A fragment of it hit me in my left cheek. It felt like being hit with a baseball bat, but the results were much worse.

"My left cheek was ripped away, the left upper jaw was gone, and teeth and gums were lying on my tongue. My left cheek was actually flapping over my ear as my blood poured out into the now four inches of dirty channel water. The tide was coming in rapidly, about one inch a minute. I washed my face in this water and luckily did not lose consciousness . . . I thought to myself, *When will I die*?"

Hal managed to crawl for the seawall and moved along it until he found a protected spot. Reinforcements were supposed to follow, Hal knew, including some with heavy weapons. But word of the slaughter at Dog Green had gotten through to commanders offshore, and the beach was shut down to further landings.

Captain Fellers—and probably two-thirds of the soldiers in Company A—had been mowed down by German machine-gun fire within minutes of landing. Roy Stevens' twin brother, Ray, did not survive. The men who were left had no leaders, no direction, no reinforcements—and very nearly no hope.

CHAPTER 19

To Hal, the beach looked as if it had been painted red. "We were left on Dog Green to fight and/or die."

With six medics trying to help, Hal recalled, "There were about four rows of dead and wounded in front of the wall." One of the aid men suggested that Hal try to head east to be evacuated.

"There was no way I was going to quit fighting. My job was to fight the enemy." Hal recited a Hebrew prayer, and stayed where he was.

And then, about eleven that morning, something remarkable happened. Hal saw fifty-one-year-old Brigadier General Norman "Dutch" Cota, pistol in hand, running up the beach from the west. Hal couldn't talk because of his wound, but other soldiers called out to the general to get down and take cover. Still, said Hal, "It was reassuring to us to see this brave man on the beach."

Like Ted Roosevelt at Utah, Dutch Cota was in the right place at the right time. And, like Roosevelt, he was fearless and dedicated to the soldiers who served under him. He drew stares and exclamations as he strode down the beach, exhorting the soldiers to move. Over the years, there have been several versions of the words Dutch Cota shouted that morning.

Captain John Raaen Jr. of the 5th Ranger Battalion, whose men (as we shall soon see) were determined to get up the bluffs to help secure Pointe du Hoc for the Allies, recalled the general shouting, " 'Rangers! Lead the way!' "

Captain Bernard S. Feinberg, a dental surgeon with the 116th Regiment, remembered Cota's encouragement as well: " 'No sense dying here, men. Let's go up on the hill and die.' And with those words, he started to tap soldiers on their butts and said, '29, Let's go!'—our divisional yell."

Said Hal Baumgarten: "The call was, 'Twenty-nine, let's go,' and we went."

U.S. troops move along a cliff on Omaha Beach.

Some of the famous words sometimes attributed to Cota may have been spoken (or perhaps were echoed) by Colonel George Taylor, commanding officer of the 16th Infantry Regiment, who landed on the beach a couple of miles east. Like Cota, Taylor strode along trying to rouse shocked and leaderless soldiers huddled against the sea wall.

According to Captain William Friedman, Taylor "looked around and in a great stentorian voice screamed, 'Get the hell off the beach! If you stay on, you're dead or about to die!' "

★

It was almost 1:30 p.m. when General Omar Bradley on the *Augusta* received a message that troops formerly pinned down were advancing up the brush-covered slopes behind Omaha, fighting their way through German defenses.

They were moving, slowly, and in small groups, but despite all odds, they were moving. What he called "the shadow of catastrophe," which had hung over their heads all day, lifted—just a little.

Radio operator Corporal John Pinder helped to make it possible for such crucial messages to be sent on D-Day. Although

Landing craft, assault troops, and tanks on Omaha Beach.

seriously wounded in the face and able to see from only one eye, he waded again and again into the sea to rescue needed communication supplies. He was hit and killed in action on Omaha Beach. John Pinder was awarded the Medal of Honor posthumously.

Despite his injuries, Hal Baumgarten was one of the men who began to move up the bluffs. He joined a small group, which he dubbed the "walking wounded." One man had a

Troops wade ashore from a landing craft, Omaha Beach.

bandaged thigh, another had blood dripping from his hand; a third seemed to be from a Ranger battalion, but Hal couldn't see the patch on his shoulder, since that was covered in blood, too.

They headed up and inland, hoping to reach the village of Vierville and then head west, along a road to the highest promontory overlooking Omaha Beach.

It was called Pointe du Hoc.

BRIEFING

We Were There

"You know, I really think that people didn't know we were there," said John Noble Roberts, an African American D-Day veteran.

But they were.

About 1,800 African Americans took part on D-Day, including men in the 327th Quartermaster Service Company and the

Soldiers of the all-black 320th Very Low Altitude Battalion prepare a barrage balloon for launch.

582nd Engineer Dump Truck Company, which worked on Utah Beach to help demolish mines and open roads.

The first unit to land in Normandy was the all-black 320th Anti-Aircraft Barrage Balloon Battalion. There were about 600 men in the 320th, which was a VLA unit, which stood for Very Low Altitude barrage balloons. Some of these balloons could be handled by as few as three or four men. It was one of the few units on D-Day deployed to both Utah and Omaha beaches.

The gas-filled barrage balloons were designed to prevent enemy planes from dive-bombing ships or other targets, since striking one of the wire cables of a balloon could severely damage an aircraft. The 320th was responsible for erecting a "balloon curtain" to protect the beaches. About two weeks after D-Day, the 320th had more than 140 balloons flying over the beachheads.

The first men from the 320th on the beach at D-Day were its medics, who set up a first-aid station. One of these was Waverly B. Woodson Jr., who was wounded by shrapnel as his landing craft approached the beach yet worked for eighteen hours straight to help others.

"All day, we medics continued to dress many, many wounded and consoled the frightened . . . With all of this going on I didn't have time to see how bad I was wounded. I know I was . . . but I only wanted to help the survivors," wrote Woodson.

"This was a horrible day for everyone. This D-Day, Army prejudices took a backseat, as far as the soldiers helping one another was concerned. However, afterwards it was an altogether different story. Even to this day, the black soldiers were never given credit for their outstanding service beyond the call of duty."

Woodson received a Purple Heart and Bronze Star for his actions on D-Day. A recently discovered memo indicates he had also been recommended for a Medal of Honor, but neither it nor a Distinguished Service Cross was ever awarded. He died in 2005, and his family has continued to advocate for recognition.

No African Americans were awarded the Medal of Honor during World War II itself. In 1993, the army commissioned a study to review whether racism had played a part. Seven Medal of Honor recipients were then identified, and Congress passed legislation to bypass the normal time limit. By then, only one veteran, Vernon Baker, was alive to receive the Medal of Honor from President Bill Clinton on January 13, 1997.

LOOK, LISTEN, REMEMBER: Read about Waverly Woodson Jr. and his barrage balloon battalion in the book by Linda Hervieux entitled *Forgotten: The Untold Story of D-Day's Black Heroes, at Home and at War.*

You can also find out more about World War II African American Medal of Honor recipients at the United States Army Center for Military History: http://www.history.army.mil/moh/mohb.html.

The story of Waverly Woodson's family's efforts to have his heroism recognized are covered in this ABC news story: http://abcnews.go.com/US/negro-day-hero-overlooked-medal-honor-lawmaker/story?id=35111460.

★★★★ DISPATCH ★★★★

John Noble Roberts

For John Noble Roberts, serving as a steward in the U.S. Coast Guard didn't mean being safe from the dangers of combat. Born in 1924 in Louisiana, John arrived in England in January 1944. On D-Day, he served on LCI (L)-93. This was a large landing craft for infantry, which could carry approximately two hundred troops. John was one of two African Americans on the ship.

After letting off their first load of troops for Omaha Beach, John recalled what happened next. "At about 10 o'clock we went back to one of the big transport ships and picked up another load of troops. It was just a short trip from the transport ship to the beach. As we went back with our second load, the tides were going out."

The troops disembarked, but the landing craft grounded on a sandbar and came under German fire. "I was taking a message from the Commanding Officer to the engine room, because the intercom was no longer working," said John. "He told me to go down to the engine room and tell them to rev the engines full to try to get us off.

"As I was coming down from where he was to the main deck, about halfway down that a shell came through and exploded underneath me. It took my leg off from the knee down. I remember hopping off the ladder down to the deck . . . Pharmacist

Mate Charles Mudgett was there, he came and put a tourniquet on . . . and that saved my life I'm sure."

LOOK, LISTEN, REMEMBER: To see a photo of John Noble Roberts, visit http://www.telegraph.co.uk/news/worldnews/barackobama/5456233/African-American-D-Day-veterans-celebrate-Barack-Obamas-trip-to-Normandy.html.

CHAPTER 20

THE RANGERS AT POINTE DU HOC

"The operation there was one of the most unusual, one of the most daring and one of the most dangerous in all of military history," said James W. Eikner, "and because of that it will always be the subject of books and movies."

Ranger Jim Eikner was talking, of course, about Pointe du Hoc. About four miles west of Omaha Beach, this steep promontory rose a hundred feet above the sea, the highest spot between Omaha and Utah, and the perfect place for defense fortifications.

Even before a gun battery was completed there, the French Resistance had smuggled out plans to alert the Allies. And when built, the emplacement held six large 155mm guns, a powerful artillery weapon with a range of up to twelve miles. This meant ships and soldiers on both Utah and Omaha beaches were within range.

No wonder Pointe du Hoc was considered by Overlord planners to be " 'the most dangerous battery in France.' "

Plans called for naval ships to bombard Pointe du Hoc on the morning of June 6. But the havoc these guns could cause meant its destruction could not be left to chance. Instead it would be left to a select, well-trained group of men, the Army Rangers.

The mission fell to Lieutenant Colonel James E. Rudder and troops from the elite 2nd and 5th Ranger battalions. "No soldier in my command has ever been wished a more difficult task," said General Omar Bradley.

Preparations began long before D-Day, when Rudder and his men trained on stony cliffs on the Isle of Wight in Great Britain, experimenting to find the best climbing equipment. The Rangers evaluated ladders used by London fire brigades. These would be mounted on amphibious trucks called Ducks, or DUKWs, brought ashore to the foot of the cliff and raised. In the end, the DUKWs foundered or were struck, and weren't much help.

Luckily, the Rangers had also devised other methods of ascending the cliffs. They brought rope ladders, as well as lightweight metal ones preassembled in sixteen-foot lengths, both of which the soldiers could bring with them right in their landing craft.

The entire Ranger group was divided into three on D-Day: Force A, Force B, and Force C, each with a distinct mission and timetable. Force A, consisting of about 225 men landing in nine LCAs, would be led by Rudder himself. "We were thankful that he was there," said Jim Eikner later, adding, "I'm sure I would not be here today if he had not led us on the assault."

The other Rangers were part of a reinforcement and backup plan. The soldiers in Force B, the smallest group, would make their way up bluffs and inland after landing on the nearest sector of Omaha, called Charlie. It was located just west of Dog Green and the important exit called the Vierville draw. And like others near that deadly stretch, these Rangers would come under heavy fire, with about half the sixty-five men killed or wounded as they struggled ashore.

The largest backup group, Force C, was to wait offshore for thirty minutes until receiving a signal from Rudder, which hopefully would come at 7:00 a.m. The code " 'Praise the Lord' " would be radioed if Rudder and his men had succeeded in taking Pointe du Hoc and its guns. The signal was " 'Tilt' " if they hadn't. If Force A failed or no signal came at all, Force C would also make an overland attack, climbing the bluffs and then heading about five miles north to Pointe du Hoc overland. If the Rangers there didn't need them right away, they would serve as backup for other forces on Omaha Beach.

Any way you looked at it, Pointe du Hoc was an ambitious, complex operation, requiring daring, luck, precise timing, and good communications. And, like most everything else at Omaha Beach that morning, it didn't go according to plan.

"Just as there was enough daylight to make out the headlands things didn't look right," recalled Jim Eikner. They were too far east—the currents had once again wreaked havoc with the LCAs.

"Colonel Rudder . . . convinced the British officer who was in charge of that craft that he was in error and made him flank right," he said. "And then we had to parallel the coastline for a couple of miles and we were within small arms range. I can remember when the first small arms hit our boat . . . and I said 'My God these guys are playing for keeps.' "

The delay cost them about forty minutes—instead of landing on the dot of 6:30 a.m., the boats arrived around ten after seven. By then, the Germans were alerted. As Jim put it, "The enemy had time enough to get up out of those underground bunkers and shake his head, clear his brain and take us under fire."

Jim was the last one off his landing craft and managed to bring in a supply of mortar shells without getting hit. Others before him had already begun the ascent, following the plan they had devised in practice. They'd shot off rockets with the grapnel hooks attached. The grapnel device dug into the ground and was strong enough to support the rope and the weight of three men. In testing, the rockets could propel the grapnels up to 200 feet in the air. And now, during the real thing, it had worked.

"We of course did this many, many times in England," explained George Kerchner, another member of the assault team. "And we could work it down in time so that a man carrying normal combat equipment and gear could scale a cliff . . . in under a minute."

By the time Jim Eikner got to the base of the cliff, several ropes had already been set. "There was a rope right in front of me and so I started up that cliff and there were two or three guys ahead of me, the enemy was leaning over and shooting at us and throwing down hand grenades by the bushel basket full."

But within the first half hour, most of the Rangers reached the top. What they found there came as a complete surprise: telephone poles designed to look like the long muzzles of big guns.

The real guns were nowhere to be seen. Where were they?

Sergeant Leonard Lomell, platoon leader of Ranger Company D, was struck in the thigh before his feet even hit the beach below the cliff. It didn't slow him down.

"It wasn't bad at all," he said some years later. "I don't know if it was a machine gun bullet or a rifle bullet. It just went through my right side through the muscle and fat, you know, if I had any fat. I've got fat now, but didn't have it then!"

Len and the other men in D Company stormed the cliff "like we play a football game. Charging hard and low. And when we got over the top, nothing stopped us. Went right into the shell craters for protection, because there were snipers around, and machine guns firing at us."

At the top, they kept going, looking to reach the coast road that ran between Utah Beach and Omaha Beach since their orders also included setting up a road block on that main road.

"We set up our road blocks and our observation post . . . And we saw these markings in this sunken road. It looked like something heavy had been over it," said Len.

On a hunch, Len went exploring. "And so Jack [Kuhn] and I went down this sunken road not knowing where the hell it was going . . . and we came upon this vale, or this little draw with camouflage all over it, and low and behold, I peeked over

this—just pure luck—over this hedgerow and there were the guns, all sitting in proper firing condition, the ammunition piled up neatly, everything at the ready, but they were pointed at Utah Beach."

In the distance, Len spotted a group of perhaps seventy-five Germans. Later, he speculated it might be a gun crew getting orders from an officer. But for now, the coast was clear. " 'Well, there's nobody here, let's take a chance,' I said. 'Jack, you cover me, I'm going in there.' "

Using the two grenades he had with him, Len knocked out two of the guns. They ran back to get more, stuffing them in their jackets. Before they finished off the others, another Ranger patrol had done the job for them.

"And we just stumbled on them. Just pure luck. It was nothing brave or calculating or by design. We were just a couple of Rangers looking for the guns. That's all."

By nine in the morning the big guns had been destroyed. "This is probably one of the most fantastic things that happened in the war, as far as I'm concerned," said Ranger George Kerchner years later.

Many would agree.

The Rangers had taken Pointe du Hoc. Keeping it proved to be harder. The Germans whom Len Lomell had spotted soon mounted a fierce counterattack. Rudder's Rangers, running low on ammunition, suffered heavy casualties through the night and the following day. But they held on to Pointe du Hoc until reinforcements began to arrive the next evening. Of the 225 men in Force A, less than seventy-five were fit for duty.

U.S. Army Rangers rest atop the cliff at Pointe du Hoc.

★

Rangers also played a critical role on the beach that day—and the next. Although Jim Eikner tried to radio Force C, the group never could decipher any radio messages. As he saw the dangers near Dog Green, Force C's leader, Lieutenant Colonel Max Schneider, redirected fourteen LCAs to land a half mile to the east until he found a safer spot on Dog White, away from the deadly guns of the Vierville draw.

Although one group of Rangers broke through to help defend Pointe du Hoc, Schneider and his men were critical in securing the beachhead and the village of Vierville throughout the night.

"I have always felt that Schneider was the unsung hero of Omaha Beach," said Herbert Epstein, a member of Ranger Force C. "He was certainly my hero, and I credit him with saving my life and countless others."

U.S. Army Rangers rest near Pointe du Hoc.

Ranger John Raaen Jr. recounted what happened when the Rangers encountered General Norman "Dutch" Cota that desperate morning.

After landing, Raaen described seeing a man coming along the beach toward them, shouting encouragement to soldiers crouched along the seawall. Raaen jumped up and ran over, telling the general that he and others in Colonel Schneider's 5th Ranger battalion had just made it to shore with few casualties. The general started toward Schneider, who snapped to attention and saluted.

"Cota asked: 'Are you Colonel Schneider of the Rangers?'

" 'Yes, sir!' Schneider replied.

"Cota then told him, 'Colonel, you are going to have to lead the way. We are bogged down. We've got to get these men off this goddamned beach.'

"After Cota finished speaking with Colonel Schneider, he turned toward the men nearby and said, 'Rangers! Lead the way!' "

They did. And those words have become the rallying cry for Army Rangers to this day.

LOOK, LISTEN, REMEMBER: Watch a video of James Eikner, Leonard "Bud" Lomell, and other Ranger veterans as they recount their D-Day experiences in the American Battle Monuments Commission's "Stories of Pointe du Hoc": https://www.abmc.gov/multimedia/videos/stories-pointe-du-hoc. Leonard "Bud" Lomell died in 2011, and Jim Eikner passed away in 2014 at the age of one hundred.

U.S. troops set up a [illegible] ox, Omaha Beac

This story shall the good man teach his son;
And Crispin Crispian shall ne'er go by,
From this day to the ending of the world,
But we in it shall be remember'd;
We few, we happy few, we band of brothers;
For he to-day that sheds his blood with me
Shall be my brother.

WILLIAM SHAKESPEARE,
HENRY V, ACT IV, SCENE 3

PART 6

AFTERMATH: MORE THAN COURAGE

"This time the challenge is not to fight to survive, but to fight to win the final victory for the good cause. Once again what is demanded from us all is something more than courage, more than endurance; we need a revival of spirit, a new unconquerable resolve."

KING GEORGE VI,
radio address to the people of Great Britain, June 6, 1944

"After it was over it seemed to me a pure miracle that we ever took the beach at all."

ERNIE PYLE, war correspondent

A view of the Beaches.

VOICES AFTER D-DAY

In the Fields

"Most of the fields were disfigured by parallel rows of tall wooden stakes which had been driven into the ground and by crashed gliders lying like the broken bodies of great prehistoric birds, for whose destruction the wooden stakes had been planted."

VERNON SCANNELL,
British soldier, 51st Highland Division

In a Village, June 7

"The rugged, independent peasants of Normandy, who refused to knuckle under to German authority, are overjoyed at the arrival of the Americans. There are 1,900 civilians still living in one village, from which the doughboys today cleared the last snipers, digging them out of basements, churches, bedrooms and shops from which they were firing through windows at our advancing troops. Most civilians had gathered in a large farmhouse at the edge of town to escape the fighting in the streets."

DON WHITEHEAD,
war correspondent

After the i verhead.

The Enemy Dead

"We climbed the steep bluffs on the bulldozed road that had cost so many lives to build and passed by a large compound filled with German prisoners-of-war. Most of these men, who were quite relieved to be out of the war at last, were standing silently looking over the great invasion fleet out in the channel . . .

"Shortly thereafter, we began to see the German dead lying in various places along the road and in various attempted hiding places along the hedgerows and remains of buildings. It was apparent that for snipers, at least, one of the worst places to fire from was up in the branches of a tree. Nearly every one that opened fire from a tree was killed almost at once and the bodies often dangled there for days . . . There was simply not much time to worry about the dead, particularly enemy dead."

ROBERT BRADLEY,
Combat Medic, 120th Infantry Regiment,
30th Infantry Division

From the Air, June 10

"I went up in a Piper Cub [small airplane] today to take a look at the wedge driven into continental Europe and what I saw was both beautiful and awesome . . . We saw armored vehicles rolling slowly along hedgerows raking the undergrowth with machine gun fire to drive out snipers while behind them came doughboys taking cover in trees and hedges as the attack moved forward . . . [the plane] swung out over the beach and

Mulberry harbor in action after D-Day.

there stood our tremendous invasion fleet stretching as far as I could see.

"Ships were moving in to discharge their cargoes and small boats scurried around, weaving white wakes about the bigger ships which were pouring more men, guns and supplies ashore."

DON WHITEHEAD,
war correspondent

On a Hospital Ship

"There were destroyers and battleships and transports, a floating city of huge vessels anchored before the green cliffs

of Normandy . . . Barrage balloons, always looking like comic toy elephants, bounced in the high wind above the massed ships, and invisible planes droned behind the gray ceiling of cloud . . . Troops were unloading from big ships to heavy cement barges to light craft, and on the shore . . . our tanks clanked slowly and steadily forward.

"Then we stopped noticing the invasion, the ships, the ominous beach, because the first wounded had arrived . . . It will be hard to tell you of the wounded, there were so many of them. There was no time to talk; there was too much to do. They had to be fed, as most of them had not eaten for two days; shoes and clothing had to be cut off; they wanted water; the nurses and orderlies, working like demons, had to be found and called quickly to a bunk where a man suddenly and desperately needed attention."

MARTHA GELLHORN,
war correspondent

Under Fire

"The fury of artillery is a cold, mechanical fury but its intent is personal. When you are under its fire you are the sole target. All of that shrieking, whining venom is directed at you and at no one else. You hunch in your hole in the ground, reduce yourself into as small a thing as you can become, and you harden your muscles in a pitiful attempt at defying the jagged, burning teeth of the shrapnel."

VERNON SCANNELL,
British soldier, 51st Highland Division

In addition to American women who were sent to war as reporters, others served as nurses. Here, Margaret Stanfill, the first American nurse to arrive in France, rolls bandages.

REPORTER'S NOTEBOOK

Those Bitter Sands: Ernie Pyle

"By the time we got there the beaches had been taken and the fighting had moved a couple of miles inland. All that remained on the beach was some sniping and artillery fire, and the occasional startling blast of a mine geysering brown sand into the air," said reporter Ernie Pyle. "That plus a gigantic and pitiful litter of wreckage along miles of shore line.

When the tide went out.

"Submerged tanks and overturned boats and burned trucks and shell-shattered jeeps and sad little personal belongings were strewn all over those bitter sands. That plus the bodies of soldiers lying in rows covered with blankets, the toes of their shoes sticking up in a line as though on drill. And other bodies, uncollected, still sprawling grotesquely in the sand or half hidden by the high grass beyond the beach.

"That plus an intense, grim determination of work-weary men to get that chaotic beach organized and get all the vital supplies and the reinforcements moving more rapidly over it from the stacked-up ships standing in droves out to sea."

A Long, Thin Line of Anguish

"There in a jumbled row for mile on mile were soldiers' packs. There were socks and shoe polish, sewing kits, diaries, Bibles, hand grenades. There were the latest letters from home . . . There were toothbrushes and razors, and snapshots of families back home staring up at you from the sand . . .

"There were torn pistol belts and canvas water buckets, first-aid kits, and jumbled heaps of life belts. I picked up a pocket Bible with a soldier's name in it, and put it in my jacket. I carried it half a mile or so and then put it back down on the beach. I don't know why I picked it up, or why I put it down again."

Always There Are Dogs

"Always there are dogs in every invasion. There was a dog still on the beach, still pitifully looking for his masters.

"He stayed at the water's edge, near a boat that lay twisted and half sunk at the waterline. He barked appealingly to every soldier who approached, trotted eagerly along with him for a few feet, and then, sensing himself unwanted in all the haste, he would run back to wait in vain for his own people at his own empty boat.

"Over and around this long thin line of personal anguish, fresh men were rushing vast supplies to keep our armies pushing on into France."

Ernie Pyle's pieces about World War II appeared in hundreds of newspapers, bringing the war to Americans back home. In 1944, he won the Pulitzer Prize for his reporting. Pyle was killed by a sniper on an island off Okinawa on April 18, 1945.

AT THIS SPOT
THE 77th INFANTRY DIVISION
LOST A BUDDY
ERNIE PYLE
18 APRIL 1945

CHAPTER 21

THE MIRACLE OF A TOEHOLD

By the end of June 6, soldiers from the 1st and 29th divisions, with help from Army Rangers, had fought their way off Omaha Beach and held positions around three villages near the sea: Vierville, Saint-Laurent, and Colleville. Paratroopers had held important roads and towns, securing the way for soldiers from the 4th Infantry Division to push inland. British and Canadian forces at Sword, Juno, and Gold had achieved at least some of their objectives.

Although the Allies did not meet all their objectives—and fierce fighting would continue—they had not been pushed back into the sea. They had secured a toehold. On D-Day plus four, General Omar Bradley moved his headquarters from the *Augusta* to the shore. The Supreme Commander, and even Winston Churchill, came to see what had been achieved by so much effort. The Mulberry harbors began to operate, and the capture of Cherbourg occurred by the end of June, followed by the opening of the port. By the end of August, the Allies had liberated Paris.

"The plans, so long made, so minute in detail, so grandiose in scale, so hazardous in execution had become history.

Omaha Beach on the afternoon of D-Day.

U.S. troops move inland.

One trembled to think of what would have happened had they miscarried," said naval officer John Mason Brown.

The toehold had been secured at an extraordinary cost, although actual casualty counts still vary. For many years, historians used a figure of 10,000 Allied casualties, including 2,500 killed. Recent research puts the total of Allied dead higher, at 4,413: 2,499 Americans and 1,914 from other Allied nations. Renowned D-Day researcher and author Joseph Balkoski uses the figures of 3,686 casualties (dead and wounded) at Omaha, and 589 casualties at Utah. There were more than 2,000 injuries and two hundred deaths among the airborne troops. The total number of German casualties for

Joint Chiefs look in the direction of a soldier pointing. Shown are Generals George C. Marshall, Dwight Eisenhower, Omar Bradley, Henry Arnold, and Admiral Ernest King.

the day is unknown, and may have ranged between 4,000 and 9,000. More than 120 vessels were lost or damaged.

Yet the numbers cannot tell the full story of D-Day. Nor can any summary of military history—the long Overlord campaign throughout 1944 that led to the heartbreak of lost battles like Market Garden, the hard-won winter ordeal of the Battle of the Bulge, the unspeakable conditions found in the liberation of concentration camps, and the final victory in May 1945.

The Allies—and Operation Overlord—persevered, thanks to skilled and talented leadership and the dedication of millions of workers behind the scenes. But most of all, thanks to

Troops march inland through fields flooded by Germans.

ordinary young men who risked and sometimes sacrificed all. This book ends with a few of their stories.

Hal Baumgarten—behind Omaha Beach

On D-Day, Hal Baumgarten, private in the 116th Regiment, 29th Division, the unlikeliest survivor of the slaughter at Dog Green, was, miraculously, moving. Along with a few other

Allied Troops in Liberated Paris, August 1944.

U.S. soldiers march in Paris Victory Parade, August 25, 1944.

battered and wounded men, he worked his way up the bluffs, roused by General Norman "Dutch" Cota's fearless example.

Hal and the other soldiers in his ragtag group encountered sporadic gun nests, snipers, and small groups of enemy soldiers. Already wounded twice on the beach—once in his left cheek and once when shrapnel penetrated his helmet—Hal was crawling to a hedgerow when he felt a stinging sensation in his left foot. It felt as though a rock had hit his foot. It wasn't a rock at all, but his third wound of the day: He had tripped a small bullet-shooting mine.

Afternoon became evening. Just after midnight, they were ambushed. Hal was wounded once again—this time through his lip, jaw, and gums. He was now alone in a ditch; six other soldiers with him had been killed. As he lay semiconscious, Hal had a strange sensation: He felt a hand on his shoulder and heard a voice, in broken English, telling him everything would be fine. He might have been hallucinating. But years later, a German veteran recounted that he had seen soldiers in that ditch and that one was alive. Hal always wondered if a German soldier had spoken to him that night.

"At 3:00 a.m. I felt like I was dying. I was cold and clammy and had a 'needles and pins' feeling throughout my whole body. I was awake, with no severe pain, even though I had been wounded four times in the last twenty hours," he said. "The last time I had eaten anything was more than thirty hours earlier. I kept drinking water from canteens that were no longer of any use to their owners."

The young soldier might not have held out much longer. Then he spotted a U.S. Army ambulance in the moonlight. Unable to yell because of his wounds, he fired his gun into the air to get attention. Miraculously, the ambulance men stopped, spotted him, and loaded him inside.

Even then, Hal's ordeal wasn't over. At an aid station on the beach the next day, German snipers began firing, killing a medic and wounding Hal yet again—this time in his right knee. It was his fifth wound of the battle.

Hal Baumgarten's injuries would require months of recovery and plastic surgery. He also had to deal with the sometimes shocked reactions to his appearance before his face and mouth were rebuilt. It taught him something. "Before that experience, I would have found it inconceivable that I could be shunned and embarrassed because of my appearance.

"I learned a valuable life lesson at that time: to look beyond the superficial in my fellow man. People should show respect, regardless of physical features, race, ethnicity or sexual orientation. This became invaluable in my later life as a physician."

Hal died on Christmas Day 2016, at the age of ninety-one. In addition to his work as a doctor, he dedicated himself to honoring World War II veterans through his speaking, writing, and commitment to the National World War II Museum. His descriptions of his ordeal on Omaha Beach inspired some of the most searing war scenes ever made, in the film *Saving Private Ryan*.

★

CHAPTER 21

William Dayton Branstrator—on a minesweeper

As Hal Baumgarten discovered when he was wounded by a sniper at an aid station, danger didn't end on June 6. William Dayton "Bill" Branstrator was a motor machinist's mate, second class, assigned to the engine room on the USS *Tide* (AM-125), a minesweeper. An experienced mechanic, he was assigned to the engine room.

The *Tide* fared well on D-Day itself. The next day, June 7, the 221-foot-long ship continued to sweep mines off the coast of Normandy. Bill (or "Branny" as he was sometimes called) was on his way down to the engine room to take care of a small job when a crewmate offered to go instead, saying, " 'Branny, you've been down below decks long enough.' "

As a result, Bill was sitting on the mess deck, taking a break to eat some cheese, when the ship hit a mine with such force the *Tide* shot out of the water.

"I went up into the air like a rocket," Bill recalled. He lost consciousness for a time, and when he came to, a crewmate asked if he was all right. "I said, 'Well, yeah, I am, but my leg hurts me so. Just straighten my leg out.'

"He looked, and he said, 'Hell, you don't have any leg from the knee down, Bill.'

"I said, 'Yeah I do, because it's up under me here by my hand.' " The bone had snapped and was bent at a horrifying angle. Bill's left arm was broken, too.

They heard men shouting to abandon ship. A crewmate grabbed Bill and dragged him to the port side, where PT-504 (patrol torpedo boat), commanded by John Bulkeley, had come alongside to rescue the crew of the sinking ship.

Bill was set down close to the commander, who was holding a megaphone and shouting orders. "When the PT boat was just getting ready to pull away from the minesweeper, he looked down at me and said, 'Are you going to make it, son?'

"I said, 'Yeah, if I just had a cigarette.' At that time, of course, I was still smoking. Nearly everybody did then."

The skipper, who'd just lit a cigarette, took it from his mouth and put it in the mouth of the wounded sailor. Bill didn't remember much after that. Back in England, Bill found out just how serious his injuries were: He had a fractured skull, a broken back, and two dislocated knees. His left arm and both legs were broken. His injuries required dozens of surgeries, and, eventually, the amputation of one leg.

Despite this, Bill Branstrator felt lucky to be alive. Only moments before he had been in the *Tide*'s engine room. Most of the men there died. "You just never know when sitting or standing in one place instead of another is going to make such a difference."

John Fitzgerald—paratrooper

In the second week of July, John Fitzgerald, now back in his original 101st Airborne Division unit, moved to an area close to Utah Beach. "It was close to the same place the division had jumped and glided into in what seemed an eternity ago. We spent most of our time cleaning our clothing and equipment.

We knew we would be going back to England soon and wanted to look our best.

"I'm sure the experience of D-Day affected each man in a different way. Each of us had learned something about ourselves, and about war. I had some time to think.

"From what I had seen, the performance of the American paratroopers had exceeded the most optimistic expectations. They were dropped into a strange land, in the black of night. Many were separated from their units, and some were completely alone. The single quality that emerged above all others was their ability to adapt to changing situations.

"They fought with a quality of courage that was outstanding. Their biggest contribution was turning the confusion caused by the scattered drop to their advantage," said John.

On July 12, John Fitzgerald boarded a landing craft for the trip across the English Channel and looked back toward shore. "I murmured a short prayer of thanks for leaving here alive. I took one last look and knew I would never forget Normandy."

In fact, it would be nearly a year before the end of the war in Europe, and fourteen months until the final surrender of Japan. Ahead for the Allied forces lay enormous challenges: breaking out of Normandy, the liberation of Paris, the Battle of the Bulge, and pursuit of the German Army to Berlin.

Those months of fighting still lay ahead, with more lives to be lost. But because of the sacrifice and courage of the men who braved the dark skies and stormed the sands of Normandy, victory was possible. They had achieved, as Ernie Pyle put it, "a toe hold." A toehold that was, at the same time, a kind of miracle of planning, execution, and raw courage.

Father Francis L. Sampson

After the invasion, Father Francis L. Sampson spent two weeks at Cherbourg, celebrating Mass in a small church in a nearby village. The little church there had suffered some damage during the battle but still stood. The pastor's house, however, had been completely destroyed.

Each Sunday, Father Sampson took up a collection for repairs from the Allied soldiers who attended Mass. "The poor priest, with tears in his eyes, tried desperately to tell me how grateful he was . . . and that this was more than his congregation had been able to contribute in a whole year."

Some of Father Sampson's duties were harder to face. As he waited for transportation back to England, a young soldier named Frederick "Fritz" Niland came to ask for help in finding his brother, who he thought was buried in the cemetery at Sainte-Mère-Église, about twenty miles away. Father Sampson had access to a jeep and drove the soldier there to check. The roster, however, showed the name of Robert Niland, not William Niland.

"'Oh gosh, Father, that's my brother too. He was a lieutenant in the Ninetieth Division,'" said Fritz. A few blocks away, at another cemetery, they found the grave of his other brother. Fritz thought his third brother, Edward, was also lost, since the family had received information that he was missing and presumed dead.

"We managed to get Fritz sent back to the states," Father Sampson noted. Fritz was assigned noncombat duties so that his parents would be spared losing all their sons. After the war, it was learned that Edward had not died but instead had been captured. He survived a Japanese POW camp and returned home to his family. (Steven Spielberg's film *Saving Private Ryan* was loosely based on the brothers' story, with Fritz serving as the model for Private James Ryan.)

In December 1944, Father Sampson himself was captured and became a prisoner of war. He survived four months in a German POW camp. He returned to active duty, served in the Korean War, and ended his military career as chief of chaplains for the U.S. Army.

After the war, Father Sampson reflected, "It didn't seem possible that these young men who had been so confident . . . and whose hands I had shaken before we boarded the planes . . . were in eternity now."

At a memorial service after the war, he asked those present to think of those who had given their lives. "See them standing before us, row after row of them . . . they all look familiar: happy, energetic American boys full of the vigor of youth.

"What now do they expect of us? What can we do for them now that they are dead? Do they ask for praise? . . . grandeur? . . . eloquence? I think not.

"No, I think they would resent any attempt on our part to place halos about their heads. But if they could look down upon our country today and see us working together for the ideals upon which our country was founded . . . if they could see us cooperating with one another in the spirit of understanding . . ."

Then, said Father Sampson, he could imagine these soldiers in heaven saying with pride, " 'That's my country; those are my people, and what I died for was worth dying for.' "

Even if most Americans never visit the white crosses in the cemeteries of France, they will never forget the men who fell here, and the debt owed those who brought down the most horrific tyrant the world has ever known.

Author and naval officer John Mason Brown ended his own reflections with a cautionary note. "We respect our heroes more for their willingness to die than for their ability to live," he wrote in 1944. But, he added, "If only men could learn to act in time. If only men could realize that the maintenance of a proud peace requires more vigilance than the prosecution of a just war.

"Yes, and equal courage. And greater character and characters . . . Because the last people on earth who want a war are the men in their right senses who must fight it."

U.S. cemetery in Normandy above Omaha Beach.

"REMEMBER THEM."

Handwritten inscription found in an autographed,
used copy of
Fragments of My Life with Company A,
116th Infantry Regiment
by John J. Barnes

John's landing craft sank before reaching shore, but the other five boats of A Company came under intense machine-gun fire on Dog Green on Omaha Beach.
John died in 2013 at the age of eighty-eight.

QUARTERMASTER'S DEPARTMENT

WORLD WAR II TIMELINE

January 1933	Adolf Hitler becomes chancellor of Germany; his Nazi Party gains prominence and he begins to assume powers of a dictator.
October 1936	Germany and Italy sign a cooperation treaty.
July 1937	Japan invades China.
November 1938	A violent attack against Jews, called *Kristallnacht*, takes place; shootings, mass deportations, and the murder of six million Jews in Germany and the countries it occupies ensue.
March 1939	France and Great Britain agree to protect Poland.
April 1939	Italy invades Albania.
August 1939	Germany and the Soviet Union sign a nonaggression agreement.
September 1, 1939	Germany invades Poland; the Soviet Union invades Poland on September 17 and the two countries divide Poland.
September 3, 1939	In honor of their agreement with Poland, France and Great Britain declare war on Germany.
April 9, 1940	Germany invades Norway and Denmark.
May–June 1940	Germany attacks France and the "Low Countries" of Europe: the Netherlands, Luxembourg, and Belgium; Germany occupies northern France and the coast; the Vichy government, a French regime which cooperates with Nazi Germany, is established in the south.
June 10, 1940	Italy attacks France and enters the war.
Sept–October 1940	Italy invades Egypt and then Greece; Germany joins the Balkan Campaign the following spring, invading Greece and Yugoslavia.

June 1941	Germany invades the Soviet Union, breaking its agreement.
December 7, 1941	Japan attacks the United States at Pearl Harbor, Hawai'i.
December 8, 1941	The United States declares war on Japan, and in the following days goes to war as an ally of Great Britain against the Axis powers of Germany and Italy.
November 1942	The United States and Great Britain launch a campaign in North Africa.
July 1943	The United States and Great Britain invade Sicily.
September 1943	The United States lands troops in Italy; Italy surrenders but the Allies continue to battle German troops in the north of Italy.
June 6, 1944	The Allies invade Normandy on D-Day.
August 1944	Allied troops reach Paris.
September 1944	The first US troops enter Germany.
October 1944	US troops land in the Philippines, having battled to win back territory taken by Japan.
December 16, 1944	The final German offensive, the Battle of the Bulge, begins.
Spring 1945	The Allies continue to drive back the Germans; by mid-April, Soviet troops have surrounded the German capital of Berlin.
April 12, 1945	President Franklin D. Roosevelt dies; Harry S. Truman becomes president.
April 30, 1945	Adolf Hitler commits suicide.
May 7–9, 1945	Germany surrenders.
August 6, 1945	The United States drops an atomic bomb on Hiroshima.
August 9, 1945	The United States drops an atomic bomb on Nagasaki.
August 15, 1945	Japan surrenders.
September 2, 1945	Japan signs surrender papers, officially ending World War II.

★ GLOSSARY ★

88MM GUN—a powerful and versatile German anti-aircraft and tank gun

AA—anti-aircraft artillery

ATLANTIC WALL—German defensive fortifications along the west coast of Europe

BATTALION—an army unit usually consisting of three or more companies

BATTERY—an artillery group that has several guns

BOATSWAIN—officer in charge of ship's equipment and crew

BOCAGE—Normandy hedgerow countryside

C-47—Douglas twin-engine transport plane

C RATION—a combat ration consisting of canned food

CAUSEWAY—a raised road above water or marshy lands

COSSAC—Chief of Staff Supreme Allied Command, the forerunner of SHAEF

COXSWAIN—boat operator

CRICKET—a metal clicking toy used to identify friendly soldiers

DD TANK—duplex-drive amphibious tank

DOUGHBOY—slang for soldier, used especially in WWI

FLAK—anti-aircraft fire

FLANK—area to the right or left

FORCE O—naval task force for Omaha Beach

FORCE U—naval task force for Utah Beach

GOOSEBERRY—artificial breakwater created off the coast of Normandy by sinking old merchant ships

HOWITZER—a short cannon

K RATIONS—waterproof boxes dipped in wax containing three meals, plus additional items, such as water purification tablets, matches, toilet paper, can opener, and cigarettes

LCA—Landing craft, assault; carries about thirty-five men

LCI—landing craft, infantry; designed to carry up to 200 troops

LCT—landing craft, tank; able to carry up to four tanks

LCVP—landing craft, vehicle/personnel

LIBERTY SHIP—cargo ships built for use in WWII

LST—landing ship, tank; can carry between 1,600–1,900 tons

LUFTWAFFE—German air force

MATÉRIEL—military materials, supplies, and equipment

MINESWEEPER—ship that can detect and disarm mines

MORTAR—a cannon loaded from the front

MULBERRIES—code name for the artificial harbors designed to allow troops, equipment, and supplies to flow into France after the invasion

OPERATION NEPTUNE—code name for the amphibious assault aspects of Operation Overlord

OPERATION OVERLORD—code name for the Allied invasion of Normandy and plan to defeat Germany

OSS—Office of Strategic Services, wartime intelligence agency and precursor to the CIA (Central Intelligence Agency)

PANZER—German tank

PHOENIX—large concrete structures used in the creation of the Mulberry harbors that were sunk to provide breakwater

SHAEF—Supreme Headquarters, Allied Expeditionary Force

ULTRA—Allied intelligence operation to decrypt intercepted enemy messages

KEY PEOPLE IN THIS BOOK

JOHN J. BARNES—Infantry soldier headed for Omaha Beach

HAROLD BAUMGARTEN—Infantry soldier on Omaha Beach

OMAR BRADLEY—General commanding the U.S. First Army

JOHN MASON BROWN—Theater critic; member of Navy Admiral Kirk's staff

DAVID BRUCE—Chief of OSS in Europe

HARRY BUTCHER—Aide to Supreme Commander Dwight D. Eisenhower

ROBERT CAPA—Photographer who landed on Omaha Beach

CHARLES CAWTHON—American captain who landed on Omaha Beach

WINSTON CHURCHILL—Prime minister of Great Britain

ROBERT G. COLE—Lieutenant colonel of the 101st Airborne Division

NORMAN "DUTCH" COTA—General who rallied the troops on Omaha Beach

WILLIAM J. DONOVAN—Head of the OSS

JAMES W. EIKNER—Ranger at Pointe du Hoc

DWIGHT D. EISENHOWER—Supreme Commander, Allied Expeditionary Force

JOHN E. FITZGERALD—Paratrooper who parachuted behind Utah Beach

JAMES M. GAVIN—General who commanded the 82nd Airborne Division

MARTHA GELLHORN—American war correspondent

LEN GRIFFING—Paratrooper who parachuted behind Utah Beach

ADOLF HITLER—Führer of Germany and leader of the Nazis

JOHN HOWARD—British major who led operation on Pegasus Bridge

ROY HOWARD—British Glider pilot at the River Orne bridge

LEONARD LOMELL—Ranger at Pointe du Hoc

ALBERT MOMINEE—Infantry soldier on Omaha Beach

BERNARD L. MONTGOMERY—British general in charge of Allied ground forces in Operation Overlord

FREDERICK E. MORGAN—British officer charged with initial planning of Operation Overlord

MARIE-LOUISE OSMONT—Normandy resident

MARVIN J. PERRETT—Coxswain on a Higgins landing craft, Utah Beach

ERNIE PYLE—American war correspondent

JOHN NOBLE ROBERTS—Coast Guard serviceman

ERWIN ROMMEL—German officer charged with Atlantic Wall defenses

FRANKLIN D. ROOSEVELT—32nd president of the United States

THEODORE ROOSEVELT JR.—General and son of President Theodore Roosevelt

FRANCIS L. SAMPSON—Catholic priest and chaplain

EDGAR A. SCHROEDER—Glider pilot who landed behind Utah Beach

JAMES MARTIN STAGG—British meteorologist

JOSEPH STALIN—Premier of the Soviet Union

BERT STILES—American bomber pilot

CHARLES H. THOMAS—Infantry soldier on Omaha Beach

HARRY S. TRUMAN—33rd president of the United States, who took office after Roosevelt's death in April 1945.

ORVAL B. WAKEFIELD—Demolition expert, Utah Beach

DAVID KENYON WEBSTER—Paratrooper who landed behind Utah Beach

DON WHITEHEAD—American war correspondent

WAVERLY B. WOODSON JR.—Medic in the 320th Anti-Aircraft Barrage Balloon Battalion

LOOK, LISTEN, REMEMBER

Links to Online Resources

Please note: While every effort has been made to include permanent links, websites and their contents do change over time. If you discover that a specific link no longer works, please try typing keywords into a search engine.

AFRICAN AMERICANS IN WORLD WAR II AND AT D-DAY

320th Anti-Aircraft Barrage Balloon Battalion
https://www.army.mil/article/119639/All_black_balloon_unit_served_with_distinction_on_D_Day

Knowlton, Brian. "Forgotten Battalion's Last Returns to Beachhead," *New York Times*.
http://www.nytimes.com/2009/06/06/world/europe/06iht-troops.html

Teacher's Guide to the documentary *A Distant Shore, African Americans of D-Day*
https://www.history.com/images/media/pdf/DistantShore.pdf

U.S. Army Center of Military History: African Americans in the U.S. Army
http://www.history.army.mil/html/topics/afam/index.html

WWII African American Medal of Honor Recipients
http://www.history.army.mil/moh/mohb.html

ARTICLES, MUSEUMS, AND GENERAL D-DAY INFORMATION

Air Mobility Command Museum
http://amcmuseum.org/history/troop-carrier-d-day-flights/

Crossword Panic of 1944
http://www.historic-uk.com/HistoryUK/HistoryofBritain/Crossword-Panic-of-1944/

D-Day Museum and Overlord Embroidery
http://www.ddaymuseum.co.uk/

D-Day-Overlord
This website offers a minute-by-minute timeline, as well as a list of films and summaries.
http://www.dday-overlord.com/en/

LEARN ABOUT GLIDERS

American Society of Mechanical Engineers: The Flying Coffins of World War II
https://www.asme.org/engineering-topics/articles/aerospace-defense/the-flying-coffins-of-world-war-ii

Higgins Boats
https://www.nationalww2museum.org/sites/default/files/2017-07/higgins-in-new-orleans-fact.pdf

Imperial War Museums: The German Response to D-Day
http://www.iwm.org.uk/history/the-german-response-to-d-day

Library of Congress: Veterans History Project, D-Day 70th Anniversary
https://www.loc.gov/vets/stories/ex-war-dday-2014.html

Minesweeping Operations
http://www.mcdoa.org.uk/Operation_Neptune_Minesweeping.htm

Mulberry Harbor
http://d-dayrevisited.co.uk/d-day/mulberry-harbour.html

National D-Day Memorial
https://www.dday.org/

National Museum of African American History and Culture
https://nmaahc.si.edu/

National Museum of the United States Army
https://armyhistory.org/about-the-museum/

National Women's History Museum
https://www.nwhm.org/womens-history/online-exhibits

National World War II Museum
https://www.nationalww2museum.org/

Naval History and Heritage Command
https://www.history.navy.mil/

Omaha Beach: 29th Infantry Division Historical Society
http://www.29infantrydivision.org/

Omaha Beach: Society of the 1st Infantry Division
https://www.1stid.org/historyindex.php

Pegasus Bridge
http://d-dayrevisited.co.uk/d-day/pegasus-bridge.html

Pegasus Museum (Memorial Pegasus Museum)
http://www.memorial-pegasus.org/mmp/musee_debarquement/

Pointe du Hoc: National Museum of the United States Army—Rudder's Rangers and the Boys of Pointe du Hoc
https://armyhistory.org/rudders-rangers-and-the-boys-of-pointe-du-hoc-the-u-s-army-rangers-mission-in-the-early-morning-hours-of-6-june-1944/

Pointe du Hoc: Rangers, Lead the Way!
http://discerninghistory.com/2016/06/rangers-lead-the-way-how-the-rangers-at-pointe-du-hoc-turned-disaster-into-victory-during-the-d-day-invasion/

Pointe du Hoc: The 2nd Ranger Battalion
http://www.wwiirangers.com/History/History/Battalion%20Pages/2nd%20Rgr%20Bn/second.htm

Sainte-Mère-Église Airborne Museum
http://www.airborne-museum.org/en/

United States Holocaust Memorial Museum
https://www.ushmm.org/

U.S. Army Center of Military History
http://www.history.army.mil/

Utah Beach
https://www.britannica.com/place/Utah-Beach

Utah Beach: 4th Infantry Division
http://www.4thinfantry.org/content/division-history

Utah Beach: 82nd Airborne Division
http://www.ww2-airborne.us/division/82_overview.html

Utah Beach: 101st Airborne Division
http://www.ww2-airborne.us/18corps/101abn/101_overview.html

Utah Beach: 502nd Parachute Infantry, 101st Airborne Division
http://www.ww2-airborne.us/units/502/502.html

SOLDIERS AND VETERANS

Harold Baumgarten
http://www.nww2m.com/2016/12/farewell-to-dr-harold-hal-baumgarten-d-day-survivor-and-friend-of-the-national-wwii-museum/

Robert B. Bradley
http://www.findagrave.com/cgi-bin/fg.cgi?page=gr&GRid=49127796

Robert G. Cole: Medal of Honor Citation
http://www.cmohs.org/recipient-detail/2685/cole-robert-g.php

Death in Operation Market Garden
http://www.ww2marketgarden.com/ltcolrobertgcole.html

Winston Churchill
The International Churchill Society
http://www.winstonchurchill.org/

The Churchill War Rooms
http://www.iwm.org.uk/exhibitions/churchill-war-rooms/churchill-museum

James W. Eikner

http://www.mystatesman.com/news/local-obituaries/james-eikner-took-part-day-helped-set-lbj-homes-with-communications/ZU8WSyyK8QvzN37B4tFNsI/

Listen to Jim "Eik" Eikner describe the assault on Pointe du Hoc

https://vimeo.com/10163948

Video about Pointe du Hoc

https://www.abmc.gov/multimedia/videos/stories-pointe-du-hoc

Dwight D. Eisenhower

The Dwight D. Eisenhower Presidential Library and Museum is located in Abilene, Kansas
https://www.eisenhower.archives.gov

King George VI

Listen to the radio address by King George VI on June 6, 1944.
https://www.youtube.com/watch?v=tY2wysVXs6Q

Roy Howard

http://www.independent.co.uk/arts-entertainment/obituary-roy-howard-1095595.html

Carwood Lipton

http://carwoodlipton.com/

Franklin D. Roosevelt

http://www.fdrlibrary.marist.edu/archives/collections/fdrspeeches.html

Bert Stiles

http://www.americanairmuseum.com/person/17046

David Kenyon Webster

http://www.davidkenyonwebster.com/

Waverly B. Woodson Jr.

ABC news story: http://abcnews.go.com/US/negro-day-hero-overlooked-medal-honor-lawmaker/story?id=35111460

REPORTERS, PHOTOGRAPHERS, AND HISTORIANS

Robert Capa

https://www.icp.org/browse/archive/constituents/robert-capa?all/all/all/all/1

WOMEN REPORTERS

American Air Museum in Britain

http://www.americanairmuseum.com/person/240041

BBC News: The Women Reporters Determined to Cover World War Two

http://www.bbc.com/news/magazine-27677889

Library of Congress: Women Come to the Front: War, Women and Opportunity

https://www.loc.gov/exhibits/wcf/wcf0002.html

★ BIBLIOGRAPHY ★

BOOKS

Alanbrooke, Field Marshal Lord. *War Diaries: 1939–1945*. Berkeley: University of California Press, 2001, 1959, 1957.

Ambrose, Stephen E. *Band of Brothers: E Company, 506th Regiment, 101st Airborne from Normandy to Hitler's Eagle's Nest*. New York: Simon & Schuster, 1992.

———. *D-Day June 6, 1944: The Climactic Battle of World War II*. New York: Simon & Schuster, 2001, 1994.

Arthur, Max. *Forgotten Voices of World War II: A New History of World War II in the Words of the Men and Women Who Were There*. Guilford, CT: Lyons Press, 2004.

Astor, Gerald. *June 6, 1944: The Voices of D-Day*. New York: St. Martin's Press, 1994.

Atkinson, Rick with Kate Waters. *D-Day*. Adapted from *The Guns at Last Light*. New York: Henry Holt and Company, 2014. [Suitable for young readers.]

Atkinson, Rick. *The Guns at Last Light: The War in Western Europe, 1944–1945*. New York: Henry Holt and Company, 2013.

Balkoski, Joseph. *Omaha Beach: D-Day, June 6, 1944*. Mechanicsburg, PA: Stackpole Books, 2004.

———. *Utah Beach: The Amphibious Landing and Airborne Operations on D-Day, June 6, 1944*. Mechanicsburg, PA: Stackpole Books, 2005.

Barris, Ted. *Juno: Canadians at D-Day, June 6, 1944.* Toronto: Thomas Allen Publishers, 2004.

Baumgarten, Harold. *D-Day Survivor: An Autobiography.* Gretna, LA: Pelican Publishing Company, 2006.

Bearden, Bob. *To D-Day and Back: Adventures with the 507th Parachute Infantry Regiment and Life as a World War II POW.* St. Paul, MN: Zenith Press, 2007.

Beevor, Antony. *D-Day: The Battle for Normandy.* New York: Penguin Books, 2009.

Beyer, Rick and Elizabeth Sayles. *The Ghost Army of World War II: How One Top-Secret Unit Deceived the Enemy with Inflatable Tanks, Sound Effects, and Other Audacious Fakery.* New York: Princeton Architectural Press, 2015.

Blumenson, Martin. *Breakout and Pursuit.* United States Army in World War II: The European Theater of Operations. Atlanta, GA: Whitman Publishing, LLC, 2012. Originally published by the Office of the Chief of Military History, Dept. of the Army, 1961.

Bradley, Omar N. *A Soldier's Story.* New York: The Modern Library, 1999, 1951.

Bradley, Robert B. *Aid Man!* New York: Vantage Press, 1970.

Brown, John Mason. *Many a Watchful Night.* New York: Whittlesey House, a division of McGraw-Hill, 1944.

Burgett, Donald R. *Currahee!: A Screaming Eagle at Normandy.* New York: Dell Publishing, 1967.

Butcher, Harry C. *My Three Years with Eisenhower: The Personal Diary of Captain Harry C. Butcher, USNR,*

Naval Aide to General Eisenhower, 1942 to 1945. New York: Simon & Schuster, 1946.

Capa, Robert. *Slightly Out of Focus*. New York: The Modern Library, 2001. Originally published in 1947 by Henry Holt and Company.

Cawthon, Charles R. *Other Clay: A Remembrance of the World War II Infantry*. New York: Dell Publishing, 1990.

Churchill, Winston S. *The Second World War. Volume Five: Closing the Ring*. London: The Reprint Society Ltd., 1954.

———. *The Second World War. Volume Six: Triumph and Tragedy*. Boston: Houghton Mifflin Company, 1953.

Cowdrey, Albert E. *Fighting for Life: American Military Medicine in World War II*. New York: The Free Press, 1994.

Critchell, Laurence. *Four Stars of Hell: The 501st Parachute Infantry Regiment in WWII*. Nashville: The Battery Press, 1982, 1974.

D'Este, Carlos. *Eisenhower: A Soldier's Life*. New York: Henry Holt, 2002.

———. *Decision in Normandy*. Old Saybrook, CT: Konecky & Konecky, 1994, 1983.

Drez, Ronald J., ed. *Voices of D-Day: The Story of the Allied Invasion Told by Those Who Were There*. Baton Rouge, LA: Louisiana State University Press, 1994.

Edwards, Kenneth. *Operation Neptune: The Normandy Landings, 1944*. Stroud, UK: Fonthill, 2015. First published in the United Kingdom in 1946.

Ellsberg, Edward. *The Far Shore*. New York: Dodd, Mead & Co., 1960.

Gavin, James M. *On to Berlin: Battles of an Airborne Commander, 1943–1946*. New York: The Viking Press, 1978.

Gawne, Jonathan. *Spearheading D-Day: American Special Units of the Normandy Invasion*. Paris, France: Histoire & Collections, 2011.

Gellhorn, Martha. *The Face of War*. New York: Atlantic Monthly Press, 1988, 1959.

Giangreco, D. M. and Kathryn Moore. *Eyewitness D-Day: Firsthand Accounts from the Landing at Normandy to the Liberation of Paris*. New York: Union Square Press, 2005.

Harrison, Gordon A. *Cross-Channel Attack*. United States Army in World War II: The European Theater of Operations. Atlanta, GA: Whitman, 2012.

Hastings, Max. *Overlord: D-Day and the Battle for Normandy*. New York: Simon & Schuster, 1984.

———. *The Secret War: Spies, Ciphers, and Guerrillas, 1939–1945*. New York: HarperCollins, 2016.

Hemingway, Mary Welsh. *How It Was*. New York: Knopf, 1976, 1951.

Hervieux, Linda. *Forgotten: The Untold Story of D-Day's Black Heroes, at Home and at War*. New York: Harper, 2015.

Hesketh, Roger. *Fortitude: The D-Day Deception Campaign*. Woodstock, NY: Overlook, 2000.

Holt, Thaddeus. *The Deceivers: Allied Military Deception in the Second World War.* New York: Skyhorse, 2007.

Howard, John and Penny Howard Bates. *The Pegasus Diaries.* Barnsley, GB: Pen & Sword Military, 2006.

Hynes, Samuel, Anne Matthews, Nancy Caldwell Sorel, and Roger J. Spiller, eds. *Reporting World War II. Part Two: American Journalism 1944–1946.* New York: Library of America, 1995.

Kershaw, Robert. *D-Day: Piercing the Atlantic Wall.* Hersham, Surrey, UK: Ian Allan Publishing Ltd., 1993.

Liddle, Peter. *D-Day by Those Who Were There.* Barnsley: Pen & Sword Military, 2004.

Liebling, A.J. *World War II Writings.* New York: The Library of America, 2008.

Loewenheim, Francis L., Harold D. Langley, and Manfred Jonas, eds. *Roosevelt and Churchill: Their Secret Wartime Correspondence.* New York: Saturday Review Press, 1975.

Master, Charles J. *Glidermen of Neptune: The American D-Day Glider Attack.* Carbondale, IL: Southern Illinois University Press, 1995.

McManus, John C. *The Dead and Those about to Die: D-Day: The Big Red One at Omaha Beach.* New York: NAL Caliber, 2014.

Messenger, Charles. *The D-Day Atlas: Anatomy of the Normandy Campaign.* New York: Thames & Hudson, 2004.

Moore, Christopher Paul. *Fighting for America: Black Soldiers—The Unsung Heroes of World War II*. New York: One World, 2005.

Morgan, Frederick. *Overture to Overlord*. London: Hodder & Stoughton, Ltd., 1950.

Morison, Samuel Eliot. *History of United States Naval Operations in World War II. Volume X1: The Invasion of France and Germany, 1944–1945*. Annapolis, MD: Naval Institute Press, 2011, 1953.

Nordyke, Phil. *Four Stars of Valor: The Combat History of the 505th Parachute Infantry Regiment in World War II*. Minneapolis, MN: Zenith Press, 2010.

O'Donnell, Patrick K. *Dog Company: The Boys of Pointe Du Hoc—The Rangers Who Accomplished D-Day's Toughest Mission and Led the Way across Europe*. Boston: Da Capo Press, 2012.

Olson, Lynne. *Citizens of London: The Americans Who Stood with Britain in its Finest, Darkest Hour*. New York: Random House, 2010.

Osmont, Marie-Louise. Translated by George L. Newman. *The Normandy Diary of Marie-Louise Osmont: 1940–1944*. New York: Random House/The Discovery Channel Press, 1994.

Pogue, Forrest C. *Pogue's War: Diaries of a WWII Combat Historian*. Lexington, KY: The University Press of Kentucky, 2001.

———. *The Supreme Command*. Washington, D.C.: Center of Military History, United States Army. 2015, 1996, 1954.

Prados, Edward F., ed. *Neptunus Rex: Naval Stories of the Normandy Invasion, June 6, 1944*. Novato, CA: Presidio Press, 1998.

Pyle, Ernie. *Brave Men*. Lincoln, NE: University of Nebraska Press, 2001. Originally published New York: H. Holt, 1944.

Pyle, Ernie and David Nichols, ed., *Ernie's War: The Best of Ernie Pyle's World War II Dispatches*. New York: Touchstone, 1986.

Rapport, Leonard and Arthur Norwood Jr. *Rendezvous with Destiny: A History of the 101st Airborne Division*. Old Saybrook, CT: Konecky & Konecky, 2001. History of the 101st Airborne Division originally published in 1948.

Rohmer, Richard. *Patton's Gap: An Account of the Battle of Normandy 1944*. Ontario, Canada: Paper Jacks, 1982.

Ruppenthal, Roland G. *The European Theater of Operations Logistical Support of the Armies: In Two Volumes, Volume I: May 1941–September 1944*. Center of Military History, U.S. Army, 1995.

Ryan, Cornelius. *The Longest Day*. New York: Simon & Schuster, 1994, 1959.

Sampson, Francis L. *Paratrooper Padre*. Washington, D.C.: The Catholic University of America Press, 1948.

Scannell, Vernon. *Argument of Kings*. London: Robson Books, 1987.

Smith, Richard Harris. *OSS: The Secret History of America's First Central Intelligence Agency*. Berkeley: University of California Press, 1972.

Sorel, Nancy Caldwell. *The Women Who Wrote the War.* New York: Arcade Publishing, 1999.

Stagg, J. M. *Forecast for Overlord, June 6, 1944.* New York: W.W. Norton, 1971.

Stanford, Alfred. *Force Mulberry: The Planning and Installation of the Artificial Harbor off U.S. Normandy Beaches in World War II.* New York: William Morrow and Co., 1951.

Stiles, Bert. *Serenade to the Big Bird: A True Account of Life and Death from Inside the Cockpit.* New York: W.W. Norton & Co., 1952.

Stillwell, Paul, ed. *Assault on Normandy: First-Person Accounts from the Sea Services.* Annapolis, MD: Naval Institute Press, 1994.

Symonds, Craig L. *Neptune: The Allied Invasion of Europe and the D-Day Landings.* New York: Oxford University Press, 2014.

Tobin, Richard L. *Invasion Journal.* New York: E.P. Dutton & Co., Inc., 1944.

von Luck, Hans. *Panzer Commander: The Memoirs of Colonel Hans von Luck.* New York: Dell, 1989.

Webster, David Kenyon. *Parachute Infantry: An American Paratrooper's Memoir of D-Day and the Fall of the Third Reich.* Baton Rouge, LA: Louisiana State University Press, 1994.

Whitehead, Don. *Beachhead Don: Reporting the War from the European Theater, 1942–1945.* New York: Fordham University Press, 2004.

Whitlock, Flint. *The Fighting First: The Untold Story of the Big Red One on D-Day*. Boulder, CO: Perseus, 2004.

Winik, Jay. *1944: FDR and the Year that Changed History*. New York: Simon & Schuster, 2015.

Yellin, Ellen. *Our Mothers' War: American Women at Home and at the Front During World War II*. New York: Free Press, 2004.

Zaloga, Steven. *The Devil's Garden: Rommel's Desperate Defense of Omaha Beach on D-Day*. Mechanicsburg, PA: Stackpole Books, 2013.

MANUSCRIPT SOURCES

National World War II Museum

Briand N. Beaudin

Dwayne T. Burns

John Desrosiers

James W. Eikner

John E. Fitzgerald

Len Griffing

George Kerchner

Carwood Lipton

Leonard Lomell

Kenneth Russell

Edgar A. Schroeder

Charles H. Thomas

U.S. Coast Guard Oral History Program (accessed 2017)
Marvin J. Perrett
John Noble Roberts

ARTICLES AND PAMPHLETS

Department of the Army. "Organization of the United States Army." Washington, D.C.: Headquarters, Department of the Army, 1994. http://www.apd.army.mil/epubs/DR_pubs/DR_a/pdf/web/p10_1.pdf

Sherwill, P. "African-American D-Day Veterans Celebrate Barack Obama's Trip to Normandy." *The Telegraph*, June 6, 2009. http://www.telegraph.co.uk/news/worldnews/barackobama/5456233/African-American-D-Day-veterans-celebrate-Barack-Obamas-trip-to-Normandy.html

Woodson Jr., Waverly B. "My Witness to D-Day, June 6, 1944," unpublished article. http://stateside.digitalnewsroom.org/wp-content/uploads/2015/11/Woodson-Waverly-Enclosed-Docs-Sent-to-Army-11.5.15.-No-PR.pdf

★ SOURCE NOTES ★

JUNE 6, 1944—JUST PAST MIDNIGHT OFF THE COAST OF NORMANDY

"'Look, men, look!' . . .": Webster, *Parachute Infantry*, 24.
"Five hundred feet below . . .": ibid.
"I stared at the men . . .": ibid.
"Oh God, I prayed . . .": ibid., 25.
"I smelled the smoke and oil . . .": ibid., 26.
"There was a wild . . .": ibid., 27.
"But this was D-Day . . .": ibid.
"I fell a hundred feet . . .": ibid.
"Just before I hit . . .": ibid., 28.
"Lost and lonely, wrestling with . . .": ibid.

AND WHAT'S A REGIMENT, ANYWAY?

General Structuring of Army Forces: "Organization of the United States Army," June 14, 1994, http://www.apd.army.mil/epubs/DR_pubs/DR_a/pdf/web/p10_1.pdf, 53.

Part 1: The Plan

"The great Allied invasion . . .": D'Este, *Decision in Normandy*, 13.
"The target date . . .": Butcher, *My Three Years with Eisenhower*, 502.

CHAPTER 1: OPERATION OVERLORD

"the German Army had been worn down . . .": Morison, *The Invasion of France and Germany*, 16.
"Just as the lift was taking off . . .": Morgan, *Overture to Overlord*, 15.
"invited" . . . : ibid., 33.
"'No hurry, old boy . . .' ": ibid.
"'Well, there it is; it won't work . . .' ": ibid., 72.
"The equipment consisted of . . .": ibid., 36.

READER'S INVASION BRIEFING: WORLD WAR II AND THE CONTEXT FOR OPERATION OVERLORD

"bloody stalemate.": D'Este, *Eisenhower*, 460.
Casablanca Conference, D'Este, *Decision in Normandy*, 33.
"The war in Italy . . .": Pyle, *Brave Men*, 151.

CHAPTER 1 CONTINUED

"the utter defeat of Germany . . .": Morgan, 71.
Advantages of Normandy: D'Este, Decision in Normandy, 35.
"The stop-watch . . .": Morgan, 239.

BRIEFING: A PREPOSTEROUS IDEA: MULBERRY HARBORS

"if momentum is not maintained . . .": Morison, 20.
"Without at least one port . . .": Morgan, 261.
"this immense puzzle": ibid.
" 'Well, all I can say is . . .' ": ibid., 262.
"There might be something . . .": ibid.

CHAPTER 2: INVASION PREPARATION: TOY SOLDIERS COME TO LIFE

"All my life . . .": Webster, 1.
By January 1944: Atkinson, *D-Day: The Invasion of Normandy, 1944*, 25.
"More than 60 percent . . .": Moore, *Fighting for America*, 174.
Norwegians at D-Day: Norwegian Royal Navy Museum, http://www.forsvaretsmuseer.no/Marinemuseet/Sjoeforsvarets-historie-1814-2014/1939-1945-Sjoeforsvaret-i-krig/I-alliert-krigstjeneste-1940-1945/D-dagen-6.juni-1944.
Invasion figures: D-Day Museum, http://ddaymuseum.co.uk.
"You know those orders . . .": Brown, *Many a Watchful Night*, 23.
"on heavy freighters dipping . . .": ibid., 24.
"to invade Europe . . .": ibid., 21.
"our tanks; our jeeps; our stretchers . . .": ibid.
Numbers in military: National WWII Museum, http://www.nationalww2museum.org/learn/education/for-students/ww2-history/ww2-by-the-numbers/us-military.html?referrer=https://www.google.com/.
C-47s: Balkoski, *Utah Beach*, 24–25.
"the vast reserve of woman power . . .": Yellin, *Our Mothers' War*, 37.
"As we Americans moved in . . .": Brown, 30.
Civilian deaths: BBC History, http://www.bbc.co.uk/history/events/the_blitz.
"Had they not stood alone . . .": Brown, 31.

BRIEFING: AFRICAN AMERICANS IN WORLD WAR II

"For American blacks . . .": Cowdrey, *Fighting for Life*, 109.
"The navy was polite . . .": ibid., 110.
NACGN: ibid., 112.
"By 1945 . . ." NWW2M, African Americans in WWII, https://www.nationalww2museum.org/sites/default/files/2017-07/african-americans.pdf.
The 761st Tank Battalion and the Tuskegee Airmen: ibid.
" 'I remember a nurse . . .' ": Cowdrey, 265.

“ ‘And, oh, yes . . .’ ”: Franklin, transcript from PBS *The War*, http://www.pbs.org/thewar/detail_5298.htm.

REPORTER'S NOTEBOOK: FOG, BLACKOUTS, AND COURAGE

“In war, one does not use a foghorn . . .”: Tobin, *Invasion Journal*, 9.
“The sausages are a joke . . .”: ibid., 37.
“The blackout comes increasingly late . . .”: ibid., 34.
“This is a timeless world . . .”: ibid., 51.
“There, indeed, they sleep” . . . “it took real courage . . .”: ibid., 49, 32.

CHAPTER 3: MEET THE SUPREME COMMANDER (AND HIS DOG)

“Germany to dominate”; “it followed that every . . .”: Harrison, *Cross-Channel Attack*, 11.
“ ‘Who will command Overlord?’ ”; D'Este, *Eisenhower*, 466.
“ ‘Well, Ike . . . you are going to command . . .’ ”: ibid., 467.
Italian campaign: ibid., 458–460.
“growled that the light was bad . . .”: Butcher, 460.
“He again took careful aim . . .”: ibid.

DISPATCH: TELEK THE (NOT SO) SUPREME DOG

“and my foot landed . . .”: ibid., 221.
“love at first sight.”: ibid., 281.
“ ‘locking up a part of my heart.’ ”: ibid., 480.
“However, I cannot control . . .”: ibid.

BRIEFING: SECRECY, DECEPTION, AND CROSSWORD CLUES

Fortitude plan: Hesketh, *Fortitude*, 15–19.
Fortitude plan: ibid.
Three goals of Fortitude: ibid., 12.
“Another case of loose talk . . .”: Butcher, 548.

Part 2: The Gods of War

“Failure would have brought . . .”: Morgan, 279.
“ ‘I thank the gods of war . . .’ ”: Stagg, *Forecast for Overlord*, 126.

CHAPTER 4: THE WEATHERMAN

“ ‘I intend to nominate you.’ ”: ibid., 10.
“Unpronounceable groups of letters . . .”: ibid., 11.
Tides: Morison, 131.
“ ‘What are the least favorable . . .’ ”: Stagg, 13.

"If every one of the requirements . . .": ibid., 14.
"With a broad smile . . .": ibid., 17.
Size of divisions: Ambrose, *D-Day*, 15.
"favorable period": Bradley, O. *A Soldier's Story*, 259.
"it could not be done . . .": Stagg, 18.
Chain of Command: adapted from Pogue, *The Supreme Command*, 159.

BRIEFING: CHOOSING D-DAY: A GENERAL AND A HISTORIAN WEIGH IN

"One of the knottiest problems . . .": Morison, 32.
"It was essential that initial assault forces . . .": ibid.
"at the mercy of the tides . . .": Bradley, O., 259.
"The first three fell on . . .": ibid.
"Even more frightening than . . .": ibid., 259–260.
"The final choice . . .": Morison, 33.

CHAPTER 5: "D-DAY CALLING"

"D-Day calling, D-Day calling . . .": Webster, 4.
Allied forces numbers: D-Day Museum, UK.
"The war room at division headquarters . . .": Sampson, *Paratrooper Padre*, 39.
"We were ready . . .": ibid.
"As General Eisenhower passed . . .": ibid., 43.
"right guy"; "refused to show . . .": ibid.
"Every piece of our clothing . . .": Capa, *Slightly Out of Focus*, 134.
"Everybody in the room . . .": Pyle, 375.
"And in more pensive moments . . .": ibid., 376.
"a shovel to dig foxholes . . .": ibid., 377.
"the old horrible life . . .": ibid.

REPORTER'S NOTEBOOK: AMERICAN WOMEN REPORTERS

"I had an arrangement . . .": Welsh Hemingway, *How It Was*, 99.
"There were four hundred and twenty-two . . .": Gellhorn, *The Face of War*, 109.

CHAPTER 6: THE DECISION TO GO

"In less than half an hour . . .": Stagg, 86.
"General Eisenhower sat motionless . . .": ibid., 98.
"The tension in the room . . .": ibid., 102.
"Within an hour . . .": ibid., 103.
"'have weighed a ton.'": Ryan, *The Longest Day*, 61.
"If the Supreme Commander . . .": Stagg, 107.
"'I am quite confident . . .'": ibid., 113.

“‘Do you see any reason . . .’ ”: ibid., 114.
“‘Well, Stagg, we’re putting it on . . .’ ”: ibid., 115.
“We could not sleep . . .”: ibid., 119.
“unsung heroes”: D’Este, *Eisenhower*, 523.
“‘a man of sharp mind . . .’ ”: ibid.
“If the invasion had been postponed . . .”: Beevor, *D-Day: The Battle for Normandy*, 216.
“‘I thank the gods . . .’ ”: Stagg, 126.

DISPATCH: IKE’S OTHER MESSAGE

“Ike wandered through them . . .”: Butcher, 566.
“I have full confidence . . .”: Eisenhower, *Order of the Day*. National Archives. https://www.archives.gov/historical-docs/todays-doc/?dod-date=606.
“This afternoon Ike called me in . . .”: Butcher, 610.

READER’S INVASION BRIEFING: OVERVIEW OF OVERLORD

D-Day figures vary by source. Atkinson, 186.
Norway to Spain: Morison, 39.
“a continuous belt of weapons . . .”: ibid., 39–40.
Rommel’s plan: ibid., 41.
“She sank soon after . . .”: ibid., 79.

DISPATCH: WATCHING HISTORY BEING MADE

“The sheer size . . .”: Watson (later Gadsden) in Liddle, 240.
“Just before going . . .”: ibid., 241.

ORDER OF THE DAY

“‘You are about to embark . . .’ ”: D’Este, *Eisenhower*, 526.
https://www.archives.gov/historical-docs/todays-doc/?dod-date=606.

Part 3: Night into Day

“‘The violence, speed, and power . . .’ ”: Balkoski, *Utah Beach*, 325.
“Of all the themes touched upon . . .”: ibid., xv.
“Enlisted men had brought . . .”: Pyle, 378.

CHAPTER 7: ACROSS THE CHANNEL BY SEA

“For the first time since Sicily . . .”: Bradley, O., 252.
Kirk: Morison, 29.
“At midnight I turned in . . .”: Bradley, O., 257.
“Just as soon as Eisenhower . . .”: ibid.

"For the second time . . .": ibid., 257–258.
"The Plan had taken over . . .": ibid., 264.
"Soon the waters of Plymouth . . .": ibid., 264–265.
"In this capricious turn . . .": ibid., 266.
"We boarded our ship . . .": Whitehead, *Beachhead Don*, 121.
"they know what lies ahead . . .": ibid., 120.
"I am a gambler . . .": Capa, 137.
" 'To help the amphibious . . .' ": ibid., 255.
"Tactically these DD tanks . . .": ibid.
"Only the lonely wind . . .": ibid., 267.
"As the skies, until recently . . .": Brown, 108, 110.

CHAPTER 8: BEFORE THE JUMP

"It was supposed to be a secret . . .": Webster, 4.
"excited way we talked . . .": ibid.
Horsa gliders: Masters, *Glidermen of Neptune*, 9–10.
"Entertainers and newsmen . . .": Webster, 5.
"It was a beautiful load . . .": ibid., 7.
"White bread and movies . . .": ibid.
" 'We've shown you this picture . . .' ": ibid., 8.
" 'We'll go in . . .' ": ibid., 9.
"First you put on . . .": ibid., 17.
"What a lousy way . . .": ibid., 18.
"Our lieutenant lined us up . . .": ibid., 19.
" 'Let's go, men . . .' ": ibid., 21.
"There was a last . . .": ibid., 23.
"The war leaders, the high commander . . .": Harrison, 274.

DISPATCH: FROM THE AIR: THEY HAD TO GO IN ALONE

"We waited so long . . .": Stiles, 111.
"We were in on it . . .": ibid., 112.
"The moon came through . . .": ibid., 113.
"Then just before we crossed . . .": ibid., 114.
"We were all thinking . . .": ibid.
"Glider Flight": Dunne, in Rapport and Norwood, *Rendezvous with Destiny*, 825.

CHAPTER 9: PEGASUS BRIDGE

Ox & Bucks: Howard, J. *Pegasus Diaries*, 17.
" 'You can have every confidence . . .' ": ibid., 89.
"If their task could be achieved . . .": Ryan, 110.
"Someone had made . . .": Howard, R. in Arthur, *Forgotten Voices of World War II*, 294.
"If I overshot . . .": ibid., 293.

"'I've got to hand it . . .' ": Howard, J., *Pegasus Diaries*, 115.
"Somehow I found I . . .": ibid.
"About forty minutes after take-off . . .": ibid., 116.
"'Prepare for cast-off . . .' ": ibid., 117.
"Suddenly we were all aware . . .": ibid.
"Never imagining that he would take . . .": ibid., 119.
"the most accurate and skilled . . .": ibid.
"I gritted my teeth . . .": ibid., 118.
"We . . . came to a sudden . . .": ibid., 119.
"There was silence . . .": ibid., 120.
"I well remember . . .": ibid., 123.
"It was a sight . . .": ibid., 126.

DISPATCH: A PANZER COMMANDER IN CAEN

"So we did not anticipate . . .": von Luck, *Panzer Commander*, 171.
"About midnight, I heard . . .": ibid., 172.
"If Rommel had been with us . . .": ibid., 174.
"In the early hours . . .": ibid.
"The example that young . . .": ibid., viii.
"For me the moment . . .": ibid., 342.

DISPATCH: LANDING! A FRENCHWOMAN'S D-DAY DIARY

"for me they represent . . .": Osmont, *The Normandy Diary of Marie-Louise Osmont*, 3.
"Everything is idyllic . . .": ibid., 37–38.
"Little by little . . .": ibid., 40.
"Coming from the sea . . .": ibid., 41.
"There's hissing and banging . . .": ibid., 42.
"The big clock, dishes . . .": ibid., 43.

READER'S INVASION BRIEFING: UTAH BEACH AND THE COTENTIN PENINSULA

Area of peninsula to hold: Ryan, 137–139.
"Utah Beach lay almost in the center . . .": ibid., 137.
Mission: Balkoski, *Utah Beach*, 94.
Pathfinders: ibid., 102–105.
Gliders: ibid., 142–144.
82nd Airborne mission: ibid., 94.
Merderet River and 82nd mission: Messenger, *D-Day Atlas*, 62–65.
4th Infantry Division on Utah Beach: Balkoski, *Utah Beach*, xvi.
"No veteran of the Utah Beach . . .": ibid., 184.

Part 4: Utah

"There was not anything . . .": Burns, Oral History Interview, NWW2M [hereafter Burns], 9.
"If all World War II . . .": Balkoski, *Utah Beach*, 115.
"The hard and difficult thing . . .": Sampson, 133.

VOICES FROM THE AIRBORNE DIVISIONS

"We loaded up our equipment . . .": Burns, 5.
"Now here we sat . . .": ibid., 6–9.
"It was now time . . .": Schroeder, Oral History Interview, NWW2M [hereafter Schroeder], 7–8.
"I heard noises . . .": Beaudin, Oral History Interview, NWW2M [hereafter Beaudin], 7.
"I noticed some German soldiers . . .": ibid., 8–9.
"In World War II . . .": Russell, Oral History Interview, NWW2M [hereafter Russell], 1, 4, 14.
"Snipers in Normandy . . .": ibid., 14.
"The drop zone . . .": Griffing, Oral History Interview, NWW2M [hereafter Griffing], 7–8.

CHAPTER 10: CRICKETS: NORMANDY BEFORE DAWN

"Each man knew . . .": Fitzgerald, Oral History Interview, NWW2M [hereafter Fitzgerald], 2.
" 'Stand up and hook up!' ": ibid.
"The heavy equipment we carried . . .": ibid.
"My legs felt as if they would go out . . .": ibid., 3.
"Tracer fire from below . . .": ibid.
" 'Go!' ": ibid.
"A blast of cool night air . . .": ibid., 4.
Evasive action and altitude of planes: Balkoski, *Utah Beach*, 113.
"I'm going to land . . .": Fitzgerald, 4.
"I felt a strange . . .": ibid.
"The peas would all land . . .": ibid., 5.
"When you put it . . .": Griffing, 2–3.
"I heard footsteps . . .": Fitzgerald, 5.
"Cloud banks forced . . .": Bradley, O., 275.
Task Force A: Gavin, *On to Berlin*, 100.
"A night jump into combat . . .": ibid., 101.
"Suddenly we entered . . .": ibid., 104.
"I began to worry . . .": ibid.
"More than 60 planeloads . . .": Bradley, O., 276.
"I should have been able . . .": Gavin, 106–107.
"For all the good they did . . .": Webster, 30.
"I was home again.": ibid., 37.
"In Normandy the dead lay . . .": ibid., 43.
"We were ready to go . . .": ibid., 43–44.
"an outstanding memoir . . .": ibid., introduction by Stephen Ambrose, xiii.

CHAPTER 11: SCENES FROM A CHAPLAIN'S D-DAY

"The plane was hit many times . . .": Sampson, 45.
"The canopy of my chute . . .": ibid., 45–46.
"By pure luck . . .": ibid., 46.
"I learned later . . .": ibid.
"We no sooner . . .": ibid.
"A German jumped . . .": ibid., 48.
"I told him . . .": ibid.
"The house was riddled . . .": ibid., 50.
"crawled off his litter . . .": ibid., 52.
"A couple of boys . . .": ibid.
"The bombs landed . . .": ibid.

CHAPTER 12: CRASH-LANDING INTO NORMANDY

"In the first hours . . .": Fitzgerald, 8.
"Perspiration broke out on my forehead . . .": ibid., 7.
"Of more than six thousand . . .": Atkinson, 72.
"I asked if anyone knew . . .": Fitzgerald, 8.
"I wanted very much . . .": ibid., 8.
"what every bold airborne leader . . .": Balkoski, *Utah Beach*, 124–125.
"I had only gone . . .": Fitzgerald, 8–9.
"I decided to join . . .": ibid., 9.
Glider missions and loads: Masters, 51.
"It was a typical . . .": Fitzgerald, 9.
"Adding to the swelling . . .": ibid., 9–10.
"In a moment . . .": ibid., 10.
"For the hard-pressed 82nd . . .": Ryan, 160.
"twelve 105mm howitzers . . .": Masters, 54.
"This stuff was like bacon grease . . .": Schroeder, 5.
"Oh, well, so at least . . .": ibid., 8.
"exactly a bed of roses . . .": ibid., 8–9.
"That, of course, was according . . .": ibid., 10.
"'Before they touched the soil . . .'": ibid., 10–11.
"favorite subject"; "I would like to . . .": ibid., 1, 11.
"Medics were working . . .": Fitzgerald, 10–11.
"Many of the troopers . . .": ibid., 11.
"While looking for water . . .": ibid., 11-12.
"his personal Alamo": ibid., 12.
"He had fought alone . . .": ibid.

DISPATCH: HEDGEROWS AND AMERICAN INGENUITY

"Like many of my fellow troopers . . .": Bearden, *To D-Day and Back*, 118.
"surprisingly difficult . . .": Gavin, 121.

"The invention came . . .": Bradley, O., 342.
"The tank backed off . . .": ibid.
"Scrap metal for the tank . . .": ibid.

CHAPTER 13: FIRST BATTLES

"The Americans could accomplish . . .": Balkoski, *Utah Beach*, 145.
Capture of Sainte-Mère-Église: ibid., 146–148.
"We were given a position . . .": Fitzgerald, 13.
"Rounds were coming in . . .": ibid., 14.
"I could not hold . . .": ibid., 14–15.
"The Germans were recovering . . .": ibid., 15.
"at the Germans . . .": ibid.
"I zigzagged through . . .": ibid., 16.
"With the last light . . .": ibid.
"Hot biscuits and ham . . .": ibid.
"The large shells . . .": ibid., 17.
"They were a welcome sight . . .": ibid.
"One night, I found . . .": ibid., 20.
"I was becoming a member . . .": ibid., 21.
"The beaches were now secure . . .": ibid.
"A lot of the guys . . .": ibid., 23.
"As soon as I could . . .": ibid.
"Evidently I became carried away . . .": ibid.

CHAPTER 14: APPROACH FROM THE SEA: VOICES FROM THE BEACHHEAD

"Everything lit up . . .": Wakefield, in Stillwell, *Assault on Normandy*, 93.
"The big guns of the battleships . . .": ibid.
"When I got out . . .": ibid.
"Soldiers of the first wave . . .": ibid., 95.
"Someone shouted the usual warning . . .": ibid.
"I don't think anything . . .": ibid.
"When we first got ashore . . .": ibid., 96.
"Of course a lot of the kids . . .": Perrett, M. Interview by Scott Price, June 18, 2003, [hereafter Perrett], 3.
"like driving a bulldozer . . .": ibid., 8.
"Every one of these . . .": ibid.
"Here I am a coxswain . . .": ibid., 13.
"But you can't . . .": ibid., 22.
" 'Look Cox, we landed at Sicily . . .' ": ibid., 23.
"He just stuck his head . . .": ibid.
"My trusty Motor Mac . . .": ibid.
" 'They're already closed . . .' ": ibid.
"I'm proud to tell you . . .": ibid., 24.

BRIEFING: HIGGINS BOATS

"Ike says that when . . .": Butcher, 275.
man who won the war . . . NWW2M, Higgins Boat Fact Sheet, https://www.nationalww2museum.org/sites/default/files/2017-07/higgins-in-new-orleans-fact.pdf.
"His employees included . . .": ibid.

CHAPTER 15: ON UTAH BEACH: STARTING THE WAR FROM HERE

"A brave, gamy, undersized man . . .": Bradley, O., 110.
" 'Hey, what outfit is that . . .' ": ibid.
" 'We're going to start . . .' ": Ryan, 206. Ryan notes that Roosevelt made the famous comment to Colonel Eugene Caffey, who contributed to his book, *The Longest Day.*
"Because the 4th Division . . .": ibid., 333.
"He broke out of the hospital . . .": ibid., 334.
"Ted died as no one . . .": ibid., 333.
"With the skill . . .": ibid., 275.
"His valor, courage, and presence . . .": Congressional Medal of Honor Society: http://www.cmohs.org/recipient-detail/2972/roosevelt-theodore-jr.php.
"By evening, 22,000 men . . .": Ryan, 263.
situation of the 82nd: Balkoski, *Utah Beach*, 268–269.
"By daylight . . .": Gavin, 111.
Turnbull: Balkoski, *Utah Beach*, 270–275.

DISPATCH: THE SPYMASTER FORGETS HIS CYANIDE

" 'Gentlemen, I find that here . . .' ": Smith, *OSS: The Secret History of America's First Central Intelligence Agency*, 183.
" 'David, we mustn't be captured . . .' ": ibid., 185.
"Thereupon, still lying prone . . .": ibid.
" 'I must shoot first . . .' ": ibid.

READER'S INVASION BRIEFING: OMAHA

"For this great seaborne . . .": Ryan, 181–182.

Part 5: Omaha

"Then we saw the coast . . .": Gellhorn, 110.
"The thought came . . .": Cawthon, *Other Clay*, 57–58.

USS *AUGUSTA* 3:35 A.M., OFF THE NORMANDY COAST

"It was 3:35 a.m . . .": Bradley, O., 267.
"The moon hung misted . . .": ibid.
"'I don't like it . . .'": ibid., 268.
"By now Overlord . . .": ibid.
"no fewer than . . .": Zaloga, *The Devil's Garden,* 76–77.
"One reason that . . ."; ineffective: ibid., 130, 188.
"'All the rockets . . .'": ibid., 189.
"At 6:10 we prepare . . .": Brown, 144.
"Not until later . . .": Bradley, O., 268.
"Seen through binoculars . . .": Brown, 148.

VOICES FROM OMAHA BEACH

"About 2:00 a.m . . .": Barnes, *Fragments of My Life*, 61–62.
"Here is a list . . .": Thomas, Oral History Interview, NWW2M [hereafter Thomas], 4.
"In my boat . . .": ibid., 54.
"The towering gray-black waves . . .": Baumgarten, *D-Day Survivor,* 59–60.
"In my own boat . . .": Eikner, Oral History Interview, NWW2M [hereafter Eikner], 8–9.
"Gradually, we began to see . . .": Barnes, 63.
"Suddenly, a swirl of water . . .": ibid., 65–66.
"There was a strong . . .": Pogue, *Pogue's War,* 66.
"We were due at 8:30 . . .": Prosser, in Liddle, *D-Day, by Those Who Were There,* 124.
"We were all wearing . . .": MacPhee, ibid., 131–132.
"Signs that things . . .": Cawthon, 55.

CHAPTER 16: SOME KIND OF PRAYER

"Waiting for the first ray . . .": Capa, 139.
"None of us . . .": ibid.
"The sun had no way . . .": ibid.
"The coast of Normandy . . .": ibid.
"The bullets tore holes . . .": ibid., 140.
"The bullets chased me back . . .": ibid.
"Above the boots and faces . . .": ibid., 141.
"I paused for a moment . . .": ibid., 148.
"I did not think . . .": ibid.
"Then things got confused . . .": ibid., 149.
"I told him . . .": ibid.
"The captions under . . .": ibid., 152.

CHAPTER 17: A SCENE OF HAVOC AND DESTRUCTION

Four companies: Balkoski, *Omaha Beach*, 129.
"The rough sea with spray . . .": Mominee, Oral History Interview, NWW2M [hereafter Mominee], 5–6.
"About 400 yards from shore . . .": ibid., 7.
"The first thing I remember . . .": ibid., 7.
"It was because . . .": ibid., 8.
"I was exhausted . . .": ibid.
"It seemed like someone . . .": ibid.
"As I sat underneath . . .": ibid., 9.
"All I could see . . .": ibid.
"the Fighting Fronts": ibid., 11.
" 'You're a rifleman now . . .' ": Thomas, 2.
"trees, farm houses, hills . . .": ibid., 3.
"The planes bombed . . .": ibid., 3–4.
"They finally got it open . . .": ibid., 5.
"Although I knew how to swim . . .": ibid.
"When I finally got . . .": ibid., 6.
"Colonel Taylor . . .": ibid., 7.
"I made the top . . .": ibid., 7–8.
"It calmed down a little . . .": ibid., 8.
"It was a gift . . .": ibid., 10.

CHAPTER 18: A THIN, WET LINE OF KHAKI

"We were in among . . .": Cawthon, 55.
"Some of the larger ones . . .": ibid., 56.
116th Regiment off course: Balkoski, *Omaha Beach*, 136.
German stronghold: ibid., 133.
"From the crests . . .": Cawthon, 56.
"its exploding horror": ibid., 57.
"The havoc they had wrought . . .": ibid., 58.
"Against the wall . . .": ibid., 59.
"While I was straining . . .": ibid.
"My overriding doubt . . .": ibid., 59–60.
"Gradually, my lungs and stomach . . .": ibid., 60.
" 'This is a debacle.' ": ibid., 61.
"In the invasion's first hour . . .": Balkoski, *Omaha Beach*, 229.
"The foot soldier . . ."; "the only salvation . . .": Cawthon, 65.
"As the morning lengthened . . .": Bradley, O., 270.
German defense numbers: Atkinson, 108–109; Austra, K. "D-Day: U.S. Army's 1st Division's Desperate Hours on Omaha Beach," http://www.historynet.com/d-day-us-armys-1st-infantry-divisions-desperate-hours-on-omaha-beach.htm; originally appeared in *World War II* magazine, July 1999.
"By 8:30 the two assault . . .": Bradley, O., 270.

DD Tanks: ibid., 98–104.

"Much of the difficulty . . .": ibid., 271.

"There was due to arrive . . .": ibid.

"The battle belonged . . .": ibid.

CHAPTER 19: "29, LET'S GO!"

"It was 6:15 a.m . . .": Baumgarten, 63.

"WN72 was the smallest . . .": Zaloga, 133–134.

Company A: Balkoski, *Omaha Beach*, 118–119.

"'I am beginning to think . . .'": ibid., 119.

"'My name is Captain Taylor Fellers . . .'": Barnes, 49.

"It was dark up on deck . . .": ibid., 62.

"It was Vierville . . .": ibid., 65.

"I had heard no noise . . .": ibid.

"There was no doubt . . .": ibid., 67.

"We had no weapons . . .": ibid., 66.

"The lowering of the ramp . . .": Baumgarten, 65.

"The sound of the German . . .": ibid., 66.

"Now I was weaponless . . .": ibid., 69–70.

"We were left . . .": ibid., 74.

"There were about four rows . . .": ibid., 79.

"There was no way . . .": ibid., 80.

"It was reassuring . . .": ibid., 81.

"'Rangers! Lead the way!'": Balkoski, *Omaha Beach*, 197.

"'No sense dying here . . .'": Feinberg, in Liddle, 121.

"The call was . . .": Baumgarten, 81.

"looked around and in a great . . .": Friedman in Balkoski, *Omaha Beach*, 198.

"the shadow of catastrophe": Bradley, O., 275.

Pinder: Balkoski, *Omaha Beach*, 200.

"Walking wounded": Baumgarten, 81.

BRIEFING: WE WERE THERE

"'You know, I really think . . .'": Sherwill, P. "African-American D-Day Veterans Celebrate Barack Obama's Trip to Normandy." *The Telegraph*, June 9, 2009. http://www.telegraph.co.uk/news/worldnews/barackobama/5456233/African-American-D-Day-veterans-celebrate-Barack-Obamas-trip-to-Normandy.html.

Number of barrage balloons: Gawne, *Spearheading D-Day*, 193.

First men ashore: ibid., 191.

"All day, we medics . . .": Woodson, "My Witness to D-Day June 6,1944," unpublished article, http://stateside.digitalnewsroom.org/wp-content/uploads/2015/11/Woodson-Waverly-Enclosed-Docs-Sent-to-Army-11.5.15.-No-PR.pdf.

DISPATCH: JOHN NOBLE ROBERTS

"At about 10 o'clock . . .": Roberts, J. Interview by C. Douglass Kroll, July 3, 2012, 6.
"I was taking a message . . .": ibid.

CHAPTER 20: THE RANGERS AT POINTE DU HOC

"The operation there . . .": Eikner, Oral History Interview, NWW2M [hereafter Eikner], 1.
French resistance: Zaloga, 170.
" 'the most dangerous battery . . .' ": ibid., 196.
"No soldier in my command . . .": Bradley, O., 269.
Ladders: Zaloga, 200–204.
"We were thankful . . .": Eikner, 5.
Ranger code messages: Balkoski, *Omaha Beach*, 171.
"Just as there was enough . . .": Eikner, 9.
"Colonel Rudder . . . convinced . . .": ibid., 9–10.
"The enemy had time enough . . .": ibid., 11.
Two hundred feet in the air: Zaloga, 204.
"We of course . . .": Kerchner, Oral History Interview, NWW2M [hereafter Kerchner], 5.
"There was a rope . . .": Eikner, 12.
"It wasn't bad at all . . .": Lomell, Oral History Interview, NWW2M [hereafter Lomell], 7.
"like we play . . .": ibid., 9.
"We set up . . .": ibid., 12.
"And so Jack . . .": ibid., 13
" 'Well, there's nobody . . .' ": ibid., 14.
"And we just stumbled . . .": ibid., 16.
Ranger casualties: National Museum of the United States Army. "Rudder's Rangers and the Boys of Pointe du Hoc." https://armyhistory.org/rudders-rangers-and-the-boys-of-pointe-du-hoc-the-u-s-army-rangers-mission-in-the-early-morning-hours-of-6-june-1944/.
"I have always felt . . .": Epstein in Balkoski, *Omaha Beach*, 174.
"Cota asked . . .": ibid., 197.

Part 6: Aftermath: More than Courage

"This time the challenge . . .": King George VI, https://www.youtube.com/watch?v=tY2wysVXs6Q.
"After it was over . . .": Pyle, 384.

VOICES AFTER D-DAY

"Most of the fields . . .": Scannell, *Argument of Kings*, 151.
"The rugged, independent . . .": Whitehead, 122.
"We climbed the steep . . .": Bradley, R., *Aid Main!*, 47–48.
"I went up in a Piper Cub . . .": Whitehead, 125.
"There were destroyers . . .": Gellhorn, 110–112.
"The fury of artillery . . .": Scannell, 165.

REPORTER'S NOTEBOOK: THOSE BITTER SANDS: ERNIE PYLE

"By the time we got there . . .": Pyle, 384.
"There in a jumbled row . . .": ibid., 391–392.
"Always there are dogs . . .": ibid., 392.

CHAPTER 21: THE MIRACLE OF A TOEHOLD

"The plans, so long made . . .": Brown, 213.
Casualties: D-Day Museum; Zaloga, 12.
"At 3:00 a.m . . .": Baumgarten, 87.
"Before that experience . . .": ibid., 99.
"'Branny, you've been down . . .'": Branstrator, in Stillwell, 126.
"I went up into the air . . .": ibid., 127.
"When the PT boat . . .": ibid., 128.
"You just never know . . .": ibid., 129.
"It was close to the same place . . .": Fitzgerald, 32.
"I murmured a short prayer . . .": ibid., 33.
"The poor priest . . .": Sampson, 60.
"'Oh gosh, Father . . .'": ibid.
"We managed to get . . .": ibid., 61.
"It didn't seem possible . . .": ibid., 53.
"See them standing . . .": ibid., 134–135.
"'That's my country . . .'": ibid., 135.
"We respect our heroes . . .": Brown, 218.

 PHOTO PERMISSIONS 

Photos ©: cover top: Naval History and Heritage Command; cover bottom: Bettmann/Getty Images; i: Everett Collection Inc./Alamy Images; iii: Robert Capa/International Center of Photography/Magnum Photos; vi: The George C. Marshall Foundation; ix: National Archives and Records Administration; 4: National Archives and Records Administration; 7: Imperial War Museum; 8: Map courtesy of the USMA, Department of History; 20: Library of Congress; 21: National Archives and Records Administration; 22: National Archives and Records Administration; 31: Library of Congress; 34: U.S. Army/AP Images; 46: Imperial War Museum; 52: Don F. Pratt Memorial Museum Collection; 54: National Archives and Records Administration; 65: National Archives and Records Administration; 68–69: Map courtesy of the USMA, Department of History; 73: U.S. Army Heritage and Education Center/World War II Signal Corps photograph collection; 76: National Archives and Records Administration; 80: The George C. Marshall Foundation; 83: The National World War II Museum; 85: Robert Capa/International Center of Photography/Magnum Photos; 86: Imperial War Museum; 91: National Archives and Records Administration; 93: National Archives and Records Administration; 95: Naval History and Heritage Command; 97: National Archives and Records Administration; 106–107: Imperial War Museum; 109: Library of Congress; 115: Naval History and Heritage Command; 122–123: Everett Collection Inc./Alamy Images; 124: U.S. Army Heritage and Education Center/World War II Signal Corps photograph collection; 126: National Archives and Records Administration; 132: The International Museum of World War II, Boston, MA; 141: National Archives and Records Administration; 148: National Archives and Records Administration; 152: PhotoQuest/Getty Images; 158: National Archives and Records Administration; 163: National Archives and Records Administration; 168–169: Naval History and Heritage Command; 171: National Archives and Records Administration; 178: Naval History and Heritage Command; 179: Naval History and Heritage Command; 182: National Archives and Records Administration; 183: National Archives and Records Administration; 185: National Archives and Records Administration; 191: John Rickard/historyofwar.org; 197: National Archives and

Records Administration; 202–203: Naval History and Heritage Command; 204: Naval History and Heritage Command; 207: Naval History and Heritage Command; 213: Robert Capa/International Center of Photography/Magnum Photos; 214: Robert Capa/International Center of Photography/Magnum Photos; 215: Robert Capa/International Center of Photography/Magnum Photos; 216: Robert Capa/International Center of Photography/Magnum Photos; 221: Naval History and Heritage Command; 225: National Archives and Records Administration; 226: Naval History and Heritage Command; 229: National Archives and Records Administration; 231: National Archives and Records Administration; 234–235: Naval History and Heritage Command; 236: Naval History and Heritage Command; 240: National Archives and Records Administration; 248: National Archives and Records Administration; 250: Everett Collection/Superstock, Inc.; 252: National Archives and Records Administration; 253: National Archives and Records Administration; 254: Naval History and Heritage Command; 256: National Archives and Records Administration; 266: Naval History and Heritage Command; 268: Naval History and Heritage Command; 269: Naval History and Heritage Command; 271: National Archives and Records Administration; 276: Robert Capa/International Center of Photography/Magnum Photos; 278: Naval History and Heritage Command; 280–281: Library of Congress; 283: National Archives and Records Administration; 284: The George C. Marshall Foundation; 287: Naval History and Heritage Command; 289: Naval History and Heritage Command; 290: National Archives and Records Administration; 291: The George C. Marshall Foundation; 292: National Archives and Records Administration; 293 top: National Archives and Records Administration; 293 bottom: National Archives and Records Administration; 302: Michael Kenney/Shutterstock.

★ INDEX ★

Note: Page numbers in *italics* refer to illustrations.

Advance Command Post at Southwick House, 59
African Americans
discrimination in U.S. Army, 17–18, 22, 24–27, 257–58
medals earned by, 258
as medical personnel, 24–25, 257
service of, 17–18, 22, 24–27, 256–58
in support roles, *20*
airborne divisions
about, xxii
aircraft on fire, 131, 141
bombs dropped by, 66, 86, 98
and C-47s, *115*, 117, 184
casualties, 125, 290
and construction of aircraft, 22
day of mission, 96–98
number of aircraft, 18, 53, 206
preassault bombings of Omaha Beach, 193, 198, 199, 200
and strategy for invasion, 116
supplies and equipment delivered by, 116
and Utah Beach, 116, 117–19 (*see also* 82nd Airborne Division; 101st Airborne Division)
voices from, 124–29
and weather conditions, 184
See also gliders; paratroopers
Allies
attempts to weaken Germany, 5, 10
at Casablanca Conference (1943), 11
declaration of war, 3, 9
invasion plan adopted by, 14
and Operation Torch, 11
participants in D-Day invasion, 67
preparedness for invasion, 6
and selection of Supreme Commander, 30
at Tehran Conference (1943), 30–31, *31*
war declared on Germany, 3
See also France; Great Britain; Soviet Union; United States
Ambrose, Stephen, 111, 151
amphibious assault (Operation Neptune)
and carpet bombing of beaches, 86
code name, 13

amphibious assault (*continued*)
and equipment and gear of troops, 202–3
first casualties of, 74
and Higgins Boats, 175–76 (*see also* landing craft)
Kirk's role in, 81
and mined obstacles (*see* beach defense obstacles)
and Royal Norwegian Navy, 18
on Utah Beach, 119, 166–74
and waterlogged troops, 237–38
See also 4th Infantry Division
anti-gas clothing, 149
armies, number of soldiers in, xxiii
Arnold, Henry, *291*
Atlantic, journey across, 19
Atlantic Wall, 5, 13, 73, *73*, 200
Axis powers, emergence of, 306. *See also* Germany; Italy; Japan

Balkoski, Joseph, xx
casualty figures of, 290
on chaos of war, 79, 121
on leaders organizing paratroopers, 145
on Sainte-Mère-Église, 157
on troops pinned on beach, 238–39
on Utah Beach invasion, 119
Barnes, John J., 202, 205–6, 246, 303
barrage balloons
and Anti-Aircraft Barrage Balloon Battalion, *256*, 257
and "balloon curtain," 257
and crossing the English Channel, *80*, 83, *83*
defensive function of, *168–69*
and fleet on Normandy's shore, *278*
Barton, Raymond "Tubby," 174, 177
battalions, number of soldiers in, xxiii
batteries, number of soldiers in, xxiii
Battle of the Bulge, 307
Baumgarten, Harold
advancement up bluffs, 251, 254–55
and Cota's leadership, 251
on failure of demolition/bombardment, 244
and slaughter at Dog Green, 247, 249–50, 292
on transport of troops to shore, 203, 205
wounds of, 249, 250, 294–95
Bay of the Seine, 66
beach defense obstacles
and Capa's experience on Omaha Beach, 212
and demolition teams, 50, 166–67, 170
and failed demolitions, 193, 232, 242, 244

landing craft destroyed by, 222–23, 246
and metal for refitting Allied tanks, 156
and meteorological considerations, 47
at Omaha Beach, 193, 242, *289*
at Utah Beach, 166–67, 170
beaches used in Overlord
locations of, 67, *68–69*
wreckage left along, 284, *284*, *289*
See also Gold Beach; Juno Beach; Omaha Beach; Sword Beach; Utah Beach
Bearden, Bob, 154
Beaudin, Briand N., 127–28
Belgium, Germany's invasion of, 9, 306
Berra, Yogi, 173
Bingham, Sidney, 238
bocage terrain in France, 132, 155
Boeing Flying Fortress B-17 Bomber, "Fort", 96
Bradley, Omar, *291*
and amphibious tanks, 87, 198
and call to battle stations, 197
command post of, 81, 288
crossing the English Channel, 81, 82
and field communications, 240–41
growing concerns of, 240–41, 242
and inland advancement of troops, 253
on paratroopers' drop zones, 134, 135
and plans for reinforcements, 242–43
on Pointe du Hoc mission, 262
and Roosevelt (Theodore, Jr.), 177, 180–81
and tanks refitted for hedgerows, 156
on tides' influence on invasion, 50
on timing of invasion, 51
and weather forecasts, 82
Bradley, Robert, 279
Branstrator, William Dayton "Bill," 296–97
brigades, number of soldiers in, xxiii
Bronze Stars, 258
Brotheridge, Den, 103, 105, 108
Brown, John Mason
on courage and peace, 301
on crossing the English Channel, 87
on distant turmoil of war, 200–201
on execution of invasion plans, 288, 290
on impact of invasion, 18–19
on naval bombardment of Omaha, 199–200
on U.S. troops in England, 23
Bruce, David, 187–89

Buckinghamshire Light Infantry, 100
Bulkeley, John, 297
Burns, Dwayne T., 121, 124–25
Butcher, Harry
  and Eisenhower's message of troop withdrawal (undelivered), 64–65
  and headquarters of Eisenhower, 33
  on security scare, 38–39
  on target date for invasion, 1
  and Telek, Eisenhower's dog, 35–36

C-47s, *115*, 117, 184
Caen, Normandy, 67, *69*, 101, 112
Caen Canal, 101, 103, 108
Camp Lejeune, North Carolina, 172
Canada
  and Dieppe raid, 4
  and Overlord participants, 67
  and Pegasus Bridge mission, 101
Capa, Robert
  accompanying troops to Omaha Beach, 84–85, 211–18
  images of Omaha Beach, 54, 212, *213*, *214*, *215*, *216*
  on preinvasion activities of soldiers, 84–85
  on preparations for invasion, 54
  on transport of troops to shore, 211–12
Carpenter, Iris, 57
Carson, Lee, 57–58
Casablanca Conference (1943), 5–6
casualties of D-Day, *248*
  airborne divisions, 125, 290
  anticipation of, 84
  arriving on hospital ships, 281–82
  Baumgarten's wounds, 249, 250, 294–95
  and cemeteries of France, 301, *302*
  in demolition teams, 242
  effect on morale of soldiers, 152
  estimates of, xx, 290
  first, 106, 108
  German, 143, *229*, 279, 290–91
  and glider landings, 147
  and hospital ships, 58, 280–82
  left by soldiers for medics, 228
  and medics, 127–28, 151, *185*, 228, *229*
  and memorial for lost paratroopers, 137
  at Omaha Beach, 71, 193, *231*, 239, 249, 250, *250*, 290
  paratroopers, 125, 151–52, 184
  at Pegasus Bridge, 106, 108
  and perseverance of troops, 254–55

and Pointe du Hoc operation, 265, 267
Pyle on, 285
remembering soldiers' sacrifices, 300–301
retrieved from battlefield, 209–10
Roberts's leg amputation, 259–60
sight of wounded and dead, on beaches, 228
and survivors, 230
treating wounded, *141*, 141–43, 151, *185*, *229*
at Utah Beach, 290
Cawthon, Charles R.
on factors affecting invasion plans, 239–40
and field communications, 239–40
on separation of troops from units, 195
on signs of problems, 210, 237
on transport of troops to shore, 203, 232–33, 237
waterlogged equipment of, 237–38
cemeteries of France, 301, *302*
chaos of war
Balkoski on, 121
and glider landings, 147
at Omaha Beach, 208, 224
as overriding theme of D-Day, 79
weather's impact on, 134
chaplains, 53–54, *54*, 139–43. *See also* Sampson, Francis L.
Charlie area of Omaha Beach, *191*, 191, 192–93
Château de Périers, 112
Cherbourg, France
and bombing mission, 96
captured by Allies, 288
location of, 67
port of, 67, 116, 118
Sampson in, 299
sealing off German access to, 118
See also Cotentin Peninsula
Chief of Staff to the Supreme Allied Commander (COSSAC), 6
Churchill, Winston
at Casablanca Conference (1943), 11
Operation Overload adopted by, 14
on readiness for invasion, 6
and selection of Supreme Commander, 31
stress experienced by, 43
at Tehran Conference (1943), *31*
trip to Normandy, 288
civilians living through the war, 112–14, 277
code name for D-Day, 7. *See also* Operation Overload
Cole, Robert G., 130, 145, 164
Colleville Draw of Omaha Beach, 220

Colleville village, 288
communications in battle, 240–41, 253–54
companies, number of soldiers in, xxiii
Company A, 245–47, 249
corps, number of soldiers in, xxiii
Cota, Norman "Dutch," 251, 270, 294
Cotentin Peninsula (aka Cherbourg Peninsula)
  beaches of, 67
  and chaos of war, 121
  geography of, 115–16
  German defense of, 116
  and Mulberry harbors, 67
  sealing off German access to, 118
  and strategy for invasion, 116
  and Utah Beach landing site, 71–72
Cowdrey, Albert E., 24–25
cows, encounters with, 127, 128–29, 131
Coyne, Catherine, 57
"crickets" (clickers) used by paratroopers, *132*, 133, 137
crossword puzzles, security scare related to, 38–39
Culin, Curtis Grubb, III, 155–56

Davis, Benjamin Oliver, Sr., 24
D-Day (term), xix. *See also* Operation Overload
D-Day Museum, Portsmouth, England, xx
deception used in Overlord planning, 37–38
demolition teams
  casualties of, 242
  explosives of, 167
  at Omaha Beach, 193, 232, 237, 242, 244
  and strategy for invasion, 50
  and tidal conditions, 50
  at Utah Beach, 119, 166–67, 170, 181, 257
  and weather considerations, 47
Denmark, 4, 9, 306
D'Este, Carlo, 1, 11
Dieppe raid, 4
disabilities, people with, 10
Distinguished Service Cross, 258
divisions, number of soldiers in, xxiii
Dog Green area of Omaha Beach, 244–55
  dire situation at, 249–50
  German defense of, 247, 249–50
  location of, *191*, 191
  medics at, 250
  and Pointe du Hoc mission, 268
  slaughter of Company A at, 247, 249–50, 292
  and Vierville draw, 192–93
Dog Red area of Omaha Beach, *191*, 191, 232–40

dogs present at invasion, 79, 285–86
Dog White area of Omaha Beach, *191*, 191, 268
Donovan, William J. "Wild Bill," 187–89
double agents, 37
Dunkirk, France, 3
Dunne, Tom, 99

Easy Green area of Omaha Beach, *191*, 191
Easy Red area of Omaha Beach
  Capa's experience on, 212–13, 216–18
  Capa's images of, *213*, *214–15*, *216*
  casualties of, 228
  location of, *191*, 191
  and tanks' inability to reach shores, 241
  transport of troops to, 224, 227–28
  troops under heavy fire, 228–30
Egypt, 306
Eighth Air Force, 200
8th Infantry Regiment, 119, *183*
18th Infantry Regiment, 179
82nd Airborne Division ("The All Americans")
  commander of, 134
  and dispersal of gliders, 147
  drop zones for, 118
  Fitzgerald's service with, 144, 145, 158, 162, 164
  goals of, 118–19
  passwords used by, 133
  in Sainte-Mère-Église, *158*
  scattered landings of paratroopers, 135–36, 183, 185
  success of, 183
Eikner, James W., 205, 261–64, 268
Eisenhower, Dwight D., *291*
  appointed Supreme Commander, 31–32
  background of, 32
  dog of, 33, *34*, 35–36
  headquarters of, 33
  and Italian campaign, 11, 32
  and landing craft, 175
  message of troop withdrawal (undelivered), 64–65
  Order of the Day, 64, *76*, 77
  preparations for D-Day, 59
  and revisions to invasion plan, 48–49
  on timing of invasion, 43, 62
  visiting with troops prior to invasion, 53–54, 64, *65*
  and weather forecasts, 48–49, 60–62
England
  blackouts in, 29
  and Blitz, 23, 29
  supply shortages in, 28–29
  U.S. troops in, 17, 19, 22, 23
  See also Great Britain

English Channel
crossing, *80*, *83*, 83–85, 87, *95*, 139
map of, *8*
and risk of seasickness, 82
and timing of invasion, 50, 51
Epstein, Herbert, 269

fear
and Capa's experience on Omaha Beach, 216–17
Fitzgerald on, 162
and Roosevelt (Theodore, Jr.), 180
Feinberg, Bernard S., 251
Fellers, Taylor, 245–46, 249
5th Ranger Battalion, 251, 262, 270
"Final Solution," 9–10
1st Infantry Division, 220–24, 227–230, 288
Thomas, Charles "Chuck" H., 224, 227–30
Fitzgerald, John E.
assisting with wounded, 151
with 82nd Airborne, 144, 145, 158, 162
encounter with Germans, 133–34
first battle experiences of, 158–64
and glider landings, 146–47
jumping, 130–32
leaving Normandy, 297–98
listed missing in action, 163
medals earned by, 164
on performance of paratroopers, 298
reunited with original unit, 162–63
as runner, 160–61
separated from unit, 132, 144–45
501st Parachute Infantry Regiment, 53, 118, 139–43
502nd Parachute Infantry Regiment, 118
505th Parachute Infantry Regiment
and capture of Sainte-Mère-Église, 157, 158
combat experience of, 117, 118
and stand at Neuville, 184
and Task Force A, 134
506th Parachute Infantry Regiment, ix–xii, 118
507th Parachute Infantry Regiment, 118, 134
508th Parachute Infantry Regiment, 118, 134
582nd Engineer Dump Truck Company, 257
foggy conditions, 28, 200
4th Infantry Division
arrival on Utah Beach, 166
and barrage balloons, *168–69*
beachhead secured by, 181
goals of, 119
inland advancement of, *183*, 288
and Roosevelt (Theodore, Jr.), 180–81

and strategy for invasion, 116
and support from paratroopers, 117
target landing sites missed by, 186
Fox, Dennis, 106
Fox Green area of Omaha Beach, *191*, 191, 220–24, 241
foxholes, 143
Fox Red area of Omaha Beach, *191*, 191, 241
France
and Allied powers, 9
bocage country of, 116, 132, 155
French Resistance, 261
German invasion/occupation of, 4, 9, 306
hedgerows of, 154–56, 159
and liberation of Paris, 57, *293*, 307
map of, *8*
war declared on Germany, 3, 9, 306
Franklin, John Hope, 26–27
Free France, 18, 67
French Resistance, 261
Friedman, William, 252
friendly fire, 142
Fuller, Margaret, 57

Gavin, James M.
drop zone missed by, 135
and hedgerows, 154–55
mission of, 136
on night jumps, 135
on scattered paratroopers, 181, 183
on success of division, 183
and Task Force A, 134–35
Gearing, Edward, 206
Gellhorn, Martha, 57, 58, 195, 280–82
George VI, King of Great Britain, 275
German military
Allies' attempt to weaken, 5, 10
Allies studying footage of, 90
artillery of, 159
and Atlantic Wall, 5, 13, 73, *73*, 200
blocked by Pegasus Bridge mission, 101
casualties, 143, *229*, 279, 290–91
countries invaded and held by, 3–4, 9
defense strategies of, 116
defense strongholds on Omaha Beach, 71, 190, 191–92, 198–99, 238–39, 241
guns destroyed by Rangers, 267
occupying civilians' homes, 112–13
panzers, 109, *109*
and prisoners of war, 279, 300
reconnaissance patrols of, 84
reinforcements from, 181
U-Boats of, 19, 28
and Von Luck, 109–11

Germany
and Axis powers, 9, 307
extermination camps of, 10
and Hitler's "Final Solution," 9
and *Kristallnacht*, 306
and Nazi Party's rise to power, 9
slave labor driving war machine of, 10
surrender of, 307
war declared on, by Allies, 3, 9
and World War I, 9
Gerow, Leonard, 156
"Glider Flight" song, 99
gliders
cargo carried by, 88, 146, 147, *148*
casualties, 147
and German defenses, 110, 150–51, 277
goals of, 66
and hedgerows, 154
landings of, 104–5, *126*, 126–27, 149, *152*
missed landing areas of, 147, 149–50
and Operation Deadstick, 100–108
and Pegasus Bridge mission, *107*
plan for, 101–2
protecting landing areas of, 146
towed by planes, 88, 103
Gold Beach
about, 70
German defense of, 70
location of, 67, *69*, 70
and Mulberry harbors, 16
objectives at, 288
and revisions to invasion plan, 49
Great Britain
and Allied powers, 9
capacity of forces, 4
and Dieppe raid, 4
and Dunkirk evacuation, 3
in early stages of war, 10
king's address to, 275
and Overlord participants, 67
paratroopers from, 107
and Pegasus Bridge mission, 100, 101, 106, 107
and review of D-Day plans, 7, 14
Royal Navy, 74, 75
6th Airborne of, 108
U.S. troops in U.K., 17–18, 19, 22, 23, 52
war declared on Germany, 3, 9, 306
See also Gold Beach; Sword Beach
Greece, 4, 306
Griffing, Len, 129, 133
groups, number of soldiers in, xxiii

Harrison, Gordon, 30, 94
hedgerows, 154–56, 159

helmets of infantry, 128
Hersh, Martin V., 153
H-hour (time of invasion), 50, 66, 198, 200
Higgins, Andrew Jackson, 170, 175
Higgins Boats, 175–76
Higgins Industries, 175–76
Hill 110, 118
Hitler, Adolf
asleep during invasion, 110
and Atlantic Wall, 73, 200
crimes of, xii–xiii
and defense of port towns, 15
"Final Solution" of, 9–10
as German chancellor, 306
racism of, xii, 24
suicide of, 307
and World War I, 9
Holocaust, xii, 9–10
Horsa Bridge, 108
Horsa gliders, 88–89, 100
hospital ships, 58, 280–82
Howard, John, 100–107, 111
Howard, Roy, 100, 102, 106
Hughes-Hallett, John, 15
Hull, Peggy, 57

infantry
arrival of, 116, *182* (*see also* amphibious assault)
and "Dogfaces" nickname, 128
equipment and gear of, 202–3
helmets of, 128
and supplies on gliders, 149
See also specific infantry divisions, including 4th Infantry Division
Inouye, Daniel, 25
Ismay, Hastings Lionel, 5, 6
Italy, 9, 10, 11, 32, 306

Japan
and atomic bombs, 307
and Axis powers, 9, 307
Pearl Harbor attack of, 3, 10, 307
surrender of, 298, 307
Japanese Americans, 25
Jewish people
and Holocaust, xii, 9–10
and *Kristallnacht*, 306
Juno Beach
about, 70
casualties at, 70
German defense of, 70
location of, 67, *69*, 70
and Mulberry harbors, 16
objectives at, 288
and revisions to invasion plan, 49

Kerchner, George, 264, 267
King, Ernest, *291*
King, William Lyon Mackenzie, 14
Kirk, Alan
command of, 19, 81
and landing craft, 242
and war correspondents, 86
Kirkpatrick, Helen, 57

Krause, Edward "Cannonball," 157
Kristallnacht, 306
Kuhn, Jack, 265

labor shortages in the United States, 22
Landing Barge School, 170, 172
landing craft
  approaching the beaches, *178*, *221*, 222, *226*, *234–35*
  bailing water from, 205
  bombers' views of, 97, *97*
  and coxswains, 172–74
  deployed, *197*
  destroyed by beach obstacles, 222–23, 246 (*see also* beach defense obstacles)
  exiting from, 206, *207*, 232, 241, *253*, *254*
  Higgins Boats, 175–76
  inflatable decoys, 38
  and Landing Barge School, 170, 172
  landing off target, 193, 232
  and meteorological considerations, 47
  number of, 18
  and Pointe du Hoc mission, 263–64
  ramps on, 172, 175, 209
  and rough seas, 198, 203, 205, 222, 227
  and seasickness, 172–73, 205, 227
  silence in, 203
  sinking of, *236*, 246–47
  and slaughter of Company A, 247
  and tidal conditions, 50, 193, 259
  transport of troops to shore, 172–74, 203, 205, 211–12, 227–28, 232–33
LCIs (Landing Craft Infantry), 217, 229, 259
LCTs (Landing Craft Tanks), 229, 242
leaked information, 37
LGBT (lesbian, gay, bisexual, transgender) people, 10
Lomell, Leonard, 265, 267
Luxembourg, Germany's invasion of, 9, 306

MacPhee, John H., 209–10
Marshall, George C., 31, 32, *291*
McKeogh, Mickey, 33
Medal of Honor, Congressional
  and African American soldiers, 258
  awarded to John Pinder, 253–54
  awarded to Robert Cole, 164
  awarded to Theodore Roosevelt Jr., 181
  awarded to Vernon Baker, 258
medical personnel
  African Americans, 24–25, 257
  and German casualties, *229*
  nurses, 25, 58, *283*

taken prisoner, 127–28
treating wounded, 151, *185*, 228
Mediterranean, Axis powers in, 10
Memorial Pegasus Museum, 108
mines
and Allied mine sweeping, 74, 296
on beaches, 284 (*see also* beach defense obstacles)
on paths, 229
Mominee, Albert, 220–24
Montgomery, Bernard, 49, 62, 79
Morgan, Frederick E., 7
headquarters of, 6
and invasion site, 13–14
plan for invasion assigned to, 5, 6, 12
and port sites, 15–16
on risk of failure, 43
submission of plan, 14
Morison, Samuel Eliot, 15, 50
mortar crew, *163*
Mountbatten, Louis, 5
Mueller, Merrill "Red," 61
Mulberry harbors, 16, 67, *280*, 288
Mussolini, Benito, 11

National Medical Association (NMA), 24
National World War II Museum, New Orleans, Louisiana, xx
Nazi Party, rise to power, 9
Netherlands, 4, 9, 306
Neuville, 505th's stand at, 184
Niland, Edward, 299–300
Niland, Frederick "Fritz," 299–300
Niland, Robert, 299
Niland, William, 299
92nd Infantry Division, 25
Norfolk House (headquarters), 45
Normandy
chosen as site of invasion, 13–14
landing zones of (*see* Gold Beach; Juno Beach; Omaha Beach; Sword Beach; Utah Beach)
map of, *68–69*
North Africa, 10–11, 32
Norway, 4, 9, 18, 67, 306

Office of Strategic Services (OSS), 187
Omaha Beach, 190–270
about, 71, 190–93
aerial and naval bombardment of, 86, 193, 198, 199, 200, 237, 241
and Army Rangers, 268–70
and beach defense obstacles, 193, 242, *289*
Capa's images of, 54, *213*, *214*, *215*, *216*
captured pillbox at, *271*
casualties, 71, 193, *231*, 239, 249, 250, *250*, 290

Omaha Beach (*continued*)
cemeteries of, *302*
challenges encountered at, 193, 210
Charlie area, *191*, 191, 192–93
cliffs of, 190, 199, 223, *225*, *240*, *252*
commander for (*see* Bradley, Omar)
and Cota's leadership, 251, 270
demolition failures on, 193, 232, 242, 244
Dog Red area, *191*, 191, 232–40 (*see also* Dog Green area of Omaha Beach)
Dog White area, *191*, 191, 268
draws (exits) from, 192, 198
eastern part of, *191*, 191, 211–18, 220–30, 241
Easy Green area, *191*, 191 (*see also* Easy Red area of Omaha Beach)
and field communications, 240–41
Fox Green area, *191*, 191, 220–24, 241
Fox Red area, *191*, 191, 241
German defense of Vierville draw, 192–93, 245
German strongholds on, 71, 190, 191–92, 198–99, 238–39, 241
goals for troops at, 193
havoc and destruction at, 224
as "Hell's Beach," 71
and inland advancement of troops, 251–53
Kirk's role at, 81
and landing craft, 193, 232, *234–36*, 241, 247, *253*
location of, 67, *68*, 190
map of, *191*
and Mulberry harbors, 16
and plans for invasion, 49, 239–40
and Pointe du Hoc cliff, 191, 193, 251, 255, 261–70
and reinforcements, 242–43, 249
rough seas of, 198, 203, 205, 212
and Schneider, 268–69
separation of troops from units, 193
and tanks, 208–9, 241–42, *253*
and tides, 193, 237
timetable of, 190
and Vierville draw, 192–93, 245
voices from, 202–10
and weapons of troops, 238
western part of, *191*, 191, 232–43, 244–55
wreckage left along, *284*, 284, *289*
101st Airborne Division ("The Screaming Eagles")
"crickets" (clickers) used by, *132*, 133, 137

Eisenhower's preinvasion visits with, 64
Fitzgerald reunited with, 162–63, 297
Fitzgerald separated from, 144–46
goals of, ix–xii, 117–18, 145
jumping, *122–23*
memorial for lost paratroopers, 137
and pathfinders, 118
Webster's reunion with, 137
116th Regiment, 191, 232–40, 242, 244–55, 292
Operation Bodyguard, 37
Operation Deadstick, 100–108
Operation Fortitude, 37–38
Operation Husky, 11
Operation Neptune. *See* amphibious assault
Operation Overload
about, 66–67, *68–69*, 70–72
airborne component (*see* airborne divisions; gliders; paratroopers)
amphibious component (*see* amphibious assault; landing craft)
beach sites (*see* Gold Beach; Juno Beach; Omaha Beach; Sword Beach; Utah Beach)
code name, 7
commander, 30, 31–32 (*see also* Eisenhower, Dwight D.)
cover operation, 37–38
date for, xix, 14
events leading to invasion, 3–5
goals of, 13, 67
H-hour (time of invasion), 50, 66, 198, 200
mission spearheading (*see* Pegasus Bridge operation)
mission to capture German battery (*see* Pointe du Hoc operation)
number of troops in, 18, 53
plans (*see* planning D-Day)
surprise component of, 14, 61, 84
toehold secured by, 288, 290, 298–99
weather delays, 60–61, 82
wounded and dead (*see* casualties of D-Day)
Operation Torch, 11
Order of the Day, 64, *76*, 77
Organization of the United States Army, xxii–xxiii
Orne River bridge, 106
Osmont, Marie-Louise, 112–14
Oxfordshire and Buckinghamshire Light Infantry ("Ox & Bucks"), 100

Panzer Commander (Ambrose), 111
paratroopers, 130–38
British paratroopers, 107
casualties, 125, 151–52, 184
and chaos of war, 121, 134
courage of, 298

paratroopers (*continued*)
"crickets" (clickers) used by, *132*, 133, 137
drop zones missed by, 134–36, 144–45, 185
drop zones planned for, 118
Eisenhower's preinvasion visits with, 64, *65*
equipment and gear of, 88, 90–91, *91*, *93*, 130
Fitzgerald on performance of, 298
and German fire, 136
goals of, 117
and hedgerows, 154
and H-hour (time of invasion), 66
jumping, ix–xi, *122–23*, 130–31, 139–40
"lost" troopers reunited with units, 162–63
parachutes of, 124–25
passwords used by, 133
and pathfinders, 117, 118, 134, 140
and Pegasus Bridge mission, 107–8
preparations for D-Day, 88–94
roads and towns secured by, 288
scattered landings of, 135–36, 183, 185, 186, 298
separated from units, xii, 132, 135, 144–45, 183, 298
and strategy for invasion, 116, 117
and tracer fire, x, 131, 139
and Utah Beach, 130–38 (*see also* 82nd Airborne Division; 101st Airborne Division)
and weather conditions, 184
Paris, liberation of, *57*, *293*, 307
Pas-de-Calais, 74
pathfinders, 118, 134, 140
Patton, George S., 25, 38
peace, courage required for, 301
Pearl Harbor attack of Japan, 3, 10, 307
Pegasus Bridge operation, 100–108
capture of bridges, 101, 105–7, *106*
casualties at, 106, 108
and landings of gliders, 104–5
mission of, 101
and paratroopers' arrival, 107–8
plan for, 101–2
as spearhead of invasion, 101
as surprise attack, 100–101
Perrett, Marvin J., 170, 172–74
Philippines, 307
Pinder, John, 253–54
planning D-Day
Allies' adoption of plan, 14
assigned to Morgan, 5, 6, 12
Brown on execution of plans, 288, 290
and challenges of Omaha Beach, 239–40

and code name for invasion, 7
compromises in, 47, 51
cover operation for Overlord, 37–38
date for invasion, 6, 48, 59
Donovan's comments on, 187
expanding number of landing sites, 49
H-hour (time of invasion), 50
meteorologist assisting with, 45–49
model of battle terrain, 84–85, *85*
and port requirements, 15–16
review of plans, 7
revisions to plans, 48–49
secrecy and deception required for, 37–38, 51, 88
and security scares, 38–39
sites for invasion, 13–14, 15–16, 66–67, *68–69*
and tide levels, 50
and weather considerations, 48, 49, 50–51, 59–63
platoons, number of soldiers in, xxiii
Pointe du Hoc operation, 261–70
battery captured by Rangers, 262–67, *268*, *269*
and bombardment plans, 261
casualties, 265, 267
cliffs scaled by Rangers, 264–65, *266*
and Cota's leadership, 251
difficulty and complexity of mission, 262, 263
and German defenses, 264, 265
as goal of assault troops, 193
location of, 191
training for, 262
poison gas threats, 149
Poland, Germany's invasion of, 9, 10, 306
prisoners of war, 127–28, 279, 300
Prosser, Austin, 208–9
Purple Hearts, 258
Pyle, Ernie
beaches described by, 284–86
death of, 55, 286, *287*
on difficulty of invasion, 275
on dogs present at invasion, 79, 285–86
on preparations for invasion, 54–55
Pulitzer Prize awarded to, 286
on "toe hold" achieved, 298–99
on war in Italy, 11–12

Raaen, John, Jr., 251, 270
racial discrimination, 17–18, 24–27, 257–58
racial integration, 175–76
Ramsay, Sir Bertram H., 81
Rangers. *See* U.S. Army Rangers
regiments, xxii, xxiii
resistance movements, 10, 261
Ridgway, Matthew B., 134
Rinehart, Mary Roberts, 57

roads
of Sainte-Mère-Église, 157
and Vierville draw, 192, 245
Roberts, John Noble, 256, 259–60
Roma heritage, Europeans with, 10
Rommel, Erwin, *73*, 74, 110, 156
Roosevelt, Eleanor, 25
Roosevelt, Franklin D.
at Casablanca Conference (1943), 11
death of, 307
and declaration of war, 3, *4*
Operation Overload adopted by, 14
on readiness for invasion, 6
selection of Supreme Commander, 30, 31–32
at Tehran Conference (1943), *31*
Roosevelt, Theodore, Jr., 177–81
Royal Norwegian Navy, 18
Rudder, James E., 262, 263
runners, 160–61
Russell, Kenneth, 128–29
Ryan, Cornelius
on fields flooded by Germans, 116
on glider landings, 147
on Omaha Beach, 190
on Pegasus Bridge operation, 101
on success of invasion, 181

Sainte-Mère-Église
as base for 82nd Airborne, 136
captured by Allies, 117, 151, 157–58, *158*, 184
at crossroads, 157
and drop zones for paratroopers, 118, 149
and 505th's stand at Neuville, 184
Saint-Laurent village, 288
Sampson, Francis L., *52*, 139–43
assisting with wounded, 141–43
on challenges of the front line, 121
duties of, 299–300
on Eisenhower, 53–54
in foxhole, 143
on jumping, 139–41
on preparations for invasion, 53
as prisoner of war, 300
and sacrifices of soldiers, 300–301
Saving Private Ryan (film), 295, 300
Scannell, Vernon, 277, 282
Schneider, Max, 268–69, 270
Schroeder, Edgar, 126–27, 147, 149–51
seasickness, 82, 172–73, 205, 227
seawalls, *179*
2nd Ranger Battalion, 262
secrecy of Operation Overload, 37–39, 51, 88
sections, number of soldiers in, xxiii

security concerns, 38–39, 51
741st Tank Division, 241
743rd Division, 242
761st Tank Battalion, 25
SHAEF (Supreme Headquarters Allied Expeditionary Force), 45, 48
ships
after the invasion, *278*, 279
and barrage balloons, *80*, 83, *83*, *168–69*, 256
and foggy conditions, 28
guns of, 166
lost or damaged, 291
minesweepers, 296
number of, 18, 195, 206
and seasickness, 82, 172–73, 205, 227
transport of troops across English Channel, 66, 83–84
See also landing craft
Sicily, Italy, 11, 307
Silver Star, 184
16th Regiment, 220–30
in eastern Omaha Beach, 191, 220–24
and tanks' inability to reach shores, 241
Taylor's leadership of, 252
transport of troops to shore, 224, 227–28
troops under heavy fire, 228–30
wounded of, *231*
snipers
and Baumgarten's wounds, 295
hiding in hedgerows, 128–29, 132
in trees, 279
Soviet Union
and Allied powers, 9, 30–31
Germany's agreement with, 306
Germany's invasion of, 10, 307
Spalding, John, 208
squadrons, number of soldiers in, xxiii
squads, number of soldiers in, xxiii
SS *Empire Javelin*, 247
Stagg, J. M. (James Martin), *46*
assignment of, 45–46
and consensus on forecast, 60
Eisenhower's trust in, 63
final forecast confirmed by, 62
reporting conditions to Eisenhower, 49, 60–62
researching optimum conditions, 46–48
Stalin, Joseph, 30–31, *31*
Stanfill, Margaret, *283*
Stanton, Henry L., 22
Stevens, Ray, 247, 249
Stevens, Roy, 247
Stewart, Jesse, 151
Stiles, Bert, 96–98
St. Laurent draw of Omaha Beach, 220
Strait of Dover, 74

Streczyk, Philip, 206, 208
Suez Canal, 11
supply shortages, 185
Supreme Commander for the Allied Expeditionary Force
  delay in assigning, 7, 14
  selection of, 30, 31–32 (*see also* Eisenhower, Dwight D.)
Supreme Headquarters of the Allied Expeditionary Force (SHAEF), 6
Sword Beach
  about, 67, 70
  casualties at, 70
  location of, 67, *69*
  and Mulberry harbors, 16
  objectives at, 288
  and Pegasus Bridge mission, 101
  and revisions to invasion plan, 49

tanks
  amphibious, 86–87, *86*
  inability to reach shores, 241–42, 285
  inflatable decoys, 38
  knocked out by German defenses, 228
  at Omaha Beach, 198, 208–9, *253*
  refitted for hedgerows, 155–56
  at Utah Beach, 162
Tappenden, Ted, 107
Task Force A, 134–35
Taylor, George A., 228, 252
Thomas, Charles "Chuck" H., 202–3, 224, 227–30
Thorson, Truman "Tubby," 198
320th Anti-Aircraft Barrage Balloon Battalion, 256, 257
320th Glider Field Artillery Battalion, 147, 149–51
327th Quartermaster Service Company, 256–57
332nd Fighter Group, 25
tidal conditions, 50, 193, 237, 259
Tobin, Richard L., 28–29
tolerance, von Luck on value of, 111
tracer bullets
  and friendly fire, 142
  and paratroopers, x, 131, 139
Treaty of Versailles, 9
Truman, Harry S., 18, 26, 307
Turnbull, Turner, 184
"Tuskegee Airmen," 25
21st Panzer Division, 109, 111
29th Infantry Division, 191, 232–40, 244–55, 288, 292

Ukraine, 10
United States
  and Allied powers, 9
  entry into World War II, 10
  ideals of, 300–301
  labor shortages in, 22
  and Overlord participants, 67
  and Pearl Harbor attack, 3, 10, 307

war declared on Germany and Italy, 3, 307
war declared on Japan, 3, 307
See also Omaha Beach; Utah Beach
U.S. Army
African Americans in, 17–18, 24, 26
equipment and supplies of, 19
and French civilians, 277
journey across the Atlantic, 19
organization of, xxii–xxiii
racial discrimination of, 17–18, 24–27
in United Kingdom, 17–18, 19, 22, 23, 52
See also specific divisions, including 4th Infantry Division
U.S. Army Rangers
and Charlie area, 191
and Cota's leadership, 251
and inland advancement of troops, 288
and Omaha Beach, 268–70
and Pointe du Hoc mission, 251, 262–67, *266*, *268*, *269*
rallying cry of, 270
U.S. Congress, 258
U.S. First Army, 50. *See also* Bradley, Omar
U.S. Navy
and mine sweeping, 74
racial discrimination of, 24–25, 26–27
USS *Augusta*, 197
bombardment of German defenses, 198, 199–200
as Bradley's command post, 81, 240, 288
call to battle stations, 197
crossing the English Channel, 81, 83, 87
and turmoil of war, 200–201
USS *Bayfield*, 173, 174, 181
USS *Osprey*, 74
USS *Samuel Chase*
and Capa, 84, 211, 217–18
crossing the English Channel, 224
preinvasion activities of soldiers, 84–85, *85*
USS *Tide*, 296
Utah Beach, 115–89
about, 71–72, 115–19
aerial and naval bombardment of, 86, 119, 166–67, 181
aerial view of, *124*, *171*
African Americans at, 257
airborne divisions, 72, 116, 125–29 (*see also* 82nd Airborne Division; 505th Parachute Infantry Regiment; 101st Airborne Division)
amphibious assault on, 116, 119, 166–74, *182* (*see also* 4th Infantry Division)
and beach defense obstacles, 166–67, 170
casualties, 290

Utah Beach (*continued*)
and demolition teams, 119, 166–67, 170, 181, 257
and Donovan's cyanide pills, 188–89
and 505th's stand at Neuville, 184
German defense of, 116, 119, 136, 183
hedgerows of, 132
Kirk's role at, 81
and landing craft, 170, 172–74
location of, 67, *68*, 71, 115–16
and Mulberry harbors, 16
number of troops in, 181
objectives at, 71–72, 116–19
paratroopers' jumps, *122–23*, 130–31, 135
paratroopers missing drop zones, 135, 144–45, 185, 186
paratroopers' missions, 116, 121, 136
paratroopers' scattered landings, 132, 135–36, 183, 185, 186
and revisions to invasion plan, 49
Roosevelt (Theodore, Jr.) at, 177–81
Sainte-Mère-Église captured/defended by Allies, 157–61, *158*
seawalls at, *179*
success of, 181
Very Low Altitude (VLA) units, 257
Vierville draw, 192–93, 245
Vierville-sur-Mer church, 244
Vierville village, 255, 268, 288
Von Luck, Hans, 109–11

Waco CG-4A gliders, 88–89
Wakefield, Orval B., 166–67, 170
Wallwork, Jim, 103, 104
war correspondents
Bradley's briefing of, 86
Capa's experience on Omaha Beach, 211–18
crossing the English Channel, 84–86
and preparations for D-Day, 54–56
women as, 57–58
See also Pyle, Ernie
war industries, 19, *20*, *21*, *22*, 22
Watson, Jean, 75
weather
and Bradley's command, 82
and chaos of invasion, 134
discussed among experts, 59–60, 62
and Eisenhower's decision, 60–61, 82
foggy conditions, 28, 200
and Germany's lack of defense, 109
and Germany's reconnaissance patrols, 84
importance of forecast, 62

and meteorologist, 45–49
and paratrooper drops, 134, 135, 184
and potential delays, 50–51
and rough seas, 198, 203, 205, 212, 222, 227
and timing of invasion, 50, 59–63
Webster, David Kenyon
jumping from plane, ix–xii
landing of, xii, 134
preparations for D-Day, 88–92
separated from unit, 134, 136–37
time in England, 52
youth of, 17
Welsh, Mary, 57
Whitehead, Don, 84, 277, 279–80
women
in communications services, 75
as nurses, 25, 58, *283*
as war correspondents, 57–58
in war industries, *21*, 22, *22*, 175–76
Women's Royal Naval Service, 75
Wood, David, 105
Woodson, Waverly B., Jr., 257–58
World War I, 9, 57
World War II
D-Day invasion (*see* Operation Overload)
declaration of war, 3, 9, 306–7
estimated casualties, 9
and Hitler's "Final Solution," 9–10
as largest conflict in history, 9
wounded. *See* casualties of D-Day

Yates, Donald Norton, 59, 62–63
Yugoslavia, 306

Zaloga, Steven, 199, 245

ACKNOWLEDGMENTS 

Anyone who writes about history owes a debt of gratitude to scholars and authors who came before. In the case of D-Day, many interviews with those who took part were conducted right after World War II or throughout the twentieth century. For this reason, works about D-Day that rely on those interviews are especially helpful, as many veterans are no longer living.

Since memories fade over time, recollections of experiences gathered soon after events are often the most useful and reliable. For this reason, I have as much as possible tried to use primary sources, oral histories, and historians' accounts close to the events of the war. I've also relied on the work of historians, especially those working in the mid-twentieth century.

I am grateful to Toni Kiser and Lisa Werling at the National World War II Museum in New Orleans for their assistance in making available transcripts of veterans' taped interviews or letters written in response to questions from historian Stephen E. Ambrose, who wrote about D-Day. Historian Michael Edwards, who works extensively with the museum, kindly agreed to read this book in manuscript form and was instrumental in correcting errors.

I'm especially grateful to Kenyon Webster, for allowing me to highlight the story of his father, David Kenyon Webster, whose memoir, *Parachute Infantry: An American Paratrooper's*

Memoir of D-Day and the Fall of the Third Reich, remains one of the most powerful accounts of a young American in World War II.

The classic book about D-Day is, of course, *The Longest Day*, by Cornelius Ryan. Although his book does not include source notes, he based it on hundreds of interviews. Thanks to Sara Harrington and the gracious archives staff at Ohio University, I had the opportunity to visit the Cornelius Ryan collection to read some of the interviews conducted in the 1950s by Mr. Ryan, including a visit with the wife of German Field Marshal Erwin Rommel. It was exciting to see Mr. Ryan's handwritten notes. The work of contemporary historian Joseph Balkoski, who has written two excellent books, *Omaha Beach* and *Utah Beach*, as well as the works of Rick Atkinson, have also been extremely helpful.

I am, as always, grateful to Lisa Sandell, my editor at Scholastic, as well as the entire Scholastic team: Lori Benton, Ellie Berger, Isa Caban, Rachel Feld, Emily Heddleson, David Levithan, Crystal McCoy, Vaishali Nayak, Lizette Serrano, Mindy Stockfield, Olivia Valcarce, Tracy van Straaten, and many others, as well as the sales team. Thanks to Keirsten Geise, Jael Fogle, and Amla Sanghvi, the incredibly hard-working and meticulous teams in design, production, and photo research and also to Robin Hoffman and the entire Scholastic Book Fairs and Scholastic Book Clubs teams.

Young readers often discover nonfiction thanks to the encouragement of parents, teachers, and librarians. As I travel across the country to visit schools and meet young readers and educators, I am inspired by the efforts of dedicated individuals everywhere to create nurturing and inclusive learning communities for children and teens. Thank you for all you do.

Thanks also to my agent, Steven Malk, for his ongoing support. I owe my interest in World War II to my late father, Russell W. Hopkinson, who fought in the Philippines. My mother, Gloria D. Hopkinson, also served. Though my dad rarely talked about his experiences, we liked to watch old television shows together (especially the 1960s series *Combat!*). My sisters, Bonnie and Janice, may have passed up this viewing experience.

Also, I wish to extend my heartfelt thanks to many wonderful friends—you know who you are. As I was finishing this project in the summer of 2017, I had special assistance from Deborah Wiles, Vicki Hemphill, Elisa Johnston, Maya Abels, Jane Kurtz, and Judy Sierra. Michael Kieran kindly put up with a hostess who rarely left her desk. This book is dedicated to a dear friend whose birthday happens to fall on June 6.

Finally, I wish to thank my family—husband, Andy; children, Rebekah and Dimitri; and son-in-law, Eric Sawyer. During the early research for this project, Oliver Hill Sawyer arrived. Months later, Oliver was able to crawl over to tear down a few towers of research books. I hope someday he will grow up to read books like this—and to love history as much as I do.

★ ABOUT THE AUTHOR ★

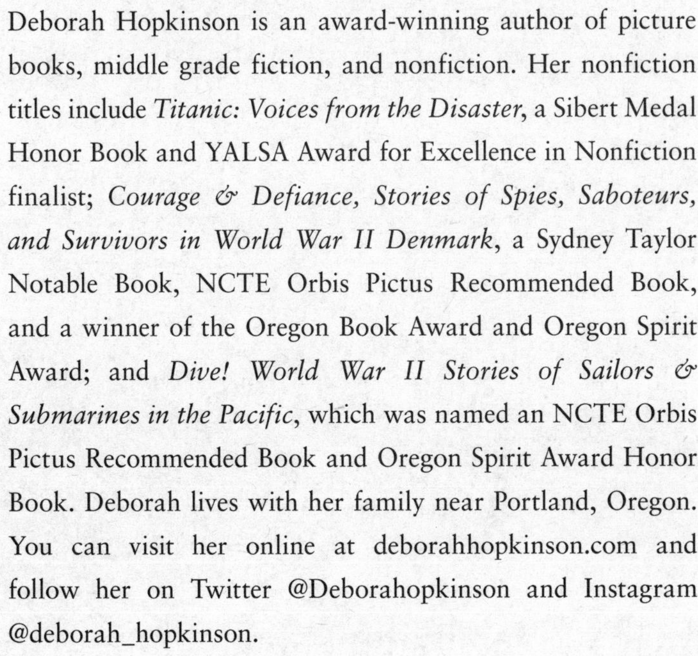

Deborah Hopkinson is an award-winning author of picture books, middle grade fiction, and nonfiction. Her nonfiction titles include *Titanic: Voices from the Disaster*, a Sibert Medal Honor Book and YALSA Award for Excellence in Nonfiction finalist; *Courage & Defiance, Stories of Spies, Saboteurs, and Survivors in World War II Denmark*, a Sydney Taylor Notable Book, NCTE Orbis Pictus Recommended Book, and a winner of the Oregon Book Award and Oregon Spirit Award; and *Dive! World War II Stories of Sailors & Submarines in the Pacific*, which was named an NCTE Orbis Pictus Recommended Book and Oregon Spirit Award Honor Book. Deborah lives with her family near Portland, Oregon. You can visit her online at deborahhopkinson.com and follow her on Twitter @Deborahopkinson and Instagram @deborah_hopkinson.